Proudhon's Sociology

Proudhon's Sociology

Pierre Ansart

Edited by Cayce Jamil
Introduction by René Berthier
Translated by Shaun Murdock, René Berthier, and Jesse S. Cohn

ISBN: 978-1-84935-519-3
E-ISBN: 978-1-84935-520-9
Library of Congress Control Number: 2023935615

AK Press
370 Ryan Ave. #100
Chico, CA 95973
www.akpress.org
akpress@akpress.org

AK Press
33 Tower St.
Edinburgh EH6 7BN
Scotland
www.akuk.com
akuk@akpress.org

The above addresses would be delighted to provide you with the latest
AK Press distribution catalog, which features books, pamphlets, zines,
and stylish apparel published and/or distributed by AK Press. Alter-
natively, visit our websites for the complete catalog, latest news, and
secure ordering.

Cover Design by Crisis

Printed in the USA on acid-free paper

Contents

Introduction

When I told Edward Castleton that I intended to translate a few chapters of Pierre Ansart's *Sociologie de Proudhon,* he asked me: why not translate Proudhon? Basically he was right, but he was reasoning like an academic. Castleton is an American researcher and teacher of philosophy and history at the University of Franche-Comté in Besançon, Proudhon's hometown. He is one of the leading specialists on the author of *What Is Property?* and is the current president of the Société Pierre-Joseph Proudhon. His remark, however, ignored one fact: Proudhon, more than anyone else, needs his thought to be synthesized so that it is accessible to readers who cannot devote twenty years to reading his complete works. This is all the more true since he is often difficult to read, even for a French reader.

This is where Pierre Ansart comes in. *Sociologie de Proudhon* is the perfect tool to lead the reader through the arcana of the thought of an author I have come to consider as one of the greatest thinkers of the nineteenth century.

The critical analysis of Proudhon's immense work is not an easy task. In *Sociologie de Proudhon,* Ansart has fortunately avoided attempts to explain Proudhon's work. He has managed to highlight the essential points of Proudhonian thought without dismissing its contradictions. None of Proudhon's works can be considered as sociological in the strict sense of the word. That was not his intention, and it certainly was not Ansart's intention to "prove" that Proudhon was a sociologist in the sense that we understand it today. However, he does give a good account of Proudhon's desire to seek objective knowledge of society. Proudhon's *System of Economic Contradictions* (1846) is an

investigation of the mechanisms of capitalist society that anticipates *Capital* by twenty years in terms of both the concepts
employed and the method of exposition.[1]

Sociologie de Proudhon, published in 1967, was originally
intended for students. The author's ambition was to make
Proudhon's social thought known but probably also to remove all
the excess from it in order to unveil the underlying thought. We
can say that what most distinguishes Marx from Proudhon is that
the former quite quickly found the structure around which he
built his thought, whereas the latter was in a permanent state of
research, which gives a seemingly contradictory character to his
work. Proudhon's thought is constantly moving because each of
his books is the result of circumstances. In order for it to appear
in its unity, Ansart has made a synthesis that restores its essential
structure, renders it intelligible, and reveals to what extent sociological concerns can be found in Proudhonian thought, whether
explicitly or implicitly.

Naturally, when one speaks of Proudhon one also thinks of
Marx. The merit of *Sociologie de Proudhon* is that it addresses the
conflict between the two men through the common sources from
which they drew. This approach is often obscured by Marxist
authors who do not want to recognize Proudhon's thought as
having any normative value.

Significantly, a year before *Sociologie de Proudhon*, Henri
Lefebvre, a "heterodox" Marxist, published *Sociologie de Marx*
as part of the same series. In my opinion, Lefebvre's book is an
indispensable complement to Ansart's. Both books, which were
made accessible to French students at the time of the strikes of
May–June 1968, had a real impact on the theoretical education of
this generation.[2]

---

1. See René Berthier, "Proudhon and the Problem of Method," *Monde
Nouveau*, June 9, 2012, http://monde-nouveau.net/spip.php?article407.

2. Henri Lefebvre (1901–91) was a French Marxist philosopher and
sociologist best known for pioneering the critique of everyday life, for
introducing the concepts of the right to the city and the production of
social space, and for his work on dialectics, alienation, and criticism of
Stalinism, existentialism, and structuralism.

The task undertaken by Ansart to reveal the common sources of the thought of Proudhon and Marx was taken up two years later with the publication of his doctoral thesis, *Marx et l'anarchisme : essai sur les sociologies de Saint-Simon, Proudhon et Marx* (Marx and Anarchism: Essay on the Sociologies of Saint-Simon, Proudhon and Marx).

Why "Marx and anarchism" when Saint-Simon and Proudhon occupy the same position?

Pierre Ansart attempts to find the sources of Marx's theory of the state by comparing his writings with those of Proudhon and Saint-Simon. In doing so, he shows both how much Proudhon's and Marx's thought are indebted to Saint-Simon's and how much Proudhon's economic thought has influenced Marx. This is why *Sociologie de Proudhon* constitutes a necessary introduction to the reading of *Marx et l'anarchisme*.

Like Proudhon, Marx made a systematic critique of utopian socialism and political economy: they attacked the same opponents. Thus, Pierre Ansart wonders if "the vigor of Marx's criticisms of Proudhon" is not due in part "to the similarity of their concerns, to their belonging to the same intellectual milieu in which the differences were all the more noticeable because they were small." On this point, I do not share Ansart's opinion. Proudhon and Marx undoubtedly had similar preoccupations, but there is nothing to say that they belonged to the same intellectual milieu.

The German intellectuals exiled in Paris tried desperately to win Proudhon over to them. Karl Marx and Karl Grün competed with each other for his good graces and to convert him to Hegelianism.

It has been said that Proudhon's knowledge of the German philosophers was superficial, that he did not undertake a methodical study of any of these thinkers, seeking confirmation of his own views in their work rather than a deepening of their thought. Marx is undoubtedly largely responsible for this image of Proudhon, but his own knowledge of Hegel deserves to be seriously reexamined. Although Proudhon's knowledge of these thinkers was limited by the lack of available translations in

his time, his understanding of them was remarkable. Most crit-
ics of the thinker from Besançon probably do not go so far as to
read chapter II of volume 2 of the *System of Economic Contradictions*,
which contains a breathtaking synthesis of the thought of Kant,
Fichte, Schelling, and Hegel.

The Frenchman and the two German intellectuals did not
have an equal relationship. At that time, Proudhon was already
famous, and Marx at least recognized him as a master. This state
of grace did not last long, however, for as soon as the *System of
Economic Contradictions* was published in 1846, their relationship
deteriorated.

Proudhon came from the people, while Marx and Grün
were academics. Proudhon was never fooled by the flattery of
the two men.

Is Proudhon's socialism so opposed to Marxism? There is no
doubt that both men attempted the same project: to create a science of the contradictions of capitalism, to show the historical
necessity of its collapse. But to say that their *project of society* was
the same would be, in my opinion, a profound mistake.

* * *

Proudhon is a complex author even for a French reader. Of
course, from a strictly academic point of view, it is obviously preferable to have a firsthand reading of his work. But the difficulty
in reading Proudhon lies not only in his language and his way of
reasoning but also in the fact that his thought seems contradictory. This contradictory character results from the fact that it is
in permanent evolution. Here is a man who says at the beginning
of his career that property is theft, and at the end of his career
he tells us that property is freedom, maintaining that he has not
changed his opinion. The twenty-three-year interval between
these two propositions was devoted to trying to solve the mystery of this contradiction. In reality, it is not property itself that
is theft. As the legitimate and sole owner of my toothbrush, I do
not see myself as a thief. What Proudhon calls theft is the appropriation by the capitalist of the value produced by the combined

and collective labor of a group of workers, which is much greater than the value that would be produced by the same number of workers individually. This is where the theft lies, because the capitalist does not pay this surplus value to his employees and instead appropriates this *aubaine*, this unearned income.

In reality, the man who said that property was theft (an unfortunate and provocative expression that is still poorly understood today) considered the question of property to be secondary.

Proudhon actually thinks that individual property has lost its importance as an institution and that society now operates solely on the basis of circulation: "Society no longer lives, as it once did, on individual property; it lives on a more generic fact, it lives on circulation." This can be seen perfectly well: we know that the crisis of 1929 took on a catastrophic turn because international trade had practically ceased.

Few readers seem to have perceived that throughout his life, and despite the different approaches he would take to the problem, Proudhon tried to show (while appearing to defend it) that property is a historical exception, a transitory form, that it has existed only for short periods of history, and that its historical function is soon to be completed.

In one of his last works, *Theory of Property*, he explains that the manufacturer does not care about being "the owner of the house or flat in which he lives with his family, of the workshop in which he works, of the storehouse in which he keeps his raw materials, of the shop in which he displays his products, of the land on which his residence, workshop, storehouse and shop have been built." What interests him is the appropriation of surplus value.

Proudhon himself complained that he was not understood. It is true that the way he presented his thoughts did not simplify things.

Often carried away by his argumentative verve, he forgot to "stick to the facts," lost himself in long digressions, and neglected the realization that the reader did not need to know everything about the chain of ideas that led him to his proof. When he wants to challenge a point of view, Proudhon often spends many pages developing the argument of the person he is opposing by pushing the latter's point of view to its extreme limits. The inattentive reader may end up believing that this is what Proudhon really thinks!

Moreover, he often resorts to reductio ad absurdum, a procedure in which he is a master, useful for showing the inanity of a line of reasoning to which he is opposed but no help in clarifying the exposition of his own theories. However, the greatest difficulty that today's reader must face is undoubtedly that of vocabulary. When he calls for "liberal, federal, decentralizing, republican, egalitarian, progressive, just" property, the word *liberal* should not be misunderstood. "Liberal" should be understood in the original sense of the word, as it has been preserved by the English language. When he speaks of socialism, it is a movement imbued with "a certain completely illiberal religiosity"; when he speaks of communism, it is absolutely not Marxism; when he speaks of "political economy," this term must be understood in the language of the time, as the economic theory of the bourgeoisie. To read Proudhon, one must therefore make the effort to enter his mode of thinking.

To complicate matters, Proudhon was an ardent polemicist and engaged in abundant debates with people who are now totally forgotten and on issues that are no longer of interest. The reader is therefore left with the choice of reading these tedious pages or skipping them without knowing whether there might have been something interesting to find after all.

At the end of his life, Proudhon stated twice that he had not changed his opinion on the substance of either the question of property or the critical analysis of capitalism. Thus, he says in his *Theory of Property* (1863): "Will, by chance, the theory of property that I am now publishing be considered a retraction? We shall see that it is nothing of the sort." He continues to say that property and theft are "two economic equivalents." As for the *System of Economic Contradictions* (published in 1846), a work that anticipates *Capital* in many respects, Proudhon declared in 1863 that he had reservations about the method used. "[But] since this reservation was made in the interest of pure logic, I maintain everything I said in my *Contradictions.*" Proudhon thus maintains the substance of his critique of property and the substance of his critique of the capitalist system. There is no reason not to follow him on these points, just as when he declared at the end of his life: "If I ever find myself a landowner, I will make sure that God and men, especially the poor, forgive me!" Proudhon did not like property, but he defended it. He was violently critical of competition but defended its principle. Why?

To answer these questions, perhaps it is necessary to recognize that Proudhon had a long-term strategic vision. From this perspective, one should not take the contradictory positions that Proudhon took at different periods of his life at face value and conclude that he simply changed his mind. One should instead understand how these different approaches are dialectically linked.

Concerning competition, Proudhon gives a striking description of the effects of competition on society and the extreme misery it causes among the people in the *System of Economic Contradictions.* He therefore knows perfectly well what is at stake. His relative defense of competition is the effect of his radical opposition to communism. But it is not the communism of Marx, of which he was unaware, but instead what was known as such at the time: doctrinaire and utopian French communism. In the years 1830-40, the main themes of what would become the anarchist movement appear as a reaction to the communist theories advocating the absolute preeminence of the community over the individual. Saint-Simon, Fourier, and Cabet are among the main ideologists of utopian socialism that the precursors of anarchism began to attack, countering with the idea that the individual and society develop in unison.

Communism was at that time a current full of good intentions and religiosity, which relied on the state to implement measures that were supposed to improve the situation of the working classes. Proudhon's *System of Economic Contradictions* contains highly critical analyses of this utopian communism, a trend that had not yet broken away from the practices of the ancien régime regarding the management of poverty and the poor, which consisted of confining the latter in highly supervised enclosures. The National Workshops of 1848, which Proudhon vigorously opposed, were a reminder of this period. The defense of the "community" by the communists appeared to the first "anarchists" as a restoration of the concentration camp system, applied to the poor.

Proudhon's recognition of a certain form of competition in society has its origin there, but it is also motivated by the sociological observation that it is impossible to eliminate all contradiction in society, that such an objective would be the death of society, and that a certain competitive spirit must be maintained in human relations. Here again Proudhon shows himself to be a true dialectician.

Concerning property, Proudhon again has an approach that is sociological, not doctrinaire. Unlike Marx, he understood that not only the peasantry but also the proletariat were attached to the notion of property. The people's feeling of fierce attachment to property is mostly due to fear of the unknown, fear of the precariousness of existence, and the individual's desire to secure a decent life for themselves and their family. Whichever way one looks at the question of property in Proudhon—"theft" or "freedom"—he starts from the fact that there is a large middle social stratum that is attached to property and is not willing to give up this idea easily. Property is an institution that is a symptom of human weakness. It is an irrational feeling that cannot be ignored if society is to be changed.

In particular, Proudhon understood that you cannot have a social revolution without the peasantry when they represent the overwhelming majority of the population. "Land ownership in France concerns two-thirds of the inhabitants," he wrote in *General Idea of the Revolution in the Nineteenth Century*. Proudhon's problem seems to be to find ways of attracting the peasantry to progressive reforms of the status of property without colliding with it head on. This is undoubtedly the key to his theories on property and the thread that links his first positions (e.g., property is theft) with those he would develop at the end of his life (e.g., property is freedom).

In *Theory of Property*, the very work in which he seems to rehabilitate property, Proudhon specifies that it is a question of "transformed, humanized property, purified of the right of aubaine."

It is hard to imagine a capitalist entrepreneur adhering to a system in which he would not have the possibility of exploiting the labor power of others. Whatever the complexity of the Proudhonian approach and the dialectical contortions he resorts to, this should be kept in mind. In *Political Capacity of the Working Classes,* his last work, he writes that despite the restrictions he was able to make on property, outside of which "it remains usurpatory and odious," it still "retains something egoistic" (to which he adds, "which is always unsympathetic to me"). This reflection is important because it was delivered at the end of his life in a text that was published after his death, and thus it reveals his point of view at a time when, in principle, he had completed his final thoughts on the matter.

For those of us who were students in 1968 and in the years that followed, Ansart was able to reveal Proudhon's thought on a very important point and one that had an important impact in practice: the theory of knowledge.

It is necessary to understand the context. In almost all intellectual spheres of society, Marxism dominated at that time, particularly Leninism, which was a distortion of Marxism as interpreted by the followers of Lenin and Trotsky—a reinterpretation that would probably have horrified Marx himself. The young Trotskyists and Maoists who came out of the universities to the working class were convinced that revolutionary theory could only come to the workers through bourgeois intellectuals. This thesis was constantly repeated, as if those who uttered it wanted to convince themselves of its veracity.

By giving us access to Proudhon's thought on this and other questions, Ansart has encouraged us to look at the direct source, Proudhon himself. He has revealed to us a more complex, more subtle, and more convincing thought than the caricatured ramblings that Lenin had actually copied word for word from Kautsky.

But, peculiarly, Ansart allowed us to realize how close Proudhon was to Marx on the theory of knowledge, the real Marx, not the Marx of his self-proclaimed interpreters. Marx would probably have said of Lenin what he said of his son-in-law Paul Lafargue, who had written a particularly boring book in which he claimed to explain Marx's economic thought: "[If this is Marxism,] I am not a Marxist."[3]

Ansart explains that, according to Proudhon, the task of the revolutionary theorist is "to participate in the revolutionary act through a labor of theoretical clarification":

> In *The Political Capacity of the Working Classes*, he expresses the relation of working-class practice to the revolutionary idea dialectically, stressing that practice implies a theory, a law of action, of which the working class becomes conscious by means of theoretical clarification. It is not a question for the working class of waiting for a truth to come from the theorist's mouth, but of extracting from itself its hidden meaning and imposing it by political struggle. The role of theorists must therefore not be overestimated: their work merely participates in a movement that goes beyond them.

If practice is an idea, adds Ansart, "we must say conversely that speech, theoretical clarification, is a form of action."

* * *

I would like to end this introduction to Pierre Ansart's book—which is really just a somewhat unorganized digression about Proudhon—by saying a few words about the question of strikes, which may not be very important in the hushed debates among academics but which has a very strong emotional impact in the

---

3. Paul Lafargue, *Le Déterminisme économique de Karl Marx* [The Economic Determinism of Karl Marx] (Paris: V. Giard and E. Brière, 1909).

discussions among militants. Proudhon's opposition to strikes is often used as a decisive argument to cut short any debate.

Proudhon's reservations concerning the usefulness of strikes are complex and cannot be summed up as "Proudhon was against strikes." The apparent paradox between his stance on strikes and the fact that the French revolutionary syndicalists claimed him is analyzed in Daniel Colson's "Proudhon et le syndicalisme révolutionnaire."[4]

How can a socialist thinker who is described as "opposed to strikes" be claimed by revolutionary syndicalist militants? This raises a first question: was Proudhon really opposed to strikes? As is often the case with the absurdities that circulate about the anarchist movement, it is Marx who is the source. Thus, when Marx reports that Proudhon was pleased that the miners of Rives-de-Gier had been repressed after going on strike, he is simply showing that he had read *Political Capacity of the Working Classes* only superficially (in fact, the quotation supposedly drawn from this work comes from the *System of Economic Contradictions*).[5] Proudhon simply says that from the point of view of the law at the time, the strike was illegal and that repression was, for the same reasons, legal. He is therefore not pleased that the miners were repressed. Proudhon underlines, moreover: "The working masses, whose noble aspirations I serve here as well as I can, [are] still, alas, only an inorganic multitude; the worker has not placed himself on the same level as the master." Here he refers to article 1781 of the civil code, which states that in a lawsuit, the word of the boss is worth more than that of his workers; a situation of which he, of course, does not approve.[6] The fact that the "working masses" are an "inorganic multitude" means for Proudhon that they do

---

4. Daniel Colson, "Proudhon et le syndicalisme révolutionnaire" [Proudhon and Revolutionary Syndicalism], http://1libertaire.free.fr/DColson20.html.

5. Marx, "Political Indifferentism," 1873, Marxists Internet Archive, Marxists.org, https://www.marxists.org/archive/marx/works/1873/01/indifferentism.htm.

6. See "A propos du Manifeste des Soixante," *Monde Nouveau*, monde-nouveau.net.

not have a collective consciousness and that they have not organized themselves.

Proudhon also points out that "these struggles of coalitions
between workers and masters . . . almost always end to the advan-
tage of the latter and to the detriment of the former."[7] He does not
dispute that the strikers act "under the impulse of a feeling of justice" ("that I do not deny," he says). What he intends to show is a
contradiction: "[in striking, the workers,] I recognize it expressly,
were not wrong, internally, to complain" (my emphasis) but at
that time "[they] exceeded, externally, their right." This contradiction is always resolved in favor of the employers: "it is found,
much more odiously, in the favor generally granted to the latter
[employers], and the repression which is the ordinary privilege of
the others [workers]." This is expressed in Proudhon's convoluted
way, but I don't think this passage needs to be deciphered.

Marx refers to a passage in *Political Capacity* in which
Proudhon writes that "the authority that shot the miners of
Rives-de-Gier was in an unfortunate situation" but had to "sacrifice its children to save the Republic." Naturally, what Proudhon
is explaining here is the point of view of the state, without
approving it. The French revolutionary syndicalists, obviously
more intelligent than Marx, understood this perfectly. Proudhon
says of strikes that they cannot fundamentally change the state
of society (which Marx also says, by the way). This is a point on
which the revolutionary syndicalists agree with Proudhon. And
on many other points: the separation of classes, the refusal of
parliamentary activity, the insistence on economic action, federalism, and more. The proximity between Proudhon and revolutionary syndicalism is probably explained mostly by the fact that
his thought is very closely linked to the thought of the workers'
movement of his time.

The question is whether this closeness between Proudhon
and the labor movement was a matter of chance or whether
there was an actual kinship. That the labor movement of his

---

7. *De la capacité politique des classes ouvrières* [The Political Capacity of
the Working Classes] (Paris: E. Dentu, 1865), 412.

time influenced Proudhon should hardly be open to debate: it is difficult to imagine a socialist thinker being impervious to his environment. Anarchist militants read a lot.[8] In France, groups of workers met to discuss Proudhon's theories and even to question Proudhon. One of these readers, Tolain, was even one of the founders of the International Workingmen's Association, although Proudhon did not share his views on workers' candidacies.[9] It is therefore not surprising that the French sections of the IWA claimed Proudhon as their own during the organization's first congresses.

Similarly, it is not surprising that the militants who helped create the Confédération Générale du Travail (CGT) and who founded revolutionary syndicalism were familiar with Proudhon's work, especially since many of them came from the anarchist movement. In "L'anarchisme et les syndicats ouvriers," published in 1895, Fernand Pelloutier speaks of Proudhon's "masterly analysis" of taxation. Émile Pouget claims to be a Proudhonist in his brochure *L'Action directe*: "Proudhon, . . . anticipating syndicalism, evoked the economic federalism that is being prepared and that surpasses, with all the superiority of life, the sterile notions of the whole political set-up."

One could argue endlessly about whether it was Proudhon who influenced the workers' movement of his time or the other way around. Such a question is of no interest whatsoever because it comes down to the chicken-and-egg argument. It is obvious that Proudhon was very strongly influenced by the workers' movement of his time, that he elaborated a general theory inspired by this influence, and that his theory, much better than those of Victor Considérant, Louis Blanc, and others, was recognized by the proletarians of the time, a recognition that provided Proudhon with new subjects for reflection. It is a permanent movement between practice and theory.

8. Gaetano Manfredonia, "Les lignées proudhoniennes dans l'anarchisme français" [The Lineages of Proudhon in French Anarchism], Les travaux de l'Atelier Proudhon, no. 11.

9. Compare "Le Manifeste des Soixante" and "A propos du Manifeste des Soixante", *Monde Nouveau*, monde-nouveau.net.

A young researcher, Samuel Hayat, explains the recognition of Proudhon's thought by the proletariat by "the structural
homology between Proudhonism and the working class."[10] The
most convincing formalization of this is due to Pierre Ansart. As
we have seen, according to him, Proudhon is not linked in an
abstract way with the workers' movement. There is a structural
homology between Proudhon's thought and certain social structures. . . . This homology is coupled with a homology of practices
with those of the mutualism of the Lyon silk workers."[11]

Contrary to what some authors assert, Proudhon's stance on
strikes did not in any way "isolate him from the nascent workers'
movement."[12] This opposition to partial strikes, considered useless and counterproductive, was shared by the whole anarchist
movement and then by the revolutionary syndicalist movement,
which had recognized Proudhon as a precursor! This is a paradox that the French CGT itself underlined at its fifth congress,
in 1900, by voting in favor of a resolution that is perfectly in
line with Proudhon: "We do not believe that we should encourage partial strikes, which we consider harmful even if they give
appreciable results, because they never compensate for the sacri-
fices made, and the results they may give are powerless to modify
the social problem."[13]

In "Proudhon et le syndicalisme révolutionnaire," Daniel
Colson addresses the reasons why "the revolutionary syndicalists

---

10. Samuel Hayat, "De l'anarchisme Proudhonien au syndicalisme
révolutionnaire : une transmission problématique" [From Proudhonian
Anarchism to Revolutionary Syndicalism: A Problematic Transmission],
http://www.academia.edu/2636763/De_lanarchisme_Proudhonien
_au_syndicalisme_r%C3%A9volutionnaire_une_transmission_probl
%C3%A9matique.

11. Ibid. Compare Pierre Ansart, *Naissance de l'anarchisme* [Birth of
Anarchism] (Paris: Presses universitaires de France, 1970), 131.

12. Michael Schmidt and Lucien Van der Walt, *Black Flame: The Revolutionary Class Politics of Anarchism and Syndicalism* (Oakland: AK Press,
2009).

13. XIe congrès national corporatif (*Ve de la CGT*) *tenu à la Bourse du
Travail de Paris* en septembre 1900 [11th National Syndicalist Congress
(5th of the CGT) held at the Paris Bourse du Travail in September 1900].

were able to recognize themselves in Proudhon even though the proposals of the two could diverge so much": "We underestimate or we completely misunderstand *the extraordinary practical and theoretical intelligence of the workers' movements of the time*" (my emphasis).[14] The revolutionary syndicalists, led by Pelloutier, were well aware that the advantages obtained by the strikes were going to be canceled out by the system, and they obviously did not blame Proudhon for not having understood that, in spite of this, the strikes served as a training ground for the working class—or as "revolutionary gymnastics," as Pouget said—something that Bakunin had understood perfectly well.

René Berthier
March–April 2021

---

14. Daniel Colson, "Proudhon et le syndicalisme révolutionnaire" [Proudhon and Revolutionary Syndicalism], http://1libertaire.free.fr/DColson20.html.

CHAPTER ONE

Method

More than one hundred years after its completion, Proudhon's work continues to generate anger or enthusiasm, whether it is treated as utopian and reformist or considered to express an authentically revolutionary thought. These quarrels over its interpretation are a continuation of the passionate discussions triggered by Proudhon's writings when they were published. In his early works, Marx interprets the first memoir on property, *What Is Property?* (1840), as a faithful expression of proletarian thought and proclaims that this declaration of war on the capitalist regime is as decisive for the labor movement as Sieyès's proclamation was for the Third Estate.[1] But a few years later, after a breakdown in relations with Proudhon, he responded to *The System of Economic Contradictions* (1846) with a lengthy critique (*The Poverty of Philosophy*) in which he treats Proudhonian thought as an expression of petit bourgeois ideology. However, in the same period, the revolutionary Bakunin, who knew the work of both Marx and Proudhon, refused to contrast them: he agreed that Marx provides a more reliable analysis of the fate of capitalism,

---

1. Marx, *La Sainte famille* [The Holy Family], *Œuvres philosophiques* [Philosophical Works], vol. 2 (Paris: Costes, 1927), 53. Translator's note: In the French ancien régime, "Third Estate" refers to the peasants and bourgeoisie, situated below the clergy (the First Estate) and the aristocracy (the Second Estate) in the social hierarchy. In January 1789, just before the outbreak of the French Revolution, French writer and clergyman Abbé Emmanuel Joseph Sieyès wrote the political pamphlet *Qu'est-ce que le Tiers-État ?* [What Is the Third Estate?], declaring: "What is the Third Estate? Everything. What has it been hitherto in the political order? Nothing. What does it want to be? Something."

but added that Proudhon's antiauthoritarian and antistatist spirit
provide the revolution with the anarchist and radical character
that Marx lacks. Today, while the Marxist tradition repeats its
founder's condemnation, theorists of worker self-management
highlight the importance of the Proudhonian critique, especially
its contribution to a self-managed and decentralized socialism.[2]

The strength of these controversies is a sign of this work's
unique, ongoing relevance. Proudhon is engaged in a series
of questions that immediately call contemporary problems to
mind, within a discussion that successively calls into question
capitalism and state communism. Undoubtedly, the terms of
debate have changed to a large extent: the *regime of property* condemned in *The System of Economic Contradictions* corresponds to
the competitive capitalism that could be seen before 1848 and
in the early days of the Second Empire, and *community* is not a
developed system but a largely utopian project that is more rem-
iniscent of the hopes of Babeuf than of Marxist communism.[3]
However, the change in the terms of debate did not erase its
underlying meaning: the critique of the anarchic and inhumane
character of the regime of property reaches any economy based
on the pursuit of private profit; the critique of the authoritarian character of the regime of community reaches any economy
based on state centralization of the means of production. Such
a difficult and uncomfortable position was bound to rankle the
adherents of the established order, as well as many socialists,
and still to this day it can only stir up irritation. Proudhon did
nothing to ease these difficulties and soothe the anger that he
provoked: at first sight, he seems to radically attack everything
he studies, in particular property, the state, and religion, setting
the revolution the task of abolishing them once and for all. He

---

2. Daniel Guérin, *L'anarchisme* [Anarchism] (Paris: Gallimard, 1965),
170 and passim.

3. Translator's note: François-Noël Babeuf, also known as Gracchus
Babeuf, was a French proto-socialist and revolutionary. In May 1776 he
led the Conjuration des Égaux (Conspiracy of the Equals), a failed coup
d'état during the French Revolution aimed at achieving absolute equality
through the collectivization of property.

proposes to apply a negative dialectic to all social phenomena, aiming to destroy all dogma, and resulting in atheism in religion, anarchy in politics, and non-property in political economy.[4] All these negations could not fail to irritate his friends and trouble those who only half understood him.

However, the diversity of interpretations also stems from the great complexity of this work, where the fury threatens to hide the nuances of the analyses. Proudhon has a strong knack for aggressive phrases, for contradiction, but none of his famous invectives adequately express his thought; for him, the phrase is just one aspect of the truth, according to the general principle that truth is not absolute but dialectical, and that a proposition must immediately be corrected by its opposite. Hence the movement of Proudhon's thought, which could assert in turn that property must be destroyed and that it must be preserved, in a constant movement that has caused some to believe that his critique was nothing but sophistry. Proudhon can only be understood if we recover, from within, the movement of his thought, which obeys its own logic and overturns received notions of traditional logic. In *The Poverty of Philosophy*, Marx is surprised that Proudhon retained only the words and not the content of the Hegelian method, and indeed, as we will show, Proudhon retains from Hegel only what illuminates his own method and refuses to submit to a school. The difficulty is compounded by the fact that he creates his methodology as he encounters new difficulties; he has not received a fixed method from an academy, or by practicing a particular science, to apply to his objects of study. He thinks like an autodidact, but in doing so he inaugurates an original way of thinking that must not be understood by comparison with traditional philosophical schools—materialism, empiricism, individualism, or idealism—or by reduction to the sciences that he strives to overcome, history or political economy.

---

4. "Our own principle, on the contrary, is the negation of all dogma; our first datum, nothing. To deny, always to deny: that is our method of construction in philosophy." *Le Représentant du Peuple* [The Representative of the People], May 16, 1848; in *Solution du problème social* [Solution of the Social Problem], vol. 6 (Paris: Lacroix, Verboeckoven (1867-71), 144.

From the outset, these preliminary difficulties encourage us to provide an outline of Proudhon's approach, even if this means temporarily neglecting the details and nuances. Proudhon develops a sociology only by means of a social and political struggle, and it is only by discussing his fights and critiques that we will rediscover the spirit of the *social science* he develops and the dialectical method he proposes.

As suggested by the famous phrase in the first memoir, "Property is theft," the first battle fought by Proudhon is directed against private property, or more precisely against profit, against capital as the source of profit, and against of all forms of aubaine, rent, and interest.[5] This ability of capital to produce an aubaine, to reproduce itself without its owner having to take part in collective labor, is theft, in right and in fact. In fact, capitalist profit can only be obtained through a misappropriation whereby the proprietor does not compensate the workers for all of their production. This theft appears in the qualitative and quantitative discrepancy between wages and social production. In offering work, the capitalist commits to providing the worker with a wage equivalent on average to individual food and maintenance costs. But from the union and harmony of works, from the convergence and organization of efforts, there results an immense force, the *collective force*, which is of a completely different order than the sum of individual works. The capitalist pays for the working days, or rather he pays as many times one day's wage as he employs workers each day; but this collective force and production, which result from the synthesis of individual efforts and exceed them infinitely in quantity and quality, the capitalist does not pay but

---

5. Translator's note: The slogan was translated by Benjamin Tucker as "Property is robbery" but is now more commonly rendered as per the text. The word *aubaine* originally referred to the right of the king of France to claim the inheritance of foreigners who died in his dominions in the ancien régime. The French term may be translated as "unearned income" or "windfall," and Benjamin Tucker's translation of *What Is Property?* renders *droit d'aubaine* as "right of increase." Finally, "rent" here covers *loyers et fermages* in the original text, *loyer* being the general term for rent and *fermages* referring specifically to land or ground rent.

instead appropriates.[6] Individualistic law maintains the fiction of individual labor and a private contract between the employer and the worker. But since all labor is made possible by the full scope of previous labor, it is fundamentally social and collective: at the time they begin productive activities, individuals are engaged in a common task and are immediately in debt to the society to which they belong. Every productive enterprise brings together individual efforts whose division and combination generate an economic and social power that is fundamentally different from the individual contribution. The fiction of wages allows the capitalist to retain the profit derived from this collective force: by paying for days of work, the entrepreneur does not fairly distribute what the workers have actually produced. Workers only receive a salary that is set according to their basic needs, but in the private property regime the actual product of their labor—the social and collective product of their efforts—is constantly diverted, stolen, by the capitalist.

Thus, the first memoir goes far beyond a simple invective against social injustice: it aims to demonstrate that the individual contract between the capitalist and the worker masks a relationship of economic exploitation, that the *regime of property* is based on antagonism between labor and capital and inevitably brings the working class and the capitalist class into conflict. In such a system, profits are necessarily concentrated in the hands of the owners, and the workers, excluded from management and a fair share, receive only the means to survive for as long as capital employs them. The 1846 work *The System of Economic Contradictions, or The Philosophy of Poverty* continues this analysis by showing how the multiple contradictions of competitive capitalism materialize from this fundamental contradiction. Each "epoch" of the system—the division of labor, machinery, competition, monopoly, taxation—gives rise to new antinomies at each

---

6. *Qu'est-ce que la propriété ?, Premier mémoire* [What Is Property? First Memoir] (1840), Œuvres complètes [Complete Works], new ed., edited by C. Bouglé and H. Moysset (Paris: M. Rivière, 1926), 215. (Unless otherwise indicated, I cite Proudhon's works in this edition).

level: economic antinomies between the increase in production and the impossibility of consumption, enrichment and poverty, arbitrary power and worker subordination; moral antinomies between the improvement and deskilling of labor, and the specialization and degradation of workers. At the end of this economic and social description, the regime of property appears as a dialectical system of antagonistic terms in which no partial reform is possible and any minor change is doomed to failure by the series of contradictions, a regime that only a radical "transformation" of the economic organization can eliminate.

This critique of the economy goes hand in hand with a critique of the relations of authority and the political relations established by the regime of competitive capitalism. Indeed, private appropriation necessarily generates social relations of authority and subjugation. Centers of production, whether workshops or factories, are organized not according to the principles of equality and reciprocity but of hierarchy and exploitation. By becoming the master of labor, the capitalist also becomes the master of people: property gives its owner absolute power over those who can only survive by offering their labor. We will see that the expansion of industry and, for example, the development of machinery, exacerbate this strengthening of authority: as labor becomes mechanized, workers find themselves increasingly subjected to technology that they cannot control and that entrepreneurs manage exclusively and against workers' interests. Political power merely perpetuates and expresses these relations of domination that are rooted in the organization of the workplace. Possessing the economic powers that property confers, the capitalist class, which owns the collective force, takes direct control of the state and uses it to maintain and strengthen its privileges. Contrary to democratic mythology, the state is not in the hands of all of society. It is not the universality of citizens: it is monopolized by the class of proprietors as economic power is monopolized by capital; the counterpart of worker oppression is political despotism.

Finally, the regime of property corresponds to a set of myths and beliefs that directly contribute to the economic system and its defense. In his great work *De la justice dans la révolution et dans l'église* [Justice in the Revolution and in the Church] (1858), Proudhon considers the social significance of Christianity in the mid-nineteenth century, at that historical moment of conflict between capital and labor, the bourgeoisie and the proletariat, the idea of justice and the idea of God. The book's overall thesis is that Christianity became the theory, the *idea* of this unequal society based on the monopolization of collective forces. Of course, religion appears as a set of dogmas and truths, but every idea originates and is realized in society, and Christian dogmas, like any shared theory, are analogous to society as a whole. In affirming the supremacy of an absolute power that transcends human beings, religion expresses relations of social and political subordination. Through the dogmas of grace and faith, it symbolizes obedient attitudes and justifies the sacrifice of individual freedom to despotic power; in denying the autonomy of collective reason, it justifies opposition to social spontaneity. The church is both the *symbol* of social relations of domination and one of the forces opposed to the revolutionary movement.

The critique of capitalist society is thus conducted at all levels of social, economic, political, and ideological reality; the distinctions that we will be forced to make between economic sociology, political sociology, and sociology of knowledge must not make us forget that these levels of reality are dialectically linked and that any analysis that separates them can only be temporary.

In short, considered in its entirety, the regime of property causes injustice and inequality, and Proudhon can assert, moving from social critique to moral indignation, that modern society is the regime of immorality. In a society where theft and exploitation are the norm and the condition of wealth, we should expect a general decline in morality, especially among the privileged classes.

Opposed to this practice and this theory of private property are the socialist theories, the many factions especially active before 1848, and their revolutionary projects. But while Proudhon considers himself a socialist, it is not to indiscriminately endorse the theories formulated in the name of socialism but instead to discuss their value and denounce—sometimes amicably, more often vehemently—the dangers that some may entail. This critique would not apply directly to Marx's work, of which Proudhon could only have a limited knowledge, but rather to the works of French socialists and communists such as Henri de Saint-Simon, Charles Fourier, Louis Blanc, Pierre Leroux, François Villegardelle, and Étienne Cabet.

First and foremost, forms of utopian socialism must be condemned since, instead of relying on a critical observation of economic society, they aim to construct an imaginary society from nothing. If it is true that the objective of the revolution is to radically transform society and decisively shift its economic foundations, it is also true that despite the disorder of the regime of property, there are necessities and tendencies that lay the groundwork for socialist society: the division of labor, competition, and monopoly have their role and purpose, which must be discovered in order to build a society whose dynamism would be maintained. Utopian theories that aim to base socialism on moral principles, fraternity, or love are especially erroneous: the new society cannot be based on a feeling but can only be built on a new organization of labor that must be determined scientifically.

Proudhon also rejects theories that, under the guise of socialist language, in reality only respect the social relations of the regime of property. Thus, he reproaches the Saint-Simonians for proposing a hierarchical constitution that would create new inequalities and a new form of feudalism.[7] He reproaches the Fourierists for respecting capitalist property: reforming production, however profoundly, will not radically alter social relations unless it first aims to abolish private property in its capitalist form.[8]

---

7. Translator's note: Saint-Simon advocated a society based on a hierarchy of merit.

8. Translator's note: Charles Fourier suggested that production should be organized into communities called "phalanxes," fostering cooperation between rich and poor. He believed that poverty, rather than inequality, was the main cause of disorder in society.

The most acute debate is therefore between communism and
anarchist socialism, or more accurately between the theory of the
community and a socialist conception of society that Proudhon
would successively name *progressive association, mutuality*, and
industrial democracy. Despite its seemingly radical character, the
theory of the community remains, in his view, a utopia. Étienne
Cabet imagines, in the name of a universal brotherhood, a society in which goods would be pooled, in which the state would
be the sole owner and manager of the economy. The state would
make decisions on activities, distribute forces and people, set pay
and the share of personal consumption, and turn all citizens into
wage earners. The authority of the proprietor would therefore
be replaced by the authority of the collectivity, and the unique
individual would be replaced by the collective person in all social
functions: production, exchange, consumption, and education.

One of Proudhon's core objections to the theory of the community would be to deny the originality of such a conception.
Instead of seeking, beyond the routines of political economy, a
socialist society where worker responsibility and freedom would
be respected, in opposing the regime of property the theory of
the community merely re-creates its forms. Instead of destroying the concentration of monopolies, the community perpetuates monopoly in the form of the state; instead of breaking the
inherent despotism of the regime of property, the community
increases the power of the government by extending a police
state to all production. The central error of communitarian
theories is to expect from increased power, from an unlimited
extension of centralized powers, what can only be achieved by
the ever-renewed initiative of the workers. Proudhon would constantly criticize factions that call themselves socialist, and especially Louis Blanc, for what he believes to be their fundamental
illusion: to expect from a reform from above what can only be
obtained by a transformation of production relations at the base.
In his works and articles written during the February Revolution
(*Confessions of a Revolutionary*, 1849; *General Idea of the Revolution in
the Nineteenth Century*, 1851), Proudhon constantly warns against
this error of principle. Strengthening the government and

granting the state the greatest power of initiative merely reproduces the routines of an oppressive society and cannot prevent
the strengthening of despotism, the growth of bureaucracy, and
the multiplication of powers opposed to production.

Through this struggle against the regime of property and
state socialism, the objectives of Proudhon's social theory and
its determination to avoid the pitfalls of centralizing doctrines
become apparent. The challenge is to escape once and for all the
contradictions of which, despite appearances, community is only
one of the terms. Since in dialectical becoming community simply
opposes property, the goal will be to escape both by overcoming
the antagonisms they entail.[9] It is indeed a matter of organizing
labor, as the socialist factions say, but instead of establishing a
new oppressive institution, labor must organize itself; that is,
the producers must create new relations, seize the means of production, and constantly manage production and distribution.
Instead of stifling worker initiative via a new form of oppression,
the means of production and control of all organs of economic
society must be returned to them completely, their freedom
fully restored. Economically, achieving such an objective would
imply giving everything diverted by the regime of property back
to society and reestablishing the whole of economic society on a
principle completely opposed to propertarian and communistic
principles. Politically, the goal of the social revolution would not
be to strengthen the state but to subject it to economic society
and the initiative of the producers.

It would be the goal of *social science* to discover the laws of
the organization of labor and to serve as a theory for the establishment of a society freed from alienation and contradiction. It
would perform critical and positive functions for revolutionary
action. It would first and foremost denounce the anarchy, despotism, and injustice of capitalist society. Whereas political

---

9. Translator's note: In philosophy, "becoming" refers to the process
of change, development, or evolution. In Hegelian dialectics, "becoming" (*Werden*) describes the movement between being (*Sein*) and nothing
(*Nichts*).

economy merely validates economic practices without concern for the human consequences of the system or the political consequences of industrial anarchy, social science will show the social significance of the regime of production, thus exposing the oppression and exploitation it causes. Instead of justifying the existing order, social science will assume the role of defending the oppressed classes and denouncing privilege. It will also aim to destroy the utopias and illusions that constantly dissipate energies and delay the coming of industrial democracy; in particular, it will show the errors of the democrats who persist in believing that a political revolution will be a necessary and sufficient means of ensuring the coming of an egalitarian society, whereas only a general transformation of economic relations will ensure the conditions for social reconciliation. This science must not be an invention, but must be a discovery of the social and economic laws revealed in history, at least partially, despite the anarchy and uncertainty of social laws. Contrary to what the utopians assert, it would be futile to aim to organize labor as if nothing in the past had heralded its future constitution: even in disorder, labor organizes itself, and spontaneous initiatives such as worker associations already provide a model for industrial democracy.[10] More generally, economic and social life have their own laws that must be discovered beyond appearances and disturbances. Thus, founded on the knowledge of necessities and laws, social science would establish the theory of socialist society and the *idea* of a revolutionary practice. It would not only be a knowledge of economic needs, but also a theory of all society's features and, since the various forms of reality cannot be separated, a theory of labor, the state, freedom, ideas, and morality. In short, it would be a theory of justice, showing the gradual rise of just relations through the anarchy of economic forces and the potential for justice to be achieved in industrial democracy. At this level, social science becomes social theory and philosophy. Indeed, revolutionary theory does not merely propose a

10. "Labor organizes itself": *Système des contradictions économiques*, vol. I, 75.

model for an economic constitution, but it also opposes all the
old ideologies and resolves all the issues they had raised without
responding to them. Revolutionary philosophy, diametrically
opposed to religion, outlines an economic and political practice,
rethinks humanity's immanent logic, defines the aims of education, develops a morality of individual and social action, and
rethinks social becoming in its meaning and in its totality.

The sheer scope of Proudhonian thought requires us to iden-
tify what pertains to sociology among the problems encountered,
and to explain the significance carried by the strictly sociological studies. If we understand positivist sociology as referring to
the study of social phenomena externally to the object observed,
which would reject any interpretative theory and describe the
actions of people and groups beyond their intentions and indications, we cannot mistake Proudhon's sociology for a sociology
inspired by positivism.[11] Proudhon engages in sociological observation as a man of action to defend the downtrodden classes: his
whole oeuvre has a militant purpose and constitutes a passionate indictment of the society of private property and oppressive authority. Far from being reluctant to theorize, Proudhon
shows that human facts reveal a logic—a dialectical logic—and
that knowing this theory is indispensable in order to understand
history precisely: while humanity is logical, economic and social
facts undergo a movement analogous to the becoming of thought,
and using this method allows a complex reality to be discovered

---

11. Translator's note: The term "positivism" has become highly
contentious since the late nineteenth century, so much so that it argu-
ably contains little value as a signifier today. Auguste Comte's original
formulation of positivism is so markedly different from the "logical positivism" of the twentieth century that became the whipping boy of philosophy that Comte's position has ironically been referred to as closer to
"post-positivism," especially since he embeds his epistemology within history (see Robert C. Sharff's *Comte after Positivism,* (Cambridge University
Press, 1995). In this particular context, Ansart appears to be referring to
the formulation of positivism put forth by Emile Durkheim in *The Rules
of Sociological Method* (translated by W. D. Halls, Macmillan Press Ltd,
1895/1982, 53-59) which argues that sociology seeks to examine "social
facts" that exert a "pressure" or "external constraint" upon individuals.

that cannot be revealed by partial observation. Theory is indispensable for social knowledge because it is inherent to human action. However, the dialectical nature of human becoming does not imply that history is inevitable and that outcomes are entirely predictable: while in his early writings Proudhon tends to treat the revolution as the "fatal" result and the necessary sublation (*Aufheben*) of economic contradictions, after 1850 he tends to question the accuracy of the laws of social evolution, and he expects revolutionary transformation from working-class initiative, action, and practice. Proudhonian sociology is not positivist in its intentions, methods, or conclusions.[12]

Proudhon's sociology is established at the levels of critique, social theory, and political theory. The critique of capitalism is simultaneously a critique of capitalist society: the study of contradictions highlights the negative consequences of the economic system and the confrontation that it provokes between social classes. Capitalism cannot be considered only as a set of processes and technologies for the production and circulation of wealth, but it is also a socioeconomic system in which class relations form the basis of economic laws and consistently result from production and distribution practices. Thus, Proudhon's fierce denunciation of injustice and poverty stems from a set of sociological observations on classes, on the action of individuals and groups, and on the social evolution of the system. The economic critique cannot be separated from a sociological reading, since the purpose of the critique is to show that contradictions of a seemingly economic nature are in reality social contradictions in which there is necessarily a confrontation between the classes holding capital and labor, respectively. Similarly, the critique of the state is less a political critique than a social critique of

---

12. Translator's note: It is worth noting that Proudhon once referred to himself as a positivist in a letter to Michelet in 1855. When Proudhon exchanged letters with Comte in 1852, he told Comte there was "a whole side of positivism that escapes you, something that can affect you, since the positive, like nature and humanity, is infinity." Quoted in Mary Pickering, *Auguste Comte: An Intellectual Biography*, vol. 3 (Cambridge: Cambridge University Press, 2009), 88.

political life: the goal is neither to analyze constitutional forms, nor to define the best possible government, but to consider the political structures within society as a whole, to link political domination with economic domination, and to analyze their causalities and dialectics. Denouncing authority, the concentration of power, and bureaucracy and collusion among the various dominant forces gives rise to sociological analyses, linking powers to the various social forces present. Similarly, the critique of ideologies, especially Christianity, not only concerns the truth or error of these intellectual theories but also links these systems with social practice to show that a theory constitutes the *idea* of a society and that, for example, a representation of sacred hierarchies is analogous to a society torn apart by oppression. The entire critical portion of Proudhon's work, whether it applies to economic society before 1848, to the February Revolution, or to society in the Second Empire, thus provides a sociological description of French society around the mid-nineteenth century.

But partial observations cannot reveal the entire social structure: only a general theory of society, whether it is called serial dialectics, dialectics, or even theory of equilibrium, will allow us to understand the conflicts of society as a whole. Partial empirical studies, such as Le Play's surveys of working-class family budgets, can provide valuable lessons, but they are interpreted differently by different schools and may equally serve as instruments for politically conservative practices. Conversely, dialectical theory will force us to understand the development of capitalist society, reconsider the system's contradictions, and thus reveal the necessity or urgency of their disappearance. Of course, theory cannot be deduced directly from partial observation, and it is characteristic of the defenders of the status quo to reject theory and isolate the terms in order to avoid the present being called into question. Knowledge of theory requires the use of logic and philosophical knowledge. But theory nevertheless expresses the very form of social reality: dialectics is not only the necessary movement of reason but is simultaneously the constant form of social activity. Thus, one cannot separate denunciatory critique, which makes more careful use of partial sociological data, from theory, which gives it meaning. Critique will constantly be linked to theory: theory will guide research and show the relations between apparently distinct facts; conversely, by sketching the outlines of a non-antagonistic society, theory will serve as an argument for critique.

Finally, this general sociology is the basis for the development of economic and political theory, for the formulation of the revolutionary project. At this level, there is an explicit separation between sociology and doctrine, between observation and the revolutionary message, but the role of social science would be precisely to erase this separation as much as possible. Whereas the utopians introduce a discontinuity between social science and political reform, revolutionary science would create a dialectical continuity between theory and practice, between the consciousness of an anarchic past and the idea of a balanced society. Indeed, all aspects of Proudhon's revolutionary project hinge on a knowledge of the social. As we will need to analyze in greater detail, the theory of worker appropriation of the management of economic society is based on the analysis of collective force. It is because the products are exclusively created by labor, by the organized efforts of people, that the product must return in its entirety to the real producers; it is because labor is social that it must be socialized. The theory of industrial democracy, of the decentralization of responsibilities and decisions, is based on a pluralist reading of society. It is because vitality and social dynamism are necessarily linked with the plurality of centers of production, and immobility with authoritarian centralization, that the totalitarianism of monopoly must be broken and relative autonomy returned to producer groups. The antistate and federalist theory is based on a set of social analyses showing the necessarily oppressive and conservative character of the centralized state, even if it is democratic. The economic-political theory will in turn clarify the sociological theory, just as deduction allows a better understanding of the principles; and while the study of Proudhon's sociology does not require a detailed exposition of his theories, it will nevertheless be useful to summarize their main points here.

There is thus a constant sociological inspiration in this great body of work. Of course, there is more to this work than social investigation. Proudhon could more clearly be remembered as an economist, historian of ideas and religions, art critic, or theorist. However, the perception of social structures and transformations is the reference point for these many works and helps shed light on their unity. Indeed, the partial studies, analyses, and theories always point to a general conception of social reality that must now be explained: it will dialectically define the object of social science and the method for studying it.

The validity and necessity of social science is based on the fact that society constitutes a real being, the *collective being*, which possesses specific features. *Society* is not an abstract word used to designate an aggregation or collection of distinct individuals: society is a living being, with particular features and laws whose originality must be recognized. Expressing this principle of the reality of the collective being as early as 1840, Proudhon essentially emphasizes two general aspects that seem inseparable to him: the vitality of the collective and the existence of a specific mode of consciousness. Without us mistaking the social being for a biological reality, society can be provisionally compared to an organism whose parts are united by constant relations and exchanges. It will be the task of social science to study the nature of this solidarity that unites the different members of the collective being, and it will be seen that its essential modality is the economic relation of exchange. We will see that, through exchange between producers and groups of producers, a social relation is established that emerges directly from the action of the participants but at the same time exceeds individuals through the solidarity it instills. But Proudhon immediately adds that the collective being is also endowed with will and reason, although these terms cannot be precisely compared to individual faculties. The living relations that are constantly being made and transformed between members of a group cannot be reduced to mechanical or material relations that a natural science could account for. Despite social divisions and antagonisms, a unity of productive activities occurs, expressing a common will, one that is real but that may not be recognized by the members of the collectivity. Similarly, we will need to develop Proudhon's thesis that the encounter and conflict of individual reasons and desires gives rise to a common reason or *collective reason* that is fundamentally heterogeneous to individual reason, although it can only emerge from the free confrontation of individuals.

Thus, the collective being exceeds the individual in essence, not only by the extent of its power and the sum of the individual contributions. By insisting on the reality of the collective, Proudhon aims to emphasize the essential heterogeneity of the social in relation to the individual. This heterogeneity emerges in particular in the reality of the collective force and in the fundamental discontinuity of this force in relation to individual effort. Indeed, in productive activity, individual forces spontaneously organize and divide equally in shared work. But this combination and division give rise to a power, a force, that is essentially different from the simple sum of individual efforts. The work produced by an organized workplace, by a group of people, is not only greater than the sum of the individual tasks but also fundamentally irreducible to them. This means that social action itself constitutes a specific type of reality of which we cannot gain knowledge solely by considering individual activity. In labor, humans participate in a task whose general meaning they can understand if the antagonisms are suppressed but that essentially transcends the individual.

The significance of these preliminary definitions emerges in the polemical conclusions that Proudhon draws from them. In repeating that the collective being has specific laws that must be recognized, he aims to show that one cannot think about the social solely in terms of individual activity or attribute collective production to individual contributions. From this definition, Proudhon states his intention to use social science to criticize individualism and economic liberalism: in demonstrating that the productive act is a collective act, he aims to show that no individual can claim a privileged share; in demonstrating that the product is fundamentally heterogeneous to the various individual contributions, he aims to show that production cannot belong to an individual but by definition belongs to all. This definition of collective force is intended to serve as an argument against the monopolization of production by one individual and, for example, by the capitalist. In his critique of the regime of property, Proudhon aims to demonstrate that capital is not productive by itself, that production is the fruit of the workers alone, and therefore that profit is a fraudulent monopolization. But more generally he will show that no individual contribution, even from the inventor or the genius, can claim a privileged share of production. All individuals who participate socially in production and consumption are immediately in debt to a collective action that they cannot claim to control or monopolize. Thus, social science implies socialist conclusions.

Similarly, this recognition of the collective being as a specific being immediately leads to a critique of the theories that Proudhon terms theories of transcendence: religions and statisms. He criticizes these doctrines for seeking principles of organization outside of social activity, as if society were to be organized from the outside by transcendent norms. In the religious tradition, it is assumed that truth and law are given to society by divine word, by revelation. In all statist theories, whether monarchist or democratic, it is assumed that order comes to the social through external discipline, based on the will of a ruler or government. Conversely, by demonstrating that society has a life of its own, that labor is organized according to its immanent needs and its own necessities, that groups form and divide according to their internal spontaneity, and that knowledge and beliefs spring from collective practice, Proudhon aims to show that all the doctrines of transcendence invert real relations and attribute the power to create social reality to something that is only the work of humans. Proudhon thus proposes a radical epistemological inversion: instead of seeking the meaning or truth of religions and political constitutions, one should examine the creative dynamism of society and understand the movement by which a society gives itself a religion or creates a state for itself. We must first highlight why a society causes a power to emerge from itself which it believes superior, show the conditions that make this alienation possible, and then examine the consequences of this creation which is at the same time an "externalization." The description of social reality as a specific reality will then help provide a basis for the critique of alienation.

This definition of social reality immediately raises the problem of the relations between the individual and the social, as well as between subgroups and the whole. This problem is all the more acute in the Proudhonian problematic, since sociological concepts seem to lead to a reduction of the individual and since Proudhon is nevertheless eager to stress that there is no social activity except through individual action and innovation. The concepts of collective force, social laws, and collective reason highlight the fundamental gap between individual action and social production, between private reason and collective reason. In the case of collective reason, Proudhon will show that the individual will, infinite in its demands and despotic by nature, is limited and, as it were, negated by social confrontation. One could therefore decide on a theoretical subordination of the individual to the collective and, in practice, a justification for totalitarianism. But these conclusions are diametrically opposed to Proudhon's. For him, this vitality of the social is in no way comparable to the life of a biological organism whose parts are integrated into a group and dominated by the whole. On the contrary, the mobility and full vitality of the social are ensured only by the liberation, and even the confrontation, of individual activities. Concluding his critique of theories of transcendence, Proudhon refuses to make society something that would transcend and impose itself on individuals but instead aims to show that the collective constantly reconstitutes itself solely on the basis of relations forged between individuals and groups. In particular, we will see that he refuses to eliminate social antagonisms and especially economic antagonisms from practice, believing that clashes of interests directly contribute to social dynamism, provided that they take place within an egalitarian society. The collective force should therefore not be seen as an objective power imposed on individuals, but its creative movement, rooted in the dynamic relationships established between individuals and groups, should be reconsidered: the collective force emerges from labor, from the forms of cooperation that producers and associations of producers constantly reproduce. Similarly, the collective reason cannot be taken for an established reason, a dogma that could assume a completely external relationship to individuals: collective reason is, in its conclusions, different and potentially opposed to private reason, but it is only created and modified through dialogue and the confrontation of reasons. It can only arise from these clashes, these conflicts, and thus from the full expression of individuals.

While society is a specific reality, a real being, it is thus neither a complete being with permanent characteristics, nor a material reality of which individuals are only a part, nor a hierarchical organism. In order to understand it, a method specific to social science must therefore be used that underlines how terms can oppose and contradict one another without destroying one another, how a reality is transformed by its own antagonisms, and how a being can be both practice and reason, reality and logic. Proudhon, like Marx, intended to explain this dialectical logic but did not find the time to do so; however, his two works in 1843 and 1846 contain the outlines, and his concrete analyses provide several examples.[13]

Recognizing the dialectical character of social reality means first and foremost perceiving its distinct elements. One of Proudhon's main concerns is to stress the extreme diversity of social elements and to link this plurality to social change, showing that dynamism depends on maintaining relative differences and independences. For example, in studying competition between producers and centers of production, he seeks to show that rivalries, despite the harm they cause in the regime of capitalist appropriation, are fundamentally beneficial and ensure economic vitality. In particular, he reproaches communist theories for ignoring this essential aspect of social reality and for risking, through a destruction of differences, a slowdown in activities. In laying out a proposal for mutualist socialism, he tries to describe

---

13. *De la création de l'ordre dans l'humanité* [The Creation of Order in Humanity] and *Système des contradictions économiques*.

an economy in which the plurality of groups would be respected and their independence ensured within a system of contracts and balances. While he emphasizes the need to re-create total equality between producers, it is without mistaking equality for identity, convinced on the contrary that diversity among centers of production and the preservation of originality are guarantors of freedom and conditions for vitality.

Proudhon distinguishes, at least provisionally, four essential "faces" or "movements" in social activity: productive labor, circulation of wealth, social rules, and collective reason.[14] Labor is the essential dynamic force, the "plastic force" of society; the division of labor and the coordination of roles determine the general relations between groups, and changes in modes of production will necessarily lead to a change in social relations. Exchange and distribution, the credit system, and capital formation directly contribute to activity as a whole, and we will see that a radical modification of credit, if implemented in full, could destroy the foundations of the capitalist economy. Legal regulations and especially economic laws describe the organization of industry and establish the conditions under which it operates. Finally, collective reason, ideas, which the conception of education and the orientation of science in particular depend on, lead to the formation of collective attitudes favorable or unfavorable to social transformations. All these components and movements mutually engender one another, and their close combination produces an organized system in which the various elements respond to the whole. This constant correspondence between the part and the whole will reveal a reciprocal relationship between the element and the general organization and allow the whole social arrangement to be described from different "points of view." Thus, to study property is to study an economic relation, but it is also to discover class relations, the political system, legislation, and ultimately an entire social philosophy within a simple element; similarly, modern society can be said to be a regime of property, a political system, or an ideology. Each of

---

14. *De la création de l'ordre*, 421–24.

these elements can be chosen as a point of view to describe the arrangement as a whole.

Secondly, the dialectical method requires us to emphasize the inseparability of the recognized terms, their independence, and the nature of their reciprocal relationship. In capitalist society, use value and exchange value, division of labor and machinery, and competition and monopoly are in constant opposition, an internal relation such that one term cannot exist without its opposite or transform without modifying it. At the level of society as a whole, all terms, relationships, and related units form a system: all the elements are linked, and all the social powers in perpetual struggle constitute a combined unit. The contradictions of the capitalist system are all integrated within a system in which all particular actions and dialectics play a part. The concept of the organism, chosen to emphasize this unity of the social, can only be understood in a nonbiological sense. Society is not an organism in which hierarchical centers would direct social activity: the action of all the elements ensures the life and vitality of the collectivity. In place of the hierarchical vision of conservative thought, Proudhon substitutes a horizontal vision of dialectics in which all dialectics participate in a common activity according to their diverse functions. Moreover, society is not organic: it is both united and divided, and in the case of capitalist society the contradictions are so strong that they prepare the terrain for the system's disintegration. Society must not even seek complete unification, and economic and political theory will confirm that social activity and freedom depend on maintaining divisions.

In *The System of Economic Contradictions*, Proudhon states his intention to show that all fundamental economic relations are relations of contradiction in which the terms are both incompatible and necessarily linked. The division of labor and machinery, and competition and monopoly, are opposed to one another, tend to destroy one another, and are at the same time dependent on one another; use value and exchange value are opposed in such a way that the growth of one is the decline of the other, but they cannot exist separately. However, the pursuit of concrete analyses leads Proudhon to abandon the simplifying nature of his stated method: studying the divergent consequences of the same economic activity reveals dialectics not envisaged in the initial system. Thus, the division of labor entails, on the one hand, worker progression in qualifications and, on the other hand, worker regression due to the fragmented nature of the work; it prepares both the equality of conditions and the failure of this equality. These antagonisms are not contradictions, despite the stated methodology, but refer to complementary relations within a system that renders them necessary. Worker progression and regression are not directly related but simply two opposite and complementary consequences of the same economic principle. Hence, under the pressure of concrete analyses, the methodology is enriched with new dialectical procedures, and Hegelian formulations are abandoned.

The originality of Proudhon's method lies in particular in his critique of the notion of sublation and in the abandonment of Hegelian syntheses. According to the methodology provisionally laid out in *The System of Economic Contradictions*, the exacerbation of a contradiction would necessarily entail its sublation in a superior term that would reconcile the antagonisms by overcoming them. The contradiction of use value and exchange value, for example, would entail its sublation in the synthesis of "constituted" value. But here too progress in his analyses leads Proudhon to overcome the dogmatism of the initial formulas: studying the antagonisms and the economic role of each term leads him to doubt the possibility of a synthesis in which the antagonism would be suppressed. Competition and monopoly are two economic principles that, in the anarchic regime of production, tend to negate and destroy one another, but one cannot imagine a system that would make them disappear: these principles are inherent, in different forms, to any system of production. The problem is therefore not to seek a principle whereby the terms of production would be negated but rather to find a balance between the terms, a superior relationship in which the form of the terms would be modified but their content preserved. *Sublation* no longer means the negation of the terms but rather

their balance, their reconciliation, in a system in which the principles would be both preserved and transformed. Therefore, the
term *contradiction* is not the most accurate to describe the antagonisms, in that it may suggest the existence of a principle superior
to the opposed terms. The terms are not contradictory; rather,
they are antinomic, and this antagonistic relation cannot entirely
be overcome. Furthermore, in Hegelian contradiction, thesis and
antithesis arise successively, the antithesis being the productive
negation that questions the thesis and constrains its movement.
In Proudhon's antinomy, the two terms are simultaneous and
equally necessary: competition and monopoly cannot disappear
in favor of a distinct synthesis; they can only counteract and balance, either with one another or with other antinomies. In other
words, "the antinomy does not resolve itself," but is transformed
by losing its destructive character.[15] According to Proudhon,
this reconciliation would in no way constitute a middle ground
between excesses, nor would it constitute eclecticism. It would
instead inaugurate a new social and economic model that would
destroy discord but preserve the movement ensured by the
antinomies.

Antinomy is in fact the very principle of life and change. It is
the conflict between terms and the multiplicity of antagonisms
that achieve society's permanent vitality. Contrary to the conservative theory of the permanence of social hierarchies, Proudhon
stresses that all social phenomena are in constant transformation,
that legal, political, and ideological forms are engaged in becoming and are susceptible to revolutionary changes. However, this
does not mean that old relations cannot be extended across
successive societies. Certain antinomies, those of authority and
liberty, and the mechanical and the spontaneous, have such a
general character that they can be understood as inherent in society. Conversely, others—the antinomy of capital and labor, of the
bourgeoisie and the proletariat—have a purely historical character and will be overcome in a reconciled society. The dialectic is
thus both a science of change and a science of continuity: it must

---

15. *De la justice dans la révolution et dans l'église*, 3rd étude, vol. 2, 155.

show what must disappear once and for all in the social revolution and what should continue in new forms, integrated within a different system.

Finally, the possibility of thinking of social reality as a dialectical whole, as a totality of antagonisms, exchanges, or balances, indicates the existence of a particular relationship between idea and reality, between reason and social practice. Indeed, a social relationship such as exchange or the division of labor arises both as a practical reality and as a particular logic: exchange is a material activity, a reality, but it can also be expressed as a mathematical "equation," a set of symbolic relationships. Not only is it possible to describe reality in language, but the logical relationship must also be held as immanent in practice: the social act is both the reality and the logical form. In constituting itself in balance or antagonism, social reality is created simultaneously in its reality and in its ideality, and it will be possible to reconsider the entire economic system as a logical system, provided that traditional logic is abandoned and the plurality of dialectics is recognized. Thus, social reality assumes a unique character that science must define precisely. On the one hand, it appears as a reality that imposes itself on the subject and that the mind cannot transform arbitrarily, but it cannot be reduced to a chaos of material forces that reason must study as an object. On the other hand, it is a logical system, in other words an *idea*, since contradiction, antagonism, balance, and equality are rational relationships, but society cannot be reduced to a system of representations. Hence the seemingly contradictory possibility of provisionally using vocabularies that evoke materialistic or idealistic philosophies. Some passages treat labor and the organization of production as a force, the predominant force, while others treat society as an idea, as if the unity of the social fabric were of an intellectual nature. Not all of Proudhon's utterances on this subject are perfectly clear, as we will see, and some, when taken out of context, seem to derive from an intellectualist theory. However, his work tends to define a dialectical conception that treats social organization as a specific type of being: society is indeed a reality, as shown by the permanence of relations of solidarity or the creation of collective

forces, but it is also an idea, since social relations reproduce a
logic whose structures are analogous to those of reason.

In short, social reality is "ideo-realist"; the goal of social
science is at the same time to rethink social activities, contradictions and their development, and the logical system that
each society constitutes.[16] This theory of social reality will allow
Proudhon to lay the foundations for a sociology of knowledge: if
a society constitutes a logical whole, it may give rise to an ideological system, a mythology, a religion whose critique will show
that it corresponds to a full expression of that society. Thus, the
critique of religion will reveal an analogy between the content of
religious beliefs and the nature of social relations and, in capitalism, a reciprocal relationship of expression and justification
between unequal economic relationships and the content of
Christian dogmas. The theory of the identity of the real and the
ideal, which we will need to clarify, will not only enable us to discover the sites where ideologies are created in society but also to
perceive an image of society in them and thus to restore relative
truth to them.

---

16. "Ideo-realist": *De la création de l'ordre*, 286n.

CHAPTER TWO

Economic Sociology

1. Critique of Property

It is through a violent denunciation of private property that Proudhon approaches his critique of the capitalist economy. Property is indeed, as the conservative theorists claim, the basis of society and the most important issue of the social problem, but it is not the foundation for a reconciled society. On the contrary, it is the foundation that is unjustifiable in theory and that leads to an unequal and contradictory society in practice. To denounce private property is to criticize society as a whole, its economic foundations and its rational justifications.[1]

What Is Property? proposes to demonstrate that individual and absolute property as defined by Napoleonic law is irrational, unjust, and "impossible" since it is a usurpation, a *theft*, carried out by capital at the expense of labor. By the term *property*, Proudhon does not mean the simple fact whereby a person uses and is responsible for an asset, but the economic fact whereby property becomes a creator of interest, a capital that is the source of all forms of aubaine. It is therefore necessary to strictly distinguish the terms *possession* and *property* in the particular sense that they have in Proudhon's language. *Possession* designates the mere fact of being responsible for and managing a property, or an instrument of production, of deriving a usufruct from it corresponding to labor supplied, without this possession implying

---

1. "The whole social question is summed up for us in property." *Banque d'échange* [Bank of Exchange], vol. 6 (Paris: Lacroix, 1848), 170.

either an absolute right of ownership or the possibility of converting these assets into interest-producing capital. *Property*, on the contrary, implies the absolute right to use and abuse regardless of any social consideration, and the possibility of using an asset to obtain a profit, rent, or interest—in other words, an aubaine. By this ambiguous term *property*, Proudhon is thus referring to land, financial and industrial capital: any wealth that may produce interest in the regime of property, regardless of how active or idle the proprietor is.[2] This form of property, shared unequally among the members of society, cannot be justified by rational arguments, and Proudhon, who here recalls Rousseau's critiques, turns the arguments of the theorists of property on the naturalness of this right against them. If property were a natural right inherent in every individual, all citizens should be proprietors since they legally have equality in rights and liberty. In reality, property is only a matter of fact; it is based on a primitive occupation or monopolization, and no theory can find a rational justification for it.

But a true denunciation of property must occur at the level of economic and social explanations, not at the level of principles. Proudhon bases his critique of the regime of property on an interpretation of social relations of production and on a theory of productive society. If a society were merely an aggregation of isolated individuals, joined together only by a political power or by a series of private contracts, monopolization of wealth might spark the indignation of the egalitarian moralist, but it would not, in fact, be theft. For theft to occur, a value must be produced that is not rendered to its true authors. It must be shown that all production is collective production, that the workers are its true authors, that the productivity of capital is only a myth, and that the capitalist is monopolizing a value that he has not produced. This is what the theory of collective force will show.

In the regime of property, it is assumed that the share of labor supplied by the worker is fairly rewarded by paying wages,

---

2. "Property is the right of aubaine; that is, the power to produce without labor." *Qu'est-ce que la propriété ?*, 245.

that labor and production correspond to the sum of individual efforts and thus that paying individual wages adequately compensates labor. However, productive activity is not an individual activity, and cooperation in tasks is not equivalent to the sum of individual efforts. The union of individual efforts in a coherent and convergent organization generates a production that fundamentally exceeds the simple numerical total of hours of labor supplied. Two hundred workers employed on the same day according to the principles of division and organization of labor create a product that is qualitatively and quantitatively incommensurable with what a single worker could produce over two hundred days. This is because the coherent union of efforts generates an "immense force," the source of social production: the collective force.[3] The fundamental discrepancy between the creative possibilities of isolated individuals and those of workers joined together in a common task shows that work is a collective act and that the collective force is a specific reality that exceeds the individual and the sum of individuals. This collective force shows the reality of the social, whereby organization and coherent division correspond to a specific mode of being.

But for the capitalist, paying two hundred days for the same worker and paying two hundred workers working together during a single day would entail the same costs, even though in the first case no profit would be made. This discrepancy is what causes the emergence of the theft performed by capital. The proprietor pays each worker as if they had merely completed an individual task, and in this conception wages are set based on the worker's basic needs for food and upkeep. But the proprietor does not pay for the collective force directly generated by the union of efforts and instead retains the entire product of this force. This discrepancy between the sums paid to workers and their collective production explains capitalist profit. Indeed, production cannot be understood as the consequence of capital, but is exclusively the work of labor and the assembled producers. A theft therefore occurs, since the capitalist monopolizes the collective

---

3. Ibid., 215.

force which comes only from the cooperation of the workers; he monopolizes their production, of which they are the sole authors and should therefore be the sole beneficiaries. The source of the inequality that enriches the capitalist and exploits the worker lies in this theft, this *accounting error* between owner and employee:[4] while the worker will receive only an average wage equal to their daily consumption and will not be guaranteed job security, the capitalist accumulates the profits of collective labor and thus secures his power and independence.

However, this notion of theft does not exhaust Proudhon's analyses on the social characteristics of property. Proudhon could indeed conclude from the fact that property is theft that it must be completely abolished, but he would not stop protesting against such an interpretation of his thought: from the unjust nature of property he would not decide on general dispossession but instead on its subordination in a new economic system. Indeed, while property, in its capitalist form, is the source of class division and worker exploitation, it is important to emphasize that in the past it fulfilled important social functions and that it alone made material development possible. Property relations enabled a more intimate union of people with their goods, the economic constitution of the family and the creation of rent, all functions that emerged in particular in the case of land property, which served as a first model for subsequent appropriations. Humans' mastery of the earth invigorated their energies and stimulated their perseverance and determination to transform what they considered part of themselves; it developed an organic relationship between humans and their possessions and resulted in subordinates becoming attached to the common heritage and its protection. Similarly, property secured the family's economic foundations and guaranteed its security through inheritance.[5] Finally, it enabled economic rent, which allowed

4. "It is in this, above all things, that what has been fitly named exploitation of man by man consists." Ibid., 216.

5. "It is above all in the family that the deep meaning of property is discovered." *Système des contradictions*, vol. 2, 196.

the owner to accumulate surpluses used to increase resources for production: whatever injustice this regime may have caused, the creation of economic rent allowed the proprietor to accumulate in order to boost production. The notion of theft must therefore be subjected to a dialectic: it appears as one aspect of the problem, which must not hide the complexity of its economic and social functions. But economic and social development has caused property to become corrupted: the old functions of property were fully realized in the old French agrarian economy, but the expansion of industry and trade have disrupted the limits of the old production and destroyed the functions previously fulfilled by property; moreover, the collapse of feudal relations has removed the obstacles that prevented monopolies from developing. Indeed, in the regime of property freed from the limits of feudalism, a nonreciprocal relationship was established between the interests of the proprietor and the public interest. In agriculture, for example, where crop rationalization, land consolidation, and the implementation of public works would be in the general interest, landowners prevent any improvements since they have no immediate interest in accepting such encroachments on their rights. Economic rent, which was previously used to increase production capabilities, becomes purely a means of enjoyment for idle owners.[6] In industry, production does not serve consumers but is organized solely with the goal of accumulating profit: the industrialist is not concerned about the quality of the product or the social risks of their production but will choose to manufacture and temporarily overproduce goods if this suits his immediate interests, without worrying about the suffering that these practices may cause for the disadvantaged classes. Property, as defined in individualistic law, breaks social relations and separates people from each other:[7] human relations between producer and consumer, doctor and patient, lawyer and client, and writer and reader are replaced by relations of money and personal

6. "Thus, property becomes an obstacle to labor and wealth, an obstacle to the social economy." Ibid., 214.
7. "Thus property separates man from man." Ibid., 220.

interest. Functions, talents, and science are transformed into market values, objects to be sold and traded. The unsociability of property is no less great when monopolies and large industrial companies are established. Large companies seeking the same goal of profit accumulation are even more fearsome than small ones, less inclined to kindness, and more inflexible in their pursuit of profit.

Thus, property creates a fundamental unsociability in economic relations and a set of contradictions in production and consumption. However, whatever its importance, property does not constitute the whole economic system.[8] It establishes a general relationship of theft, exploitation, and despotism, but it is only one aspect of a whole system made up of a set of contradictions.

2. The System of Contradictions

Going beyond the limited problem of property, Proudhon proposes to demonstrate in his 1846 work *The System of Economic Contradictions, or The Philosophy of Poverty* that the whole economic system is made up of antagonistic terms and forces, and that these contradictions tear economic society apart and cause working-class poverty and subordination. Indeed, while Proudhon uses the expression *economic contradiction* to specify that he intends to study conflicts concerning labor and the production and circulation of wealth, the meaning he gives this expression has more to do with socioeconomics or economic sociology than with political economy. Contradiction does not arise from a system whose means and ends exclusively concern production and circulation but rather from a totality whose terms are in conflict. The opposition of capital and labor can be

---

8. Property "does not constitute the whole system. It lives in an organized milieu, surrounded by a certain number of corresponding functions and special institutions . . . which, consequently, it must reckon with." *Théorie de la propriété* [Theory of Property] (Paris: Lacroix, 1866), 176–77.

described in economic terms, but it reflects the general division of society between proprietors and non-proprietors, bourgeoisie and proletariat. In his descriptions, Proudhon constantly moves from economic analysis, such as analysis of value or taxation, to analysis of the underlying antagonisms and social relations. He intends to denounce classical political economy by demonstrating that it masks the human consequences of the regime of property, but in doing so he reconsiders economics in terms of its position in society by showing the social confrontation that lies behind economic confrontation. Sometimes the analysis focuses on particular technical or financial problems, on the division of labor or on the balance of trade, and sometimes it relates these partial phenomena to the objectives of society as a whole and its conflicts. The book's goal is less to list the system of economic contradictions than to study the social system of contradictions and thus to denounce it, to demonstrate that the regime of property inevitably brings the social classes into conflict and causes the monopolization of wealth, poverty, theft, and exploitation.

Contradictions exist at two levels: between different economic terms or "epochs" and within each term considered. After an initial discussion of the theory of value, Proudhon distinguishes ten successive epochs: division of labor, machinery, competition, monopoly, taxation, balance of trade, credit, property, community, and population. At the level of general contradictions, each term is in antagonism with the preceding term: thus, the introduction of machinery contradicts the division of labor, while monopoly is dialectically opposed to competition. Marx did not fail to notice the artificial nature of some of these dialectics: for example, he notes that machinery, rather than reducing the division of labor, may instead cause it.[9] And, indeed, the successive placement of these ten "epochs" and some of the contradictions arise more from concern for logical exposition than from fidelity to observation. However, Proudhon's methodology, however debatable it may be in this work, allows the fundamental

---

9. Karl Marx, *Misère de la philosophie* [The Poverty of Philosophy] (Paris: Costes, 1960), 166-67.

contradictions of competitive capitalism to be shown in stark
relief. Thus, the dialectic of competition and monopoly underlines the need for antagonism between the two terms: each term
fulfills necessary functions but must be set against its opposite. In
the regime of property, competition is as essential to production
as the division of labor, which it corresponds to and confirms; it
makes it possible to establish value and ensures the spontaneous
dynamism of the economy through the freedom and confrontation of producers. The 1789 Revolution, by enabling free competition, only fulfilled one useful requirement of the social economy.
But this freedom contains its own destruction due to the conflicts
and ills it causes. It inherently implies monopolization, its opposite, since each center of production tends to become an exclusive producer: faced with the difficulties and losses generated by
competition, capitalists inevitably tend to combine forces. But by
giving industrial feudalism absolute power over wealth and labor,
the creation of monopolies inevitably leads to price increases and
higher unemployment. The economic system thus finds itself
torn between two equally necessary antagonistic principles whose
contradiction cannot be resolved in the regime of property: the
implementation of competition alone is just as impossible as the
total dissolution of conflicts within an exclusive monopoly. This
results in a permanent conflict between the two principles, bringing economic and social destruction.

It is above all the study of the contradictions inherent in each
term, each "epoch," that attracts Proudhon's attention and highlights the negative consequences of the economic system. Each
economic principle yields two types of socially opposite consequences—one positive and the other destructive—and Proudhon
tries to demonstrate that the proprietary system inevitably carries these contradictions within itself, which no partial remedy,
no "palliative," can overcome. Thus, the division of labor is a
prerequisite for increased production: the segregation of tasks
allows an increase in production that is disproportional to individual production. Furthermore, specialization promotes professional progression and seems to promote personal creativity.
Socially, by integrating each worker within a collective activity,

it lays the groundwork for equal conditions. However, contrary to this primary purpose, the division of labor simultaneously produces the opposite consequences.[10] By restricting labor to a segregated activity, division leads to professional regression, reducing humans to purely mechanical activity and degrading workers. Artisans, masters of their tools and knowledge, give way to unqualified workers. This degradation of labor leads to longer working days and a relative fall in wages, since the employer cannot avoid employing unqualified workers for lower wages. The expansion of the division of labor tends to create a proletariat much more subordinated to owners than qualified workers were. Thus the division of labor, intended to lead to economic development and progress, in fact results in worker enslavement and poverty; more precisely, it produces both of these consequences and makes poverty the very consequence of labor. Not only is this division a source of advantages and disadvantages that economists have highlighted, but it is also in itself a contradictory law, an *antinomy* whose inverse terms tend to destroy each other.[11] It reveals an inevitable relationship in industrial development between the goals pursued and their negation, the creation of things and human regression, and wealth and poverty. The same contradiction can be found in different forms with the development of machinery. Machinery symbolizes human freedom and power over things. It expresses both creative intelligence and mastery over things. It should have the immediate effect of reducing labor effort and removing obstacles to the conquest of nature. In reality, the development of machinery has the effect

---

10. "Division, in the absence of which there is no progress, no wealth, no equality, subordinates the workingman, and renders intelligence useless, wealth harmful, and equality impossible." *Système des contradictions*, vol. 1, 138–39.

11. "We cannot fail to recognize in the division of labor, as a general fact and as a cause, all the characteristics of a law; but as this law governs two orders of phenomena radically opposite and destructive of each other, it must be confessed also that this law is of a sort unknown in the exact sciences,—that it is, strange to say, a contradictory law, a counter-law, an antinomy." Ibid., 140.

of continuing the worker degradation initiated by the division of labor; the greater the proliferation of machines, the more they must be served by a growing number of operators and "degraded workers:" machinery tends to degrade workers by reducing them from the rank of artisans to the role of operators.[12] In doing so, it increases worker subordination by causing industrial companies to expand: in the artisan's workshop, the relations established between producers were relatively egalitarian, and artisans treated each other equally as partners. With the rise of machinery and the expansion of companies, these egalitarian relations completely disappeared; the power of entrepreneurs grew as the independence of equal partners disappeared. Regressing from the rank of equal partner to employee, the worker loses any possibility of resisting an infinitely superior force. Machinery establishes a despotic relationship between human and machine and at the same time a hierarchical relationship between the industrialist and the workers: it establishes a type of relation that will serve as a model and support for political relations of subordination. Moreover, although the development of machinery is intended to increase production and therefore amplify social wealth, in reality it supports and extends poverty through unemployment. Every mechanical development leads to the elimination of some workers and the reduction of jobs; in the face of these difficulties, the economists respond that these new inventions will offer new opportunities for work, but this compensation is only made slowly, whereas the elimination of jobs is immediate and constant, thereby maintaining poverty and pauperism. Finally, the development of machinery tends to deepen the severity of crises by promoting underconsumption: by increasing unemployment and thus limiting consumption, industrial production inevitably restricts opportunities, dooming it to repeated crises.

The Proudhonian critique is pursued against each of the antinomies of the proprietary economy. Competition is the expression of productive spontaneity and the sign of freedom, but left to its own devices it reinforces pauperism and huge

---

12. Ibid., 194.

wealth inequality. Monopoly promotes productive stability but gives overwhelming power to industrialists and results in worker servitude. Taxation and credit are intended to compensate for the harm caused by industrial development, but in reality they raise costs for workers and increase the fortunes of the wealthy. Thus, *The System of Economic Contradictions* ends with a dramatic description of a society lacking in solidarity, given over to disharmony and contradiction: not only is production surrendered to uncoordinated activities, to all kinds of exploitation and theft, but also, since any attempt to modify the system is inevitably woven into the fabric of contradictions, it can only reinforce social tensions and injustice.

Beyond the particular contradictions, the division of society into two antagonistic classes corresponding to capital and labor is both the constant social framework of the antinomies and their consequence. Indeed, economic principles, developing in a society whose general principles are theft and the exploitation of labor, always result in the reinforcement of social antagonism. The division of labor and the expansion of segregated tasks, by turning artisans into operators, cause work and workers to regress, provoke a fall in wages, and widen the gap between rich and poor. Machinery, by subordinating the worker to instruments and technologies monopolized by capital, reinforces the owner's power and establishes insurmountable relations of submission and hierarchy. Monopoly, by giving capital full freedom to earn profits without regard for the public interest, intensifies this theft of the collective force carried out by all owners. Indeed, monopoly openly performs this *accounting error*, this discrepancy, between the sum of individual wages and the sum of the values produced. According to Adam Smith's axiom, since every value is only worth the labor that went into it, the worker's fair remuneration would be their fair share of the wealth produced, taking into account the costs and surpluses to be retained. This axiom is radically denied by monopoly, which, deciding arbitrarily on the share of profits, gives the worker a wage that is unrelated to the values produced and thus prevents the proletariat from ever being able to buy back their product.

Thus, each epoch of the economic system ends up confirming the division of society into two antagonistic classes and the social and economic exploitation of the proletariat. Socially, the mechanisms of the economy engage the proletariat in a hopeless situation of subordination: degradation, stupefaction, and submission to hierarchies snatch from workers the share they once had under artisanal production. Economically, the extortion of wages by capitalist theft radically prohibits the working classes from consuming what it produces. Since, as Proudhon affirmed in *What Is Property?*, capitalist interest is nothing but a theft, a deduction made directly from wages, producers must be deprived of a portion of their labor. For capitalist profit to be made, producers must be fundamentally unable to buy back what they produce. If the workers received the whole of their production, after taking into account the surplus derived from all labor and that must be deducted from wages, property would in principle disappear immediately. In the regime of property, the proletariat is therefore condemned not to consume, labor is deprived of what it produces, and thus its poverty is offset by the wealth of the owners.

Proudhon, who describes the dynamics of the antagonisms with precision, is less precise in his indications of the likely development of the proprietary economy. However, it is clear from his analyses that the entire system carries within itself a double contradictory movement of destruction and recomposition: on the one hand, crises, impoverishment, and falls in profit cause tensions and prepare the system's collapse; on the other hand, the transformation of property and the pricing of products herald the coming of an economic society based on radically different principles.

In capitalist anarchy, crises are regular and inevitable, since the mass of products cannot be consumed in their entirety. During periods of activity, society as a whole works and produces as if all classes could buy back their production; entrepreneurs, for whom large-scale production is an opportunity for increased profits, push for maximum growth. But the more we produce, the more we prepare for crisis, since in a society in which the products cannot all be bought, sales inevitably run up against shortages in demand. Crisis will affect small peasant producers less dependent on the right of aubaine moderately but will hit the industrialists and the workers they employ mercilessly. Thus, after the failure of the 1848 revolution, Proudhon believes that industrial development leads to crises even more violent than in the past: the concentration of capital, the increase in the number of wage earners, the demise of the rural population, the submission of agriculture to financial forces—all these factors, by concentrating economic power into a small number of hands, encourage the repetition and extension of crises.

Proudhon does not affirm that pauperism necessarily increases in line with economic transformations but rather that it cannot disappear, since it is organically linked to the mechanism of capitalist monopolization. However, the increase in the number of wage earners, the concentration of capital, and the decline of the peasantry lead him to think that poverty would spread to larger groups, thus confirming the antinomy that links a rise in poverty to a rise in wealth.[13]

Finally, among the signs of the collapse of the regime of property, Proudhon retains the economic law of the reduction of interest: the proliferation of capital loans, their reciprocal competition, and their increasingly easy circulation would inflict a gradual fall in interest rates. And since this theft is the fundamental reason for social antagonism, this inevitable decline would lead to the collapse of the proprietary economy.

But while the system of private property carries within itself the causes of its own ruin, and despite the contradictions that tear it apart, it also brings transformations that herald features of the socialist economy.

Private property is challenged not only by socialist utopias but also in theoretical and practical terms within the regime of property itself. As early as the eighteenth century, when the physiocrats called for land property alone to be subject to taxation

---

13. "The increase of misery in the present state of society is parallel and equal to the increase of wealth." *Système des contradictions*, vol. 1, 89.

and for industry to be declared free, they were calling for labor to be promoted and proprietary monopoly to be attacked.[14] Similarly, the liberal economists who demand that laissez-faire be taken to its logical conclusion—for all obstacles to freedom of production and trade to be abolished—are merely fighting the old monopolies and hope to multiply the forms of individual possession. Moreover, by affirming that labor is the only measure of value, Adam Smith and David Ricardo denounce the theft carried out by property on labor, and they define the principles of a true economy in which values would be established based on the labor that produced them. In practice, the debate is no less crucial: in the face of the obstacles posed by absolute property against the public interest, the public authorities must declare the right of expropriation, thereby denying the fundamental principle of property; by making such decisions, society negates the very principles on which it claims to be based: the absolute legitimacy of property and the sovereign right to use one's goods. These practices betray the contradictory character of property and its "impossibility" in right and in fact; but they also herald its inevitable abolition and the disappearance of the aubaine, in a society that would fully recover what is diverted from it by the system of property.

Similarly, the fall in profit rates and the movement of values toward their natural price herald what Proudhon refers to as the "constitutionality of value." In the regime of property, the assessment of values seems to depend only on the arbitrariness of transactions, and some economists indeed argue that supply and demand are the only rules for determining value. In reality, as Smith and Ricardo have shown, since labor is both the principle and the efficient cause of value, it is possible to ground values empirically and discover their law. In all the products that make up wealth, each value must be proportionate to the quantity of

---

14. Translator's note: The physiocrats were French economists such as François Quesnay (1694–1774), the marquis de Mirabeau (1715–1789) and Anne-Robert-Jacques Turgot (1727–81), who believed that labor and commerce should be freed from all restraint and interference, and that land is the source of all wealth.

labor supplied in its production.[15] This fair relationship is continually disturbed in random transactions in which capital finds an opportunity to carry out theft, but through the oscillations between supply and demand the value of each product tends to be established according to the quantity of labor supplied. The possibility of setting a fair price corresponding to production costs will constitute a decisive point for Proudhon's economic theory: in order to establish equal relations between producers, products must be exchanged at their value, excluding all of the anomalies generated by the proprietary system. The spontaneous tendency of value to its "constitution," even within capitalist anarchy, prefigures the establishment of egalitarian relations and at the same time indicates their possibility.

Thus, the study of economic contradictions shows the system's antinomies, society's inability to achieve its own ends in the regime of property, and the reality of economic laws that industrial democracy cannot escape. The social revolution must therefore "transform" economic and social forms: as Proudhon writes, "a *force majeure* must invert the current formulas of society," but this revolution must also be based on objective economic laws of which capitalist anarchy gives an inverted image.[16] The challenge posed is therefore neither to deny economic principles such as competition or the division of labor, nor to conquer economic forces in order to make them serve the interests of a new class, but to submit social and economic powers to collective labor. It is necessary that labor, "by a scientific combination," "subject capital to the people and deliver power to them."[17]

3. Industrial Democracy, Positive Anarchy

We will not explain in detail Proudhon's socioeconomic doctrine, which is more ideological than sociological, but will seek to grasp

---

15. *De la création de l'ordre*, 311; *Système des contradictions*, vol. I, 105–18.
16. *Système des contradictions*, vol. I, 348.
17. Ibid.

its principles and broad outlines to the extent that they are based on and confirm the sociological theory.

The decisive importance of the economy in the social totality is a key theme that motivates the whole debate against the advocates of political reform. Proudhon constantly denounces the illusion that a political reform could alter social relations and constitute a real revolution by itself; the revolution must above all be social—socioeconomic—and only the transformation of relations of production, the organization of labor, can radically destroy the regime of property and exploitation. Proudhon adopts Saint-Simon's sociological intuition that the real forces of society are not political powers but rather economic forces of industry. The "constitutive unit" of society is neither the family nor state power but the workshop; and the relations established between workshops, between proprietors and workers, and between producers and consumers are the only ones that inform society as a whole.[18] The traditionalists, by making family the base and the model of social organization, propose an image of society that all modern development tends to destroy: the family, with its organic unity and relations of subordination, served as a model for ancient and feudal societies based on relations of sovereignty and authority, but modern democracy tends precisely to destroy this type of organization. When the utopians dream of seeing society constituted as a large family whose members would all be united in brotherhood, they are committing the same error, ignoring that the foundation of society, the workshop, is not a homogeneous unit but rather a sort of alliance in which each person is constrained by the law of their interests. The economists have shown the importance of economic functions, but they have not understood that all social relations depend on them, and they have refused to question the nature of the state, as if economic and political functions were distinct. But as Proudhon shows as early as his first memoir, studying the economic relation of private property in fact means studying the most general social relation: that which divides society into proprietors and workers. It also means revealing the

18. "The constitutive unit of society is the workshop." Ibid., 238.

nature of the political relationship between governors and governed and determining the meaning of the moral ideas of justice and injustice. In short, to pose the problem of property is to pose the problem of the social constitution as a whole. Indeed, the workshop is not only a site of production but also the social site of production in which particular human relations of equality or subordination are established; the relations between centers of production are not only economic relations but also relations between social groups. As we see in the example of machinery, relations of authority are instilled in the workshop, and this is where the source of relations of political authority are found: *power, authority,* and *sovereignty* are just other names for economic subordination created by capital, monopoly, and property.[19]

For the revolution, it is therefore not a question of conquering power or introducing political reform but rather of revolutionizing the basis of society by overturning its foundations, the entire system of the social economy. In short, it is a question of organizing labor in all its forms: subjectively, objectively, and synthetically, according to the vocabulary that Proudhon uses in *The Creation of Order.* To consider work subjectively would be to practice the science of organization, society, and progress; to consider work objectively would be to study its achievements and results, production, wealth, and trade; and to consider work synthetically would be to discover the rules of economic law and to define the rules of sharing and distribution, of equal justice for all. This scientific program is at the same time a revolutionary program, since the goal of social transformation would be to reach all these areas: the creation of a new social organization and of a new form of production and distribution. In doing so, the organization of labor would directly result in the reconstitution of society.

The study of economic contradictions has highlighted the intensity of the antagonisms inherent in the anarchy of the regime of property, suggested their synthesis, and stressed the necessity and purpose of each term. Faced with these antagonisms, political economy and utopian socialism give two equally

---

19. Ibid., 195.

unsatisfactory answers: political economy asserts that the antag-onisms and harms they entail are inevitable and that there is no other law than maintaining the antinomies. Conversely, utopian socialism responds that in a fraternal community, all conflicts would disappear as a result of equal submission to the collective power. Both agree in denying that a *social science* could be estab-lished, denying the existence of laws inherent in the economy and society. But contrary to the skeptical assertions of political economy, the oscillations between the principles highlight the reality of constants and laws inherent in economic activity: it is thus false that value has no rule and that it depends only on the chance and luck of markets. The principle and law of value is the quantity of labor supplied, and this principle is only not realized in the regime of property because of the anarchy introduced by capitalist theft. Similarly, while competition causes ruin and destroys itself, it also ensures the vitality of trade and the speed of inventions. Therefore, the fundamental principle of the social economy should be dialectical synthesis, understood as a dynamic balancing of opposites and not as a destruction of antagonisms.

The mistake of communist utopias is the desire to annihi-late antinomies by means of a new authority and to destroy the dynamic of contradictions in a governmental synthesis; the social movement can only be ensured if free exchanges are maintained between the various sites of social production and between the various autonomous producers. The solution to the social prob-lem does not consist in destroying producers' autonomy but in establishing balances between them that will both socialize and emancipate labor. The mistake of liberal economists is to claim that the economy is based on a simple factor, property, thereby denying dialectics and their laws: by retaining only one term that inevitably proves to be intrusive and despotic, economists prevent themselves from discovering the constant social movement that destroys the principle by submitting it to a dialectic. Propertarian theory and communist theory commit the same error—one by denying the dialectic, the other by confusing synthesis with doc-trinaire unitarism—leading to the same result, whereby the econ-omy and society are founded on constraint and force. Creating an economic society that meets worker aspirations and economic laws would require maintaining the autonomy and plurality of centers of production while making freedoms reciprocal and balanced. This decentralized, nononauthoritarian economy—in which the workers, whether independent or joined together in worker companies, are the sole masters of their production and thus the sole masters of society as a whole—would achieve *positive anarchy*.[20] In proclaiming himself an anarchist, Proudhon intends to signify that in right and in fact the socialist economy—which in his vocabulary is called progressive association, mutuality, or agro-industrial federation—must eliminate command and constraint and restore to the producers alone the social power alienated in property and the state. The very activity of this autonomous organization of associated workers would dissolve any false and external authority, property, government, or religion. The implementation of the negative dialectic, a dialectic of antagonisms in an antiauthoritarian balance, would result in the true emancipation of workers, the dissolution of all economic or political absolutism.[21]

Three principles justified in the socioeconomic analysis would be realized in this industrial democracy: equality, freedom, and responsibility. The equality of producers stems from the principle that the act of production is a collective act and not, as the propertarian theory claims, an individual endeavor. The theory of collective force has shown that the union of efforts gives rise to a power qualitatively heterogeneous to the sum of individual efforts: no worker, whether entrepreneur or proletarian, can claim the result as theirs alone. Thus, the product can only be monopolized by a theft since it is fundamentally the property of all.[22] The workers who participated in production—who are its

---

20. *Solution du problème social*, vol. 6, 87.

21. "Negative dialectic": An expression that Georges Gurvitch uses precisely to characterize the Proudhonian dialectic. *Dialectique et Sociologie* [Dialectics and Sociology] (Paris: Flammarion, 1962), 105.

22. "All capital, whether material or mental, being the result of collective labor, is, in consequence, collective property." *Qu'est-ce que la propriété ?*, 238.

sole authors, since capital produces nothing by itself—must be
its sole beneficiaries. More precisely, since every group of workers uses means that were amassed by previous labor, and is thus
indebted to society, collective production must return to its true
authors: all the workers. As participants in an eminently collective endeavor, all workers are fundamentally equal, all fulfilling
diverse and necessary functions. To this principle, the defenders
of the hierarchy of functions, such as the Saint-Simonians, object
that unequal capacities and talents justify and guarantee unequal
conditions. This, Proudhon says, is only a prejudice maintained
by those who have an interest in maintaining it. In asserting that
abilities are unequal and that this justifies wage inequality, it is
assumed that labor is a war in which prices are fought over and the
most able are rewarded;[23] however, if labor is indeed a struggle, it
is not a struggle between producers but rather a war of all against
nature, in which functions are mutually coordinated and united.
Thus, the collective nature of labor instills equality: the worker
and the entrepreneur are equally associated in an activity in which
they are united. Proudhon does not conclude that absolute equality of wages must be an imperative rule and that it must establish
the norms for distribution: on the contrary, he accepts that the
principle of paying in proportion to the labor supplied is necessary and in accordance with the law of equality. But he intends
to show that the nature of labor, a social activity that involves all
participants in an exchange of services, requires all producers to
be considered as equal partners. Since all functions in common
activity are fundamentally associated and necessary, with wages
to be paid only for services rendered, remuneration must be considered equal, at least as allowed by the ills or irregularities for
which society must take responsibility. The principle of wages
does not lie in the arbitrary estimate imposed by privileges and
prejudices, but in labor time, of which the unit is the working day.
In affirming that every product is worth what it costs, that every
product is worth the labor assigned to its production, political
economy itself indicated that there could be no criterion other

---

23. Ibid., 219.

than labor time, thereby affirming the equality of working days, regardless of their nature.[24] Thus, the labor movement and the elimination of proprietary parasitism instill an equality of conditions that will be achieved by the association of workers.

The second principle that the industrial republic must realize is freedom. In the regime of property, the freedom proclaimed is only a lie: it only benefits the proprietor, whose will is neither controlled nor limited, while the proletarian is free only to work and to be exploited—or not to work and to die of hunger. These contradictions, which the liberal economists regard as true economic laws, are in reality only a fateful system whose consequences are inevitably suffered by the workers. In proclaiming the defense of freedom, the economists are in reality only bowing to fate. And it is once again by sacrificing freedom that the communist utopias would like to achieve equality: here too, communist utopias do not free themselves from the propertarian routine but merely replace the despotism of property with the despotism of the community. However, the goal of a reform cannot be to destroy freedom but must be to socialize it.[25] The economic tool of this socialization of freedom will be the establishment of economic contracts between different producers and between producers and consumers, and the organization of economic forces under the "supreme law of the contract." The social contract, directly opposed to Rousseau's definition, is the act by which two or more individuals decide to organize a means of exchange among themselves for a given time: they bind themselves to each other and mutually guarantee a certain quantity of services or products.[26] This economic contract, which Proudhon makes one of the fundamental conditions of positive anarchy, would satisfy the requirements for both equality and freedom. In this type of contract, there is necessarily a reciprocal interest between the contracting parties: in the political contract, as Rousseau describes it,

---

24. "So that political economy affirms at its birth . . . equality of conditions and fortunes." *Système des contradictions*, vol. I, 129.

25. "We are not to kill individual liberty, but to socialize it." Ibid., 97.

26. *Idée générale de la révolution au XIXe siècle* [General Idea of the Revolution in the Nineteenth Century], 188.

the citizen alienates a part of their freedom to a random counter-party, but in the social contract both contracting parties commit to an equal exchange, the extent of their respective rights being determined by the size of their contributions. Moreover, this social contract is freely debated and agreed on by all participants: no external authority intervenes to constrain the contracting parties. Each person agrees voluntarily and only for the services or products expressly stipulated in the agreement, retaining their full freedom and finding only an increase in freedom in this egalitarian and free contract. This social contract, the true foundation of the industrial republic, would achieve both solidarity and freedom, the separation and socialization of freedoms. Whereas the political contract, whether monarchical or democratic, had the institution of an authority as its goal, and thus the restriction of individual freedom as its consequence, the social contract, having the purpose of establishing free exchanges, would be conditional on and result in respecting the true autonomy of the producers.

Ultimately, this freedom which Proudhon wants to see fully respected is a freedom manifested in the act of production, an organizing freedom. What he denounces in the regimes of property and community is the worker's inability to be personally involved in and responsible for the activity. The proprietary system, especially as seen in the development of the division of labor and in the expansion of machinery, prevents the worker from taking part in the organization of labor. Securing producers' freedom would restore their responsibility for managing their own production, transforming working conditions into "responsible stewardship," another meaning of positive anarchy.[27] For individual producers such as small farmers, autonomous management will occur once proprietary exploitation ceases, since the contract will only relate to exchanges and the farmers will be free to manage their production freely.[28] But in large industries such

27. *De la création de l'ordre*, 422.
28. In fact, management of the agricultural enterprise would be entrusted to the father of the family, since Proudhon justifies paternal authority and violently professes antifeminism. This defense of the patriarchal family did not fail to attract many criticisms. Recall that, while

as mines, railways, or factories, the principle of responsibility must also be realized by transferring industry to a worker-owned company.[29] Rather than belonging to a capitalist owner, industrial enterprises must become the property of worker companies, responsible for freely managing and exercising their production according to the rules of competition and contract. The workers will then cease to be employees but will share the organization's gains and losses, have a deciding voice on the board, and choose temporary leaders, thus actually participating in their industry's activity. In addition, the education that they will receive will enable them to explore different jobs and cooperate in all parts of collective labor.

These principles of equality, freedom, and responsibility merely describe Proudhon's general intention: to radically invert the forms of social vitality. In the regime of property, just as in the theory of the community, workers find themselves subjected to an authority that seizes the right to manage the economy by reducing workers to the rank of operators and employees. Similarly, in political theories, whether monarchical or democratic, it is assumed that politics is the site where social life is instigated and that citizens' rights must be alienated to a governing hierarchy. Conversely, anarchy requires governmental hierarchy to be replaced by economic organization by giving independent producers and associated producers management of the economy and therefore management of society as a whole. Rather than expecting social life to fall down from the powers that be, anarchism intends to allow social life to spring up from its own foundations, to "break through" from below.[30]

The model and practical means of achieving this Industrial Republic evolve somewhat from 1840 to 1865, without the fundamental principles being called into question. Before 1848,

---

advocating for the family, Proudhon stresses that it would be a mistake to make it the constitutive social cell. In his opinion, relations of authority that are constituted in the family must in no way be transposed into social life.

29. *Idée générale de la révolution*, 276.
30. *Système des contradictions*, vol. I, 242.

Proudhon notes in his *Carnets* the plan for an association that he would refer to indiscriminately by the terms *progressive association*, *worker association*, *progressive society*, *mutualism*, and *mutuality*. He intends to urge workers to decide for themselves to form associations between producers and consumers according to the principle of the reciprocal exchange of products. The association would start from the basis of the theory of exchange whereby goods are exchanged in kind, products for products (in reality, labor for labor). Producers would agree to associate with each other in order to exchange their products at cost price, the cost corresponding to the quantity of labor contained in the good. Thus, workers would immediately be assured of demand, of being able to produce and receive, and would not have to wait to amass capital: the company would create its own capital as it accumulates labor. The exchange of products at cost price would cause a reduction of prices by eliminating proprietary theft and the different forms of aubaine, and this would lead to the company's rapid expansion. Proudhon then hopes that the association's expansion would turn it into a relentless war machine destined to smash the entire regime of property: the proprietors, unable to compete against a low-cost company and retain their own customers, would be subjected to a new economic regime which would thus seize the whole of society, either peacefully or by force. At that time, he stresses, the essential condition for the proper functioning of this worker company would be the creation of a perfect form of economic accounting. Indeed, since each producer and production site must maintain an accurate account of its exchanges, its debt, and its assets, which must be transparent to all, the creation of a rigorous form of accounting would appear as an essential condition for the fair functioning of the economy.

It is in applying these principles that Proudhon would found a Bank of the People in 1849, devised to establish mutual credit and the equal exchange of products among producers. This bank, founded without capital, would act only as an intermediary between different producers and between producers and consumers: instead of lending capital and demanding interest, it would ensure the circulation of exchange notes secured by products. Each member, individual or collective producer, without committing their capital, would obtain an equal claim in value to the product of their labor and would agree to accept the notes as payment for their goods. Thus the exchange notes, instead of being secured by cash, would be secured by products already manufactured or in the process of being manufactured, and insured against any depreciation. In Proudhon's mind, this complete overhaul of the rules of circulation would have the effect of eliminating interest and thus undermining the foundations of property: since it would not have to commit capital, the bank would ensure credit and circulation by receiving only a commission to cover operating costs. Eliminating interest would cause the parasitic extortion carried out by capital to disappear and would thus result in the liquidation of the whole regime of property, the disappearance of the power of gold, and the elimination of social exploitation. Since capital is made available to workers free of charge, economic society would now only consist of producers exchanging their products at cost price.[31]

The experience of the 1848 Revolution would draw Proudhon's attention to the need to propose a total reform of society, which, instead of proceeding gradually, would proceed synthetically in all economic and political aspects. Resuming his earlier themes of the social pact, the theory of mutuality, reciprocity, economic decentralization, and social spontaneity, he declares the theory of industrial federation as the foundation and counterweight to political federation. This federalist conception of the economy does not alter his previous conclusions but rather incorporates them into a universalist vision concerned with respecting both the freedom of the producers and the various forms of solidarity.

Proudhon thus envisages a plurality of associations diversified according to the types of labor. In agricultural labor, which

---

31. *Organisation du crédit et de la circulation et solution du problème social* [The Organization of Credit and Circulation, and the Solution to the Social Problem]; *Banque d'échange* [Bank of Exchange], *Banque du Peuple* [Bank of the People]), vol. 6, 89–312.

least requires the cooperative form, the individual producers, while being able to associate for certain tasks, would keep their independence and would only be centralized by the mutuality of insurance and credit systems. In his last work on property, resuming and correcting his theory of possession, Proudhon affirms the utility of property, provided that it is controlled and limited by society and cannot cause aubaines to reappear.[32] Property thus conceived would be an invincible obstacle to the abuse of power and guarantee producer freedom. Similarly, in commerce and small industry, enterprises would keep their reciprocal independence under conditions of mutuality, responsibility, and social security. On the contrary, any industry, operation, or enterprise that requires the employment of a large number of workers of different specialties would become the site of a worker company responsible for management and production. These different workplaces, founded according to industry and profession, would expand into national federations that would combine mutual independence and necessary coordination. Agro-industrial federation would consist of all of these groupings, a federation that would replace the false centralizations of the regime of property and the communist utopia.

Whatever the evolution of Proudhon's thought, from progressive association to federalism, from the theory of possession to that of socialized property, these reform projects confirm the general theory of society as set out in *What Is Property?*: if society is a unity and reality by itself, it must be freed from its obstacles by destroying the political and economic oppressions imposed by governmental despotism and capitalist theft. It is necessary to restore to society as a whole—to its producers—what has been usurped by the false system of property. But if society is made whole by the reality of the collective force, it is given life only through the labor of individuals and groups freely united in collective activity: it is therefore necessary to respect the independence of individuals and groups and to ensure the conditions for free, nonantagonistic competition.

---

32. *Théorie de la propriété.*

CHAPTER THREE

Sociology of Social Classes

1. Antagonism Between Social Classes

The socioeconomic analysis has shown that the monopolization of profit by capitalist owners constitutes the fundamental fact of economic society and inevitably causes antagonism between capital and labor. The effect of the regime of property is not only to maintain the division between proprietors and non-proprietors, but it also generates a relationship of exploitation between these two classes, since the profit that ensures the renewal of capital is obtained only by diverting what naturally belongs to the workers. Social division therefore originates from an economic mechanism that cannot be distinguished from a class relation: the relation between capital and labor is homologous to the relation between proprietors and workers, or in other words the bourgeoisie and the proletariat. Further analyses and historical studies devoted to the activity of different classes in conflict reveal that this economic origin is not sufficient to distinguish a social class, but they confirm the paramount importance of this relation of economic exploitation and the need to define a class first as an economic class.

This fact of the division of society into antagonistic classes is not an unprecedented historical phenomenon: for example, the societies described in the Bible or in Roman society were also divided into various social classes, according to either the functions they performed or their share of property. The struggle between labor and capital is not dissimilar to the old struggles between the plebeians and the patricians. However, the bourgeois and working classes are constituted on historically new foundations and are distinguished in particular from feudal castes. Indeed, in feudalism, the three castes or "categories" of nobility, clergy, and the Third Estate corresponded to three different functions, and the workers were supported by a collection of guilds that protected them. In this social system, landlords and their workers maintained relationships that directly brought them together and caused their interests to coincide.[1] By proclaiming political equality and industrial freedom, the 1789 Revolution gave workers independence without providing them with any protection. Whereas in the feudal system workers had been involved in the guild as in a family, they and their capitalist entrepreneurs now only had private relations defined by an individual contract. The 1789 Revolution, by shattering the social order of the past, freed the regime of property from its shackles and enabled the spontaneous development of liberal economics; but the development of this economic system, with its economic contradictions and its mechanisms of monopolization, resulted in division into two classes, one living exclusively from its labor, the other living from revenue and the various forms of aubaine. Once the feudal barriers had disappeared, the economic mechanisms and the organization of labor, as established in the regime of property, inevitably caused the division of society into two classes, one exploited and the other consuming profit. Of course, this socioeconomic division does not suffice to account for all social relations and all historical events—during political changes, we will see specific groups such as the army and the church intervene—but the division between the holders of the instruments of production and the employees constitutes the fundamental separation in society and explains why the working classes achieve revolutionary *political capacity*, as Proudhon says in 1864.

Although Proudhon did not seek to formulate a definition of social class in the regime of property, his writings reveal a constant socioeconomic definition. Bourgeoisie and proletariat are

---

1. *De la capacité politique des classes ouvrières*, 94–95.

differentiated by their opposite participation in economic society, their type of work, their source of income, and their ownership or lack of property. The theory of collective force has shown that workers were the only producers, the only participants in the real social force, and that the idea of capital as a productive factor was an illusion: since the bourgeoisie lives only from its income, it is opposed to the proletariat, as the parasite is opposed to the host. Workers live from their wages, surviving only through the individual remuneration given by the entrepreneur in exchange for labor time; conversely, capitalists live from profit, from the theft endlessly carried out against labor and the workers. The workers' deprivation and lack of property is therefore only one aspect of their situation, just as capitalist appropriation must be considered within the relationships that unite and antinomically put capital and labor in conflict.

These indications, though fundamental, do not exhaust the definition of class. Indeed, while engaged in its economic situation and practice, a class tends to constitute a "separate type" with its habits, morals, ideas, and political projects, revealing a psychology peculiar to it.[2] Thus, considering the history of the bourgeoisie, Proudhon points out that at the time of its conflict against nobility, the bourgeois class had a particular style, habits, and literature, characteristic of a confident, rising class; he adds that, in his eyes, the bourgeoisie became corrupt, rotten, and unable to fulfill the guiding role in the new society.

As explained in Proudhon's final work, *The Political Capacity of the Working Classes*, a class is not just a collection of individuals playing identical roles in production and displaying a shared culture and psychology, but may also act as a unit in political life and intervene as a subject of a social practice.[3] A class being passive during a period of history does not necessarily prove that it cannot assert itself as an agent of history: just as the 1789 Revolution marked the moment when the bourgeoisie triumphed over the feudal order, the 1848 Revolution marks the moment when

---

2. *De la justice dans la révolution et dans l'église*, 6th étude, vol. 3, 139.
3. *De la capacité politique des classes ouvrières*, 90.

the working classes begin to constitute a class, signaling their transformation into a creative class. For Proudhon, this coming to autonomous practice is subject to two preconditions: self-consciousness and theoretical clarification. For a class to achieve the political capacity enabling it to create a new economic and political order, it must imagine its place in society, the functions it performs, and the roles it plays. This implies that the individuals it consists of must see themselves as members of this collectivity and become conscious of themselves as belonging to this class. This self-consciousness is at the same time consciousness of a value: in discovering its identity, a conscious class perceives its "dignity," its autonomous value, and consequently sees itself as justified in claiming its rights and defending its interests against the opposing classes. This first condition required for achieving political capacity entails the second: for a class to be able to act politically, it must proclaim an *idea* that relates a class to its being. The theoretical clarification that a class must achieve is in fact the imagination and expression of its own social existence: in formulating its idea, the class imagines and states the *law of its being*.[4] It expresses its particular constitution within the society to which it belongs and discovers what it is and therefore what it wants. This theory, proclaimed and formulated in terms of the understanding, cannot therefore be a utopia: for a class to recognize itself in theory, it must express its reality, its existence and experience, and its actual relations with the state and other collectivities. This consonance with experience allows the class to perceive its present and future, formulate its real goals, and bring together an understanding of present conditions and an imagination of its goals in the same theory.

In this transformation of the class through self-consciousness and theoretical formulation, Proudhon places particular emphasis on the separation of classes as a fact and as an idea: for a class to achieve political capacity, it must consider its differences with other classes and see itself as distinct. Self-consciousness is consciousness of its autonomy and its opposition to rival classes: for

---

4. Ibid.

the working class, becoming conscious of its role means finding itself to be distinct from the bourgeois classes, disassociat-
ing its interests, and therefore refusing to be conflated with the
bourgeoisie. To proclaim its idea and formulate its being and its
experience is to assert its own reality in opposition to other social
realities, to claim its difference. Self-consciousness includes the
desire to differentiate oneself: consciousness means consciousness of difference, and it is from this awareness of being different
that an autonomous and effective practice is born.[5]

In the regime of property, this distinction and opposition
between classes is inscribed in the very foundations of the economic system by the nature of property. In proclaiming his intention to defend the cause of the working classes as early as 1838,
Proudhon affirms the existence of a distinction and opposition
between the working classes and the privileged classes:[6] he would
refer to this opposition as "war" and "endless struggle" between
labor and capital. However, he does not exactly conclude that
society is founded on class confrontation. The relation that both
unites and separates capital and labor, before being a relationship
of struggle, is first and foremost one of economic exploitation.
This proprietary theft explains the temporary clashes, alliances,
and strikes, but these struggles are only the passing manifestations of a fundamental socioeconomic relationship. By monopolizing the fruits of collective force, the proprietor steals the labor
of others, takes possession of a product made by the worker; in
doing so, he prevents producers from buying back what they
have produced and inevitably condemns part of the proletariat to
poverty and famine.[7] This exploitation is a permanent war: every
act of production within the regime of property entails a monopolization of labor and contributes to the inevitable condemnation of the proletariat. This relationship between the bourgeois
and the workers is maintained only by force, by a binding

---

5. "To distinguish oneself, to define oneself, is to be." Ibid., 237.

6. *Lettre de candidature à la Pension Suard* [Application for the Suard
Pension], May 1838, 16.

7. "Every man who makes a profit has entered into a conspiracy with
famine." *Qu'est-ce que la propriété ?*, 272.

subordination that prevents workers from recouping their product: this extortion is carried out by force, within a society founded on a relationship of violence.

However, the terms *theft*, *extortion*, and *exploitation* better express Proudhon's thought than the terms *struggle* or *war*. If there is indeed a war between capital and labor, it is an unequal struggle in which workers are inevitably the victims. The struggle comes down to an endless alliance of capitalists against labor: the proprietors form a kind of confederation directed against the workers, who are dispossessed of the economic and political tools that would enable them to resist. Proudhon thinks—and this is a point he often stressed—that worker alliances and strikes are economically inefficient and cannot transform the workers' conditions: they may temporarily improve some workers' situation, but the increase in prices they cause merely erases the benefits temporarily obtained. Within the regime of property and the conditions imposed by this system, worker resistance is comparable to "palliatives" that inevitably fail to destroy the general form of economic relations. Exploitation is in fact less the result of an action carried out by a class than a relation inscribed within the socioeconomic system as a whole. Neither the bourgeoisie nor the proletariat are its direct authors, and it is not the actions of individuals but instead the system as a whole that must be condemned. By using armed force to quell strikes, the capitalist entrepreneur is undoubtedly only defending his own immediate interests, but more precisely he is expressing a verdict delivered by the whole system that condemns the proletariat to submission and misery: exploitation is not rooted in the particular will of a class but rather in the general organization of a system based on theft.

However, this fundamental conception of a society torn between two antagonistic classes representing capital and labor does not express the whole of Proudhon's thought. If he were merely commentating on this social war, we would not understand how he could, in some texts, expect a revolutionary practice from a bourgeoisie he so fiercely denounced. It would be easy to put Proudhon at odds with himself on this point and to contrast different quotations: after having shown in 1840 that the bourgeoisie could in no way accept worker emancipation, how could he claim, in 1851, that the bourgeois have always been the boldest revolutionaries?[8] These contradictions, however, are more superficial than real and express the fluctuating historical situation, rather than a hesitation in Proudhon's thought.

The radical division of society into two antagonistic forces is only ostensibly clear: it does not express all the social complexities and intricacies of groups, and in particular it says nothing about the situation of peasants, small entrepreneurs, and artisans. In reality, the definition of capital as a monopolizing force cannot be applied unilaterally to the whole bourgeoisie: according to the terms of the definition of property, small industrialists and traders find themselves in an ambiguous situation. To the extent that small industrialists participate directly in production by their own labor, they should be counted among the producers, and the salary that pays for their labor time is, like the working wage, a share of the cost price. Conversely, to the extent that they use their working instruments to accumulate interest extorted from the labor of the workers, they benefit from capitalist theft. It is not, in fact, possession that defines exploitation but rather property as a source of profit. As long as artisans and those running small industries act as nominal owners of the working instruments and contribute directly to production by their efforts or knowledge, they count among the producers, experiencing more or less the same risks and problems.

After affirming the fundamental split between capital and labor, Proudhon is therefore led to distinguish between two distinctly different classes within the bourgeoisie: the *grande bourgeoisie*, which he calls *industrial and mercantile feudalism*, and the middle class.[9] In this perspective, there are not two antagonistic

---

8. "The bourgeoisie will accept anything over the emancipation of the proletariat." *Deuxième mémoire* (1841), 75. "To you, the bourgeois, I dedicate these new essays. You have always been the boldest, the most skillful revolutionaries." *Idée générale de la révolution*, Dédicace [Dedication] (1851), 93.

9. "*The middle class.* It consists of entrepreneurs, bosses, shopkeepers, manufacturers, farmers, scholars, artists, etc., living, like the

classes but rather three: industrial feudalism, the working bourgeoisie, and the working classes. The *grande bourgeoisie* accurately
fits the definition given for capitalist exploitation: holding the
major means of production, it creates monopolies for its own
benefit, grows its capital without contributing to production, and
takes control of the state in order to transform it into a tool to
defend the economic system. From this exploitative bourgeoisie,
we can only expect a politics directly contrary to worker emancipation. The case of the middle class, a class partly working
and partly benefiting from aubaines and financial speculation, is
much more complex: it will be necessary to investigate whether
the economic contradictions will put it in a revolutionary situation to escape the threats to which it might also fall victim.

Like the petite bourgeoisie, the peasantry is not sufficiently
distinguished by social dichotomy in the regime of property.
Consisting mostly of small farmers who own their plots, it is
not directly threatened by capitalist exploitation and does not
directly benefit from monopolization. In his projects for agro-
industrial federation, a decentralized and coordinated economic
system, Proudhon does not envisage the expropriation of agriculture but, on the contrary, continued possession of the land
and the return of instruments of production to peasant families.
This respect for peasant possession has led Proudhon's work to
be interpreted as a socialist defense of the peasant class, and it
is true that the proposed reforms intend to preserve the family
forms of peasant production.[10] But Proudhon does not imagine that the peasant class in the regime of property can reach

---

proletarians, and unlike the bourgeois, much more from their personal
product than from their capital, privileges, and properties but distinguished from the proletariat in that they work, in vulgar terms, for themselves, they are responsible for their estate's losses and the exclusive
enjoyment of their profits, whereas the proletarian works for hire and is
paid a wage." *La Révolution sociale démontrée par le coup d'etat du deux décembre*, 125.

10. Aimé Berthod, *Proudhon et la propriété, un socialisme pour les pay-
sans* [Proudhon and Property: Socialism for the Peasants] (Paris: Giard &
Brière, 1910).

self-consciousness and lead an autonomous revolutionary struggle: he expects only the working classes to succeed in leading the
"Marianne of the fields" by demonstrating the identity of their
interests.[11] Indeed, in commercial relations, since the peasant
class does not directly participate in capitalist profit, it is driven
to re-create, at its own scale, the thefts and manipulations that
characterize exchange relations in the mercantile system, which
lacks in solidarity. If Proudhon defends rural possession, it is
without any illusions about the consequences of small property
on the consciousness of the peasant class: small property, narrow
and closed in on itself, tends to prevent peasants from becoming aware of their true interests, and commercial practices attract
them to forms of theft and exploitation.[12] Thus, the peasant class
is in an ambiguous situation that simultaneously brings it closer
and pushes it away from industrial workers. Its true interests,
including the reconstitution of property based on the principle
of mutuality, are identical to those of the working class; the deep
aspirations of the peasantry, who intend to possess the land, are
not in contradiction with the aspirations of the working classes,
who intend to seize the instruments of labor. But peasants are
threatened by the defects of small property as organized in the
regime of property. Proudhon adds, in 1864, that the French
peasants have not rid themselves of the Napoleonic myth: they
continue to see Napoleon III as the symbol of the revolution
that freed them from feudal law.[13] It will be up to the working

---

11. "Thus the cause of the peasants is the same as that of the industrial workers; the *Marianne* of the fields is the counterpart of the *Sociale* of
the cities." *De la capacité politique des classes ouvrières*, 69. Translator's note:
Marianne is the personification of the French Republic and its values of
liberty, equality, and fraternity.

12. "The peasant, who makes up the vast majority of France, is
the most abominable class, the most selfish, the most devoid of gen-
erous instincts, the most venal, the most stationary, the most enraged
owner." *Carnet, no. 6*, vol. 2 (Paris: M. Rivière, 1847), 294.

13. Translator's note: Louis-Napoléon Bonaparte (1808–1873), the
nephew of Napoleon I, was the last monarch of France. As a result of the
Revolution of 1848, France became a republic for the second time, and
elected Napoleon III as president. In December 1851, he seized power

classes to show them the identity of their interests and to dispel this political myth.[14]

Thus, despite the historical importance temporarily assumed by secondary classes, the fate of the revolution lies in the confrontation between the bourgeoisie and the proletariat.

2. The Bourgeoisie

Before 1789, the bourgeoisie formed a coherent unit, constituting only one section of feudal society and fighting against the nobility and the clergy. From the outset, the establishment of communes expressed the constitution of urban populations as a conscious class. This self-consciousness was vigorously maintained for as long as the bourgeoisie had to fight and define itself against the privileged classes.[15] Sieyès's pamphlet on the Third Estate expresses this consciousness and this desire to become the whole of society. During this period prior to the revolution, the bourgeoisie, demanding progress, liberty, and equality, had an *idea*, a political will; but, because of its coherence and self-consciousness, it also had a spirit, a style. It is this old bourgeois spirit that inspired the great writers of the nineteenth century and subsequently the revolutionary assemblies.[16]

But once the bourgeoisie became everything, once the classes that forced it to define itself by separation disappeared, it began to lose its sense of self. Class consciousness gave way to the dispersion of individual interests and the sole pursuit of

---

by force and founded the Second French Empire, in which he reigned until 1870. Proudhon was imprisoned for three years starting in 1848 for publicly insulting Napoleon III.

14. "It is the industrial democracy of Paris and the big cities that took the initiative, to look for the points of connection that exist between it and the democracy of the countryside." *De la capacité politique des classes ouvrières*, 69–70.

15. "The bourgeois class distinguished itself, defined itself, felt itself, affirmed itself by opposition to the privileged or noble classes." Ibid., 99.

16. *De la justice dans la révolution et dans l'église*, 6th étude, vol. 3, 147.

private profit. As the liberal economists put it, the individualistic doctrine of laissez-faire, the anarchic confrontation of interests, served as theory. Subsequently, the contradictions and vices that were in fact inherent in its nature flourished. Proudhon in 1860 paints a caustic picture of bourgeois psychology, nature, and attitudes. While peasants produce wealth by their own labor and workers obtain a wage by manual labor, the bourgeoisie have striven from the outset to avoid labor and to extract profit from trade and trafficking. First it comprised traders, lenders, bankers, and financiers—when the bourgeoisie created an industry, it was less as industrialists than as merchants—and did not create profits so much as divert them, not to integrate with the working class but to speculate. By increasing its properties, the bourgeoisie's sole aim was to collect, as an intermediary, the profit derived from commercial transactions: premiums, interest, usury.[17] The bourgeoisie's idol is not art, justice, or God, but wealth. Its sole concern is, in its own words, to do business—that is, according to the economic definition of property, to defraud.

The political attitude of the bourgeoisie stems from this exclusive concern: whatever the situation, the bourgeoisie is concerned only with safeguarding its interests without considering either the principles or the social or national consequences. Despite its declarations to the contrary, members of the bourgeoisie are only weakly patriotic: they will accept their national territory being annexed if it suits their interests, preferring to see the country invaded by a foreign nation rather than led by a party that would threaten them.[18] The bourgeois are thus unpatriotic and even less democratic: they fear any system that would give power to the people and threaten their privileges. In truth, the political system matters little to them: they accepted the monarchy, the coups of 18 Brumaire and December 2, 1851, and constitutional monarchy, and in 1783 they would have agreed to

---

17. Ibid., 141.

18. "Self-interest above all! Did we not hear, in 1848, the conservatives say: 'May the Cossacks come rather than the Republicans'?" Ibid., 142.

come to terms with the nobility if the upper classes had deigned to grant them a share of the profits. They are prepared to tolerate despotism, provided that the despot ensures their share of the privileges and does not scare them: they supported Bonaparte's dictatorship until the Continental Blockade.[19] If it could share the advantages and sinecures formerly reserved for the nobility, the bourgeoisie would accommodate itself to various forms of government. However, it prefers the parliamentary system to despotic power, not because it considers it more moral or just, but because it enjoys greater security in constitutional guarantees. It appreciates maintaining order above all and is afraid of disorder—not financial chaos, abuses, or general corruption but rather demonstrations and riots that cause stocks to decrease in value.[20]

The bourgeois value everything according to its market value and measure their respect based on the wealth of the owner: what they admire in people is not their merit but rather their property. In moral terms, they like to think that the primary value is that of best interests, and utilitarianism, which confuses morality with rules of business, suits them perfectly: it teaches them to focus first on how they are regarded and what other people think, which matter much more in business than duty or virtue.

In philosophy, the bourgeois fear systems and intellectual rigor. Accustomed to reconciling and compromising, they take pleasure in eclecticism which spares them from making judgments and going into depth. Intellectually and morally, they are advocates of the *juste milieu*: they call themselves Christian but also Voltairian;[21] they respect priests but fear their power; they

---

19. Translator's note: The Continental Blockade, or Continental System, was a trade embargo imposed by Napoleon against Great Britain. It was proclaimed in 1806 and prohibited French allies from trading with the British.

20. "Its soul is like the stock market: the slightest disturbance alarms it; the annihilation of moral life does not affect it." *De la justice dans la révolution et dans l'église*, 6th étude, vol. 3, 145.

21. Translator's note: Refers to someone who advocates for the ideas of Voltaire (1694–1778) who criticized the Church and promoted civil liberties.

are nonreligious but think that religion is necessary; and they are suspicious of authority but defend it, thereby ensuring that their material interests, the only things that matter, will be protected through these contradictions.

This political skepticism was perfectly apparent from 1830 to 1848. During the July Revolution, the popular masses had brought down the government, but in reality they had only served as a militia for the bourgeoisie who claimed the victory in full. The bourgeoisie had no idea what form of government it wanted to support; it only knew clearly what it did not want.[22] The bourgeoisie absolutely refused a legitimate monarch who would find their principle elsewhere. It no longer wanted a nobility and aristocracy whose titles eluded it. It cared little for the establishment of a new republican regime. It completely refused any social reform that would have favored the proletariat and harmed its own interests. Its exclusive concern was to ensure the security of business and to establish a social regime whose sole end would be to increase bourgeois wealth.[23] This was the *thought* of the reign of Louis-Philippe:[24] the government of self-interest. This does not mean that the bourgeois idea was to

---

22. *Confessions d'un révolutionnaire*, 98–99.

23. "What does it want, then, this devious, troublesome, ungovernable bourgeoisie? If you urge it to answer, it will tell you that it wants business; the rest is worthless." Ibid., 99.

24. Translator's note: King Louis-Philippe I came to power thanks to the barricades that overthrew the previous king in 1830 and abdicated after the barricades that overthrew him in 1848. His reign was characterized by the establishment of a restricted parliamentary regime and by the accession of the bourgeoisie to manufacturing and financial affairs, allowing an economic boom of first importance in France. His abdication in 1848 resulted from the inability of the French elite to adapt to the changes of the time. Mikhail Bakunin, who is a remarkable analyst of the period of the Monarchic Restoration that followed the French Revolution, explains that it was under the reign of Louis-Philippe that the merger of the former aristocracy and the rising bourgeoisie was accomplished. "It was precisely during the reign of Louis-Philippe that the spirit of the new class was also formed, under the auspices of the clergy." Bakunin, *L'Empire knouto-germanique et la révolution sociale, 1870–1871* (Paris: Champ libre, 1982), 322.

promote the interests of all and the well-being of all producers, which would only be made possible by solving the social problem; the bourgeois idea intended only to propagate the morality of self-interest, to spread political and religious indifference to all classes, and to destroy the parties. What this means is that the bourgeoisie declined as a conscious class holding collective interests, giving way only to economic needs known to lead to the aggravation of contradictions.

Thus, from February 1848 Proudhon became concerned about the fate of this new revolution, which from the first day he says was made "without an idea," without a coherent revolutionary project that would prepare for success.[25] All his previous analyses led him to believe that the bourgeoisie was unable to solve the real challenge facing society—economic reorganization— and that the working classes, while rightly posing the problem of the organization of labor, had not yet achieved sufficient cohesion and consciousness of the necessary means to solve the social problem. During this revolutionary period, Proudhon's judgments about the traits of the bourgeoisie and its possible development combine with polemical indications and reform projects. At first reading, he seems to waver between two incompatible attitudes: sometimes he affirms and seems to justify class struggle, while on other occasions he calls for reconciliation. In founding the newspaper *Le Représentant du Peuple* [Representative of the People], Proudhon proposes to fight for the social revolution, for the emancipation of the working classes, and from March he accuses the provisional government of abandoning the proletariat's cause, of restoring the proprietary status quo and the power of the bourgeoisie. After the riots of June, he defends the Parisian workers in the midst of general hostility: on July 31, at a famous meeting in the National Assembly, he proclaims from the top of the tribune the principle of class struggle and his fidelity to the proletariat's cause. However, at the same time, he affirms the urgency and therefore the possibility of reconciliation between

---

25. "They have made a revolution without an idea." *Carnet, no. 6*, vol. 2, February 24, 1848.

the middle classes and the working classes, writing on several occasions that economic reform is not possible without the participation of the bourgeois class.

These divergences are largely due to rapidly changing circumstances and do not contradict an overall judgment that remains unchanged. Prior to the February Revolution, Proudhon, distinguishing between the high and middle bourgeoisie, treated the class of industrial and financial feudalism as the most conservative class and the one most hostile to any social reform; he radically denied this class the possibility of achieving a revolutionary theory, but he did not completely deny the middle class such a possibility. From this time on, he attributed the initiative of social change to the working classes, but the boundaries between these classes were sufficiently imprecise that the petite bourgeoisie was partly included among the workers.[26] Thus, in 1848, while provisionally affirming that the proletariat could find the means of its emancipation within itself, Proudhon strives in his articles to reassure the middle class and differentiate it from the *haute bourgeoisie*.[27] The bourgeoisie, he writes, must be cut "in two" so that the middle bourgeoisie can be led to participate in the economic revolution against the large proprietors. He recommends that his collaborators advocate for "reconciliation" of this bourgeoisie with the proletariat and show the advantages that socialist ideas could provide the bourgeoisie.[28] This is why the two great

---

26. "Workers, laborers, men of the people, whoever you are, the initiative of reform belongs to you . . . you alone can accomplish it." *Avertissement aux propriétaires* [Warning to the Proprietors] (1842), 245.

27. "Yes, the working class possesses in itself the means to achieve its emancipation." Argument to la Montagne, *Le Peuple*, November 20, 1848, in *Mélanges*, vol. 17, p. 202. "First of all to separate the financial and manufacturing aristocracy, that is the bank, the stock exchange, the mines, the large factories, the construction sites such as Le Creusot—in short, all the industrial and mercantile feudalism of the real bourgeoisie, which is the middle class." Letter to Darimon, August 15, 1850, *Correspondance*, vol. 3, 322.

28. "The moment has come to show the bourgeoisie what is advantageous for it in socialist ideas." Letter to Darimon, February 14, 1850, ibid., 97.

works during this period include appeals to the bourgeoisie: *Confessions of a Revolutionary* (October 1849) ends with a post-script affirming that the revolution could take hold within the middle class, and *General Idea of the Revolution* (July 1851) begins with a dedication addressed to the bourgeoisie, reminding it of its revolutionary past. During this phase of history, Proudhon believes that social reforms are likely to succeed only if they are supported by the most progressive part of the bourgeoisie. This is not just a ruse: Proudhon would not stop asserting, contrary to widespread prejudices, that the establishment of a social-ist or mutualist regime would be favorable to the interests of the working bourgeoisie by freeing them from the oppression of capitalism and the threats posed by economic anarchy. But he also thinks, in 1848, that this economic oppression was felt enough for the middle class to participate in the revolutionary movement: repressed by big capital and humiliated by its own representatives, the true bourgeoisie has objective potential to withdraw from reactionary politics. In 1850 Proudhon was able to note this conscious awakening among small owners, industri-alists, and traders.[29]

However, the fact remains that social reform is posed by the working classes, that it must be demanded by them, and that they will be its greatest beneficiaries. Proudhon's attitude is therefore different depending on whether he is addressing the working classes or the middle class: to the working classes, he aims to denounce the myths of which they are partly victims and their vain confidence in authority; to the middle class, he aims to prove the validity of socialism. Whatever the possibilities and inclinations of the petite bourgeoisie, it must be snapped out of its routines and led to goals that belong first and foremost to the working classes. Thus Proudhon sometimes passes from promise to threat: on July 31, 1848, he makes a formal demand to property to proceed with social liquidation, and when he

---

29. "The middle class, small trade, small industry, small rural and urban property, are passing en masse to the Republic. Everything is changing." Letter to Guillemin, December 17, 1850, ibid., 383.

is pressed to explain the meaning of this proposition, he adds that "in case of refusal" the proletariat would carry out this liquidation without the support of the bourgeoisie, in other words against it.[30]

The unfolding of the 1848 Revolution would eventually convince Proudhon of the futility of his attempt and gradually make him skeptical of the revolutionary potential of the middle class. Rather than joining the proletariat and satisfying its demands on the right to work on economic organization, the middle bourgeoisie was, as Proudhon writes in 1851, an "accomplice" of the reaction: instead of joining those with whom it could be reconciled, it allied with its own enemies, the members of the class of industrial feudalism. However, the failure of the 1848 Revolution cannot be explained solely by this conservative attitude of the middle classes or even only by conflict between the three social classes. Analyzing French society in its different dimensions, Proudhon notes that alongside the division of the nation into three main classes, account must be taken of the political, religious, administrative, military, and legal forces whose power drew them toward conservatism, largely altering the dynamics between classes.[31] The clergy, large in number and in wealth, and considered as the organ of public and private morality, exerted a "hidden" force on the population and was often therefore irresistible. The army, not having a direct relation with the nation and the national guards, was entirely in the hands of the central power. The centralized administration, including the police, education, public works, and finance, employed a huge body of civil servants governing people and industries. The judiciary extended its supreme arbitration on private interests and social relations in perfect cooperation with the church, the public administration, the police, and the army. These combined forces constitute a "weight," a "straitjacket" that grips the French people as a whole and hampers its intellectual

---

30. *Discours prononcé à l'Assemblée Nationale* [Speech to the National Assembly], 370.

31. *La Révolution sociale*, 123–26.

and productive spontaneity.[32] But while the administration, the clergy, and the army recruit their upper hierarchy from the *haute bourgeoisie*, they do not limit themselves to a specific social class, but spread in different forms to all classes or, conversely, separate from them as in the case of the army, which finds itself "out of place" in the nation. The middle classes face new obstacles to their emancipation in these different hierarchies; they were both victims and accomplices.

The Second Empire confirms and aggravates the split between industrial feudalism and the middle classes that the reign of Louis-Philippe had already signaled. The term *feudalism* refers both to a new economic system, a new type of bourgeois capitalism, and the social class that benefits from it. Economically, this social system, which comes after industrial anarchy while retaining its defects, is distinguished by an enormous increase in capital, the expansion of monopolies, and the concentration of property in a small number of hands. Capital, formerly divided among many enterprises, becomes concentrated in industrial infrastructure, particularly railways, and develops in unprecedented fashion, leading to a decrease in capital in all other domains.[33] Agricultural industries and rural property lose their importance, leading to the subordination of agriculture to financial powers, the impoverishment of agricultural production, and mass unemployment of day laborers. Desertion of the countryside leads to an increase in rent in major cities, and therefore an increase in profits for the proprietors and an increase in costs for the majority of the population. Continuing tax increases continue the economic centralization that began during the Restoration. Finally, capitalist concentration encourages the proliferation of cash for

---

32. "Thus the French people, in their deep masses, with the centralization that grips them, the clergy that preaches to them, the army that surveils them, the legal order that threatens them, the parties that tug at them, the capitalist and mercantile feudalism that possesses them, resemble a criminal thrown in prison, watched night and day." Ibid., 127.

33. *Manuel du spéculateur à la Bourse* (Paris: Lacroix, 1853), vol. ii, 393–98.

the purposes of speculation. All these factors contribute to the progressive concentration of capital and the instruments of labor within a new economic centralization, increasing the wealth of a small number and widening the gap between the privileged and the producing classes.

This tiny minority constitutes the "upper class" that may be compared to a new nobility due to its small number and parasitic nature. Proudhon lists, among its members, the leading figures in industry, trade, agriculture, finance, and science, and the managers of large companies whose income comes mostly from interest or privileges; he adds to these two categories the senior officials of the public administration, the judiciary, the clergy, and the army, their high salaries making them part of this first social class.[34] In 1853 Proudhon believed that this social class intended to establish a militaristic economic regime that he termed the Industrial Empire.[35] Indeed, industrial feudalism merely continues the previous capitalist anarchy, retaining its contradictions and pursuing its own movement of concentration: it combines the anarchy of competition with the expansion of monopolies, and the exploitation of labor with the overwhelming power of a minority. The resulting contradictions cause a shift toward even greater centralization, which is intended to stifle threats of social war. The Political Empire, which has become the Industrial Empire, would achieve extreme social subordination within a monolithic system, absorbing and dominating all industrial activities with the complicity of the privileged class.[36] This parasitic minority cannot stand in the way of such a development:

---

34. Ibid., 400-401.

35. Ibid., 5-7, 399-408.

36. Georges Gurvitch underlines that here Proudhon foresees the possibility of capitalism transforming into fascist totalitarianism. *Les fondateurs français de la sociologie contemporaine* [The French Founders of Contemporary Sociology], vol. 2, *Proudhon* (Paris, Centre de documentation universitaire, 1955), 54. Translator's note: Proudhon's analysis is all the more remarkable because economic historians place the appearance of the first monopolies at the time of the international industrial depression of the 1870s and 1890s.

since the upper class shares in all the advantages of the system, it is concerned only for the increase in its profits and embodies, par excellence, the conservative party; in the face of peril, it would only seek a leader, an unprincipled savior.

Capitalist concentration, occurring during the Second Empire, weakens the middle class while enriching the upper class. The expansion of large industrial, commercial, and financial companies crushes small businesses. Tax increases, risks from stock market fluctuations, and foreign competition place small industrialists and traders in an insecure situation, causing them to disappear. Moreover, the high wages offered by large companies discourage the exercise of formerly free professions. Proudhon thus detects, in the socioeconomic changes following the coup, a progressive weakening of the middle class by a process of proletarianization of its members. Free profession gives way to subordinated activity: the increasing difficulties faced by small enterprises force the petite bourgeoisie to join the ranks of the salariat. At the extreme of this evolution, which only happens gradually, the middle class would collapse, giving way to a social system in which only the *haute bourgeoisie*, the civil service, and the salariat would survive.[37] This economic weakening can only lead to a political weakening. Conscious of its material decline, the middle class loses all faith in political combinations and passes from despair to indifference;[38] members of this class, some of whom claimed to be the social bedrock of representative government, now, under the Second Empire, make up only a precarious class, a kind of transitional phase from old industrial freedom to proletarian slavery. In 1858, when he publishes *Justice*, Proudhon, abandoning the few hopes he had put in these classes in 1848, states that they cannot have the mind for government: being intermediate classes devoted to trade, the middle

---

37. "The middle class will extinguish itself day by day, attacked from the front by the rise of wages and the development of the public company; from the side by tax and foreign competition or free exchange; and finally replaced by the public sector, the *haute bourgeoisie* and the salariat." *De la capacité politique des classes ouvrières*, 230.

38. *Manuel du spéculateur à la Bourse*, vol. II, 401.

classes have neither strength nor self-consciousness, and cannot assume leadership of the social movement.[39]

The emergence of a class consciousness, of a *political capacity of the working classes*, merely confirms and completes this decline of the bourgeoisie. Whereas in 1789 the bourgeoisie was conscious of itself and its interests, wanting to be everything in society, in 1864 it was nothing more than a mass of divergent interests. The situation had completely reversed: the people who were only a multitude had achieved consciousness and a theory, while the bourgeoisie had stopped thinking of itself as a class. However, Proudhon does not conclude from this new situation that the proletariat must seek the annihilation of the middle class. The proletariat must relentlessly fight against the *haute bourgeoisie*, which would inevitably block the social revolution, but it must offer the middle class an alliance and lead it in carrying out the *working-class idea*.[40] This alliance is justified for practical and theoretical reasons: the middle class, whatever its political emptiness, possesses the instruments of economic progression, the technical and scientific knowledge of which the workers are deprived. The alliance of the working classes and the middle classes can ensure the success of the revolution, which is hampered by the ignorance of the majority of workers. Theoretically, this alliance does not contradict the revolution's ultimate objective, which is not the extermination of a class but instead the extermination of inequalities and privileges within a reconciled society. But this politics proposed to the working classes assumes that, despite the difficulties, members of the middle class remain receptive to proletarian theory. The middle class no longer forms a coherent unit and a conscious class, but Proudhon, however fierce his critique, maintains that objective conditions place the petite bourgeoisie in such a situation of insecurity and subordination that it may agree with the revolutionary intentions of the

---

39. "No matter what has been said, there is not, there cannot be, a government of the middle classes; the reason is in their very middleness. They have the spirit of trade; they do not have the spirit of government." *De la justice dans la révolution et dans l'église*, 5th étude, vol. 3, 147.

40. *De la capacité politique des classes ouvrières*, p. 192, 231, and passim.

working classes. Ultimately, sympathies and traditions remain among the members of the middle class that the proletariat can awaken without in any way abandoning its own objectives.

3. The Working Classes

Proudhon's work can be read as a journey toward recognition of the political capacity of the working classes, as an increasingly systematic justification for the proletariat's emancipation by itself. Starting from a socioeconomic analysis of private property, Proudhon concludes his work with a call for an autonomous proletarian politics. However, this is only the political journey: these conclusions are based on a set of sociological indications concerning the working classes' objective and subjective situation and practical possibilities. Proudhon refuses to offer a utopian recipe or panacea, claiming that mutualist democracy expresses both the real needs and the idea of the working classes. It is therefore important for him to know what these classes, which he often designates by the generic term *people*, are and what they really want, and in particular to answer the question of whether the proletariat is revolutionary by itself and up to the task of enacting the social reforms that alone will ensure the establishment of an egalitarian society.

Proudhon's answers to these questions come as no surprise: on the one hand, he proposes to "express what the *people* think" and considers himself the organ, the expression of popular collective reason;[41] on the other hand, he often displays the same critical rage against the working classes as against the bourgeois classes. With Proudhon we do not find the tender sympathy that many nineteenth-century writers express toward the people's poverty, but a harshness of tone and judgment unexpected for a socialist thinker. For him, the true spontaneity of the people must not be confused with the passing opinions and prejudices it may express. As early as 1848, Proudhon affirms, as he would

---

41. *Carnet, no.* 5 (1847), vol. 2, 137.

repeat in different terms in his final book, that the proletariat ("the people") carries within itself a truth, a reason, a revolutionary purpose;[42] but at the same time, he says, it does not know itself and is not conscious of its idea, its true interests, adhering instead to bourgeois doctrines and using political means contrary to its needs.[43] Similarly, the people have a genuine experience of the political economy, and in a certain sense they are the only ones who possess this knowledge, but they must be made to discover and learn it.[44]

Consequently, Proudhon assumes an attitude of great independence from the working classes while proclaiming his unwavering belonging to the proletariat's cause and his willingness to defend and justify popular acts, whatever the circumstances. He absolutely refuses to "flatter" the people demagogically and accuses many theorists of this failing: for him, all popular ideas and votes should not be blindly approved; on the contrary, it is necessary to denounce, even brutally, everything that emanates from the people but does not really belong to them and that is not the expression of their true spontaneity. The people are not necessarily always a force for liberation and are not inherently the savior or messiah of modern times. If they are one day, it will only be after a clarification of ideas resulting from a struggle and implemented by a practice to which the revolutionary theorist contributes.

This confusion, ignorance, and corruption that the working classes carry in themselves is rooted in their economic situation. The regime of property not only places the workers in a relationship of subordination but also carries out a true degradation of their character. The division of labor, by wresting from people the initiative of their work and the synthesis of artisanal production, condemns producers to individual degeneration. As the division grows, the workers become, in Alexis de

---

42. "I do not speak to the people in the name of my own science; I speak to it in the name of its own reason, which I seek to produce." Ibid., 176.

43. "For . . . it is the collective reason not to know itself." Ibid., 137.

44. Ibid., 151.

Tocqueville's words, weaker and more narrow-minded.[45] Forms of labor inevitably influence the ideas and habits of the person involved: workers' subservience to the machines they depend on inevitably leads to their debasement in a manner comparable to that caused by ancient slavery. More generally, in the regime of property, which is justified by religion and supported by the state, workers are subjected to a system that radically despises them: classified, registered, numbered, victims of a permanent inquisition, entitled to subsidies and public charity, workers are treated by all of society with a brutal or philanthropic disrespect. The poverty that weakens wills, the fragmented work that stupefies minds, the absence of education: the whole system consigns the proletariat to material and moral "infamy."[46] Undoubtedly, a clear awareness of their situation would immediately turn proletarians into revolutionaries, but the system prevents, or at least strongly constrains, this awareness and on the contrary leads workers to accept their situation.[47]

In 1860, Proudhon writes the most violent and desperate pages on the proletariat's revolutionary potential.[48] He bitterly recalls the failure of the February Revolution, angry at the support that Napoleon found among some of the popular classes, and he denounces working-class passivity with extreme fury, highlighting the psychological and cultural obstacles to self-emancipation. Proudhon thus writes that the salariat, however different from serfs or slaves, retains their features and may be compared to the plebeians. Although employees no longer belong to a master, they are not really freer than serfs: they are mercenary workers, deprived of initiative, excluded from management, and denied all material and moral independence. In

---

45. *Système des contradictions économiques*, vol. 1, 143.

46. Ibid., vol. 2, 197.

47. "If, by some impossibility, the proletarian could reach a certain degree of intelligence, he would make use of it in the first place to revolutionize society and change all civil and industrial relations." Ibid., vol. 1, 199.

48. *De la justice dans la révolution et dans l'église*, 8th étude, vol. 3, 459–79.

this subordination, we must seek the reasons for this political passivity that the working classes have shown for so long. Limited to physical labor, the people accept their lot without being able to question whether the poverty to which they are condemned might be the result of a temporary injustice. Accustomed to depending on their business owner, they seek protection and patronage from them, naively believing that their boss is their friend. Their situation of dependence conveys to them, as to all the weak, an "instinct of obedience" that diminishes their consciousness of being subordinated.[49]

In the same text, Proudhon adds that the people are also victims of mystifications in which they spontaneously become accomplices. Stripped of all assets, they enjoy in their imagination what they are excluded from: they revere their homeland, national glories, and Napoleonic victories, as if they were the beneficiaries. This identification with the master will make them applaud a sovereign or tyrant, an image of force and possession. While the bourgeois think about their interests, the people enthuse over military conquests, regardless of whether they are favorable or harmful to the nation. In religion, the people remain unconcerned for theology and spirituality and invent the image of the good God, an expression of their submission.

In these satirical remarks, we must allow for provocation. Proudhon, who wants to write for the revolutionary workers, seeks to provoke the surge of pride that would come from an awareness of past submission. But in his view there is no doubt that the docility that the proletarian classes have shown is due in part to these ideological obstacles, this internalization of a situation of dependency. The worker, ensnared in a social constitution that is made against them, is a being "denatured by the law of labor and bourgeois exploitation."[50]

However, these indications are only provisional: they concern only one period and one aspect of proletarian psychology, whereas the Proudhonian method leads to a historical sociology

49. Ibid., 462.
50. Ibid., 461.

of classes, rethinking class in terms of its becoming and its transformations. In Proudhon's view, 1830, 1848, and 1864 are the
main dates that mark the transformation of the masses into a
conscious class, of the plebeians into a political class. The 1789
Revolution was not provoked by a popular movement but rather
by disagreements among the upper classes who sought to obtain
the support of the people against the old regime; during this
period, popular protests were not the expression of a consciousness that made demands: while the bourgeoisie felt itself to be
and presented itself as a ruling class, the people did not assert
itself as a revolutionary power, as a deprived class demanding
the reinstatement of its rights. Undoubtedly the intervention of
the masses was more direct in 1830, when again the movement
wanted by the bourgeoisie, supported only by the people, was
immediately claimed by the bourgeoisie once success was assured
and the participation of the lower classes proved unnecessary or
dangerous.

Thus, when Proudhon wrote his first works from 1840
to 1848, he did not affirm that the working classes, whom he
defended, were fully able to carry out the radical transformation of social relations mentioned in *The System of Economic
Contradictions*. The working classes can bring about this upheaval
and take the initiative: the realization of "progressive association"
would be carried out by workers and small artisans such as the
canuts of Lyon.[51] But the conception of this project means that in
order to achieve social emancipation, the working classes must
undergo a practical and ideological transformation; they must
free themselves from paternalistic and communistic illusions and
undertake organizational action themselves rather than waiting
for salvation from other classes as before. The distance between
theory, which Proudhon presents as the expression of worker
thought, and effective practice is therefore considerable. In fact,
the theory of progressive association is presented as a plan for

---

51. Translator's note: The canuts were Lyonnais silk workers who
staged major revolts in 1831, 1834, and 1848. Their mutual workers' associations inspired Proudhon's mutualism.

reform, a project that Proudhon recognizes will be extremely difficult to carry out because of the workers' passivity and ignorance.

The historical significance of the February Revolution would for the first time pose the question of the right to work, the organization of labor, or in other words the subordination of capital to labor.[52] But Proudhon attributes February's events more to the collapse of a system unable to resolve its contradictions than to a coherent action by the working class, hence his concerns once the crisis erupts and his fears of seeing the failure of a movement that is not the product of a coherent will. Not only are the revolutionary forces not broken, the revolutionary leaders themselves lack a social theory, are lost in political and Jacobin traditions, and risk taking the people in a direction that is not their own. Proudhon's activity would therefore not be directed only against conservative forces, against the moderate or authoritarian tendencies of the provisional government, but also against certain nonrevolutionary tendencies in the working classes. At the same time, Proudhon proclaims himself the expression of working-class thought, giving his newspaper the task of being the organ, the voice of the people, and he indicates that the newspaper will aim to create worker unity, a unity that does not yet exist.[53] The newspaper's aim will be to question the proletariat, observe its manifestations, and interpret its acts, but it will also act as a guide, and Proudhon hopes that the success of his publication will redirect the workers, especially the Parisian workers, toward a genuinely revolutionary practice. In this period, speech is an action and is immediately effective. Every article is both analysis and action. When Proudhon repeats that he affirms the autonomy and emancipation of the masses, he does not mean that the masses

---

52. "The revolution of February proclaimed the *right to work*, that is the predominance of labor over capital." *Toast à la Révolution* [Toast to the Revolution], vol. 17, 149.

53. "In founding *Le Peuple*, an organ of working-class thought, we have come to constitute the unity of workers in the presence of the anarchy of privileges, to pose the revolutionary idea, the progressive idea, in the face of reactionary projects, regressive ideas." *Manifeste du Peuple* [Manifesto of *Le Peuple*], September 2, 1848.

are emancipated but that they must emancipate themselves by transforming themselves;[54] moreover, the goal of his practice is to organize the workers, to help them overcome their isolation by making them aware of the necessary means for their emancipation. Thus he would provisionally write that the working class possesses the means for its emancipation, but these words must be taken more as exhortations than as assertions, corrected immediately by prompts to action.[55] The proletariat must carry out its emancipation by means of an organization that belongs to it in its own right, it must emancipate itself; in other words, this is a task to be achieved, and its success is uncertain.

In addition, the failure of the revolution, as bitter as it may have been, was not a complete surprise for Proudhon, as he was aware of the weaknesses of the labor movement. The fall of the revolution would force him to take stock of the workers' possibilities and would lead him to emphasize two weaknesses in the labor movement: the persistence of Caesarian myths and errors of judgment with regard to class hostilities. While the bourgeoisie is skeptical, distrustful, and invents quibbles against the authorities, the proletariat dreams of a simple and unified power that nothing would stop; it distrusts the complicated guarantees given to individuals and groups, repudiates federalism, and dreams of unity, centralization, and communism; and thus the people did not stand in the way of Napoleon III, who embodies this imaginary unity.[56] Moreover, accustomed by their subordinate condition to believing that there can be a good boss, a good bourgeois, a good sovereign, the people do not immediately

---

54. "We affirm what the founders of the state never believed: the personality and autonomy of the masses." *Résistance à la Révolution* [Resistance to the Revolution], *La Voix du Peuple* [The Voice of the People], December 1849, in *Mélanges*, vol. 19, 12.

55. "Yes, the working class possesses within itself the means to achieve its emancipation. . . . The proletariat, if it wants to free itself from capitalist exploitation." Argument to la Montagne, November 20, 1848, ibid., vol. 17, 202.

56. "It delights in large pieces: centralization, the indivisible republic, the unitary empire. By the same cause, it is communist." *De la justice dans la révolution et dans l'église*, 8th étude, vol. 3, 470.

distrust an emperor. By presenting himself as the enemy of ideologies and parliamentarians, Napoleon III flattered a popular prejudice and found himself in keeping with a certain popular instinct. Here Proudhon denounces what he had repeatedly criticized throughout the February Revolution: blind confidence in the power of the state and the fundamental mistake of expecting economic reform from a political reform. But during the struggles of 1848 he mostly blamed this prejudice on the democratic leaders: he was forced to recognize that this prejudice was also prevalent among the workers.

The second criticism concerns the inappropriateness of class hostilities. In February 1848, the middle class and the people were reconciled in the revolution, and the social reform would have been possible by uniting these two factions of the working world against the upper classes. However, the two tendencies, equally republican, were unable to understand their mutual interests, the middle class out of fear of socialism and the popular classes out of distrust of the middle classes.[57] This disastrous distrust would favor the election of Louis-Bonaparte: voting for the Empire was considered a vote against the bourgeoisie but was in reality a vote for industrial feudalism, and popular prejudices supported the *grande bourgeoisie*'s fears and its preference for a military savior.

Thus, from 1840, the terms of the problem did not change for Proudhon: could the people, or more precisely the working classes, assert their revolutionary project, their *idea*? Could they achieve an autonomous practice and a spontaneous organization, declaring themselves separate from bourgeois society and against the entire regime of property? They demonstrated this possibility several times in 1848, but the Second Empire showed how weak and relatively quickly these impulses were diverted. This is why the presentation of worker candidacies to the 1863 elections, especially the *Manifeste des Soixante* [Manifesto of the Sixty] (February 1864)—in which workers expressed their

---

57. "The people distrust the middle class." *Manuel du spéculateur à la Bourse*, vol. II, 405.

desire to present worker candidates and conduct a social struggle independent of the upper or middle bourgeoisie—seemed to Proudhon to be decisive signs of a new working-class consciousness. The manifesto, signed by sixty Parisian workers, asserted that the workers could not count on representatives from the upper classes to defend their interests and express their will. The text stated that this working-class will was oriented not toward mere political reforms but toward the proletariat's social emancipation by means of economic transformations. Proudhon could recognize his own terms in this manifesto: domination of capital, wage labor, social emancipation of the proletariat, justice; more precisely, he found the idea that he constantly defended: the realization of an economic revolution by the action of the workers themselves and the expansion of mutualist companies.

Responding to this manifesto in *The Political Capacity of the Working Classes*, Proudhon explains at length the decisive importance of the proletariat's coming to class consciousness. For a social class to gain political capacity and become the subject of social action, three conditions are required: first, the class must acquire consciousness of itself, its place, its role, its functions, and consequently its demands; second, it must affirm its *idea* and express and imagine "the law of its being"; finally, it must achieve a practice in accordance with its theory.[58]

The first condition, the acquisition of self-consciousness, was met during the 1848 Revolution: whereas the previous revolutions were political revolutions in which the proletariat served only as a temporary tool for the bourgeoisie, in 1848 the working classes proposed their own demands—the right to work, social revolution—thus affirming their consciousness of their distinctive nature. The *Manifeste des Soixante* was a new sign of this: in aiming for worker candidacies, the workers signified that they must be represented as a class.[59] In positing the principle that bourgeois representation could not defend their interests and express their will, they affirmed that the working class constituted

---

58. *De la capacité politique des classes ouvrières*, 89–90.
59. Ibid., 93.

a social unit with its own rights and demonstrated through their presence and expression that their class had reached self-consciousness. The demand for worker candidacies fundamentally expressed the desire to distinguish themselves, to separate themselves as a class from the bourgeoisie. Such a claim could only cause a scandal in the eyes of the privileged classes, who feigned to believe that the 1789 Revolution, by breaking up the classes, had destroyed social divisions, and that all citizens shared in the same equality, differing only by profession. Through an act of separation, the workers affirmed on the contrary that society was still divided into classes and, moreover, that these classes were in a relation of antagonism. In doing so, they gained consciousness of their situation, since the nature of the regime of property is to exclude the proletariat from bourgeois solidarity, but in gaining consciousness of their situation of exclusion they gave their class the initiative of political action.

The second condition required for political capacity, the expression of an *idea* that would stand in contrast to the theories of rival classes, the proletariat achieves, albeit imperfectly, and Proudhon gives the revolutionary theorist the task of participating in this clarification. Of course, the social question was not first asked by the workers: it was initially formulated by economists, by upper-class intellectuals such as Saint-Simon, Sismondi, Fourier, Pierre Leroux, V. Considérant, Louis Blanc, Cabet, and Flora Tristan.[60] But the working classes did not submit to any socialist school; a revolution is not the work of any one person but a general process accomplished spontaneously in all parts of the political body by replacing an entire social system with a new one. It is this system that can be called an idea and is both a form of society and a representation of this form. When the bourgeoisie enacted the Great Revolution, it possessed a social idea corresponding to its self-consciousness, the idea of *human rights*. By this idea, the nation's sovereignty was affirmed, royalty was reduced to a function, nobility was abolished, religion was relegated to a private opinion, and economic freedom

---

60. Ibid., 105–9.

was assumed. In 1864, in an empire in which the bourgeoisie had surrendered parliamentary guarantees to the state, the bourgeois classes no longer had a thought or a will:[61] their exclusive concern was to acquire profits and seek new means for exploitation; the bourgeoisie was no longer a class that thought and wanted, worked and controlled, but was instead a mass of traders, a "rabble."[62] The working-class idea was asserted in the face of this ideological vacuum; like the idea of any class, it is nothing more than the "notion of its own constitution," the expression of working-class existence:[63] to be adequate, the idea must only be the formulation of the reality, constitution, and action of the class itself.

And again, Proudhon tried to show how the idea of community, as realized by the Luxembourg Commission in 1848, contradicted true working-class thought; he continued by repeating that the working-class idea aimed to create a mutualist, federalist, and anarchist society. The Luxembourg school, by restoring an absorbing centralization, an undivided power, an association in which all individual thought was deemed to be separatist, merely repeated the old absolutism. While authoritarian communism corresponded to the "instinct" of the masses, in that, failing a conscious awakening, they might desire to submit to an omnipresent power, it could not convey working-class thought. Rather than expressing working-class thought, communism suppressed it by reducing the masses to general servitude, ostensibly founded on a dictatorship of the proletariat. Proudhon notes, in the *Manifeste des Soixante*, the importance given to mutual credit companies and the notions of freedom of labor, credit, and the elimination of wages in an egalitarian society. These statements are opposed in every way to bourgeois and communist conceptions: instead of repeating a hierarchical social model whose principles would be authority and state power, true working-class thought envisages the creation of a social system of equilibrium

---

61. Ibid., 100.
62. Ibid.
63. Ibid., 91. We will return to this problem in chapter 5.

and reciprocity, a "system of balances between free forces."[64] The content of working-class thought is not authority or charity but justice, which would be realized in industrial democracy, a society based on the principle of mutuality, and subjected to the jurisdiction of all workers.

But while the first two conditions required to reach political capacity—self-consciousness and revolutionary theory— have been fulfilled, as of 1864 the working classes have not yet arrived at an appropriate political practice; they cannot yet deduce from their *idea* the political conclusions that will enable them to impose their project on society as a whole. And here too, Proudhon strives to make a contribution to the proletarian movement by defining a revolutionary practice. As he has repeatedly stated in his previous writings, he reaffirms that strikes cannot be an instrument of struggle: in addition to their economic futility, they express a pattern whereby instead of imposing a radical social reform, the workers are limited to their subordinated condition, expecting their employers to resolve their hardships.[65] The action of working-class democracy must aim above all at class separation. It must affirm its independent existence and refuse to be in permanent thrall to the bourgeois classes. This separation, expressed in particular by the refusal to support bourgeois Opposition candidates in elections, constitutes a political "weapon" that allows a class to become a distinct faction.[66] It is the act by which a class makes itself by defining itself. However, Proudhon does not further specify the particular means or circumstances necessary for the revolutionary act because, for him, *coups de force* and riots are merely periods of acceleration of history. When the proletariat discovers the limits of political action and the urgency of an economic revolution, it faces a much broader task than a riot: the task of promoting the autonomous economic organization of the class itself, not by the

---

64. Ibid., 124.

65. *Système des contradictions*, vol. I, 151–52, 184, 267; *De la justice dans la révolution et dans l'église*, 8th étude, vol. 3, 467–68; *De la capacité politique des classes ouvrières*, 372.

66. *De la capacité politique des classes ouvrières*, 237.

creation of limited associations but by a general action aimed at imposing the social revolution.

However, Proudhon defends himself against inciting civil war: social antagonism must only be temporary. The goal of working-class practice is neither to prolong class antagonism nor to implement an inverse form of exploitation, but to ensure that class divisions and classes themselves disappear. Without proposing the formula of "classless society," Proudhon constantly develops its idea: because class division is based on the regime of property and the contradiction between capital and labor, the establishment of industrial democracy would have the effect of eliminating class antagonism and the very notions of bourgeoisie and proletariat. The destruction of capitalist theft, by eliminating both the source of profits and the wage system, would erase the distinction between bourgeoisie and proletariat and would restore social equality in the balancing of functions. This disappearance of classes would not correspond exactly to the conquest of global society by a class: Proudhon could write in *The Political Capacity of the Working Classes* that the proletariat, like the bourgeoisie in 1789, will impose its social project on all society, but it will only do so by destroying itself, since wages are only a reality in the regime of property. The classless society, a reconciled society, would be neither proletarian nor bourgeois. It should not maintain any of the defects inherent to classes but would consist of workers participating equally, according to their various functions, in management and production within a spontaneous organization.

CHAPTER FOUR

Anarchism and Sociology of the State

It was through his critique of the state that Proudhon was to shock his democratic and socialist contemporaries the most. While Louis Blanc, Étienne Cabet, and Louis August Blanqui remain influenced by the Jacobin tradition, Proudhon strives to show not only that the tools of the revolution must be sought in economic reorganization but also that the goal of the revolution lies beyond any improvement in political forms.[1] The goal of the revolutionary struggle cannot be the creation of a new state, however good it may be, but must be destruction of the centralized state—in other words, the end of politics. Of course, around 1840 the Jacobin ideology did not constitute a systematic body of theory; rather, the term connotes a set of attitudes and concerns that Proudhon opposes point by point. To the tradition of national unification as a tool for destroying privilege, Proudhon responds by defending the Girondin tradition and federalism as a tool of freedom and equality.[2] To the principles of political cen-

---

1. Translator's note: Jacobinism is a political doctrine that defends popular sovereignty and the indivisibility of the French Republic. It takes its name from the Jacobin Club, whose members were established during the French Revolution in the former Jacobin convent in Paris.

2. Translator's note: In the mythology of the French Revolution, the Girondins are seen as supporters of federalism as opposed to the centralism advocated by the Jacobins. It is from this point of view that Proudhon places himself. In reality, the situation is a little more complicated. The Girondins were a moderate political group founded in 1791 by a few deputies from the provincial bourgeoisie, several of whose instigators came from the Gironde (Bordeaux region). The Girondins, most of whom were members of the Jacobin Club, were in the majority in the 1791 Legislative Assembly, where they opposed the supporters of

tralization and the strengthening of power, he responds with a critique whereby any increase in political strength has the effect of breaking revolutionary spontaneity. To the expectation of a revolution from above, he responds with, as he puts it, the principle of a revolution "by the initiative of the masses."[3] To concern for politics, he substitutes concern for society but also the critique and critical negation of the state. He thus inaugurates a theory and invites a practice that, after him, would constantly fight with or run into the Marxist tradition.

From the outset, however, Proudhon seems to come up against a difficulty of principle: he tries to demonstrate that the state has fulfilled necessary social functions in the past, in particular in the historical phenomenon of war, but nevertheless concludes that the state is a mystification and that society must annihilate it or at least subordinate it in a federal organization. The transition from social analysis to anarchist theory seems all the more delicate, since the spontaneist theory of the social leads him to emphasize the functional nature of all great human creation.[4] Whether it is a question of religion or the state, it is important to set aside false explanations that reduce them to accidents or illusions: just as religion cannot be explained by the malice of priests or the ignorance of the faithful, the state cannot be explained only by the violence of a class or the mystification of citizens. Saint-Simon was able to reconcile this thesis of the

---

the constitutional monarchy. The Girondins refused both a return to the ancien régime and economic and social reforms favorable to the working classes. During the National Convention, the Girondins formed the right wing of national representation. They abolished royalty and proclaimed the First Republic. Frightened by the radicalization of the population of Paris, particularly after the massacres of September 1792, the Girondins withdrew from the Jacobin Club. On June 2, 1793, a riot led by the sansculottes drove the Girondins out of the Convention. Twenty-one of them were tried and executed by the Revolutionary Court. Others tried to stage a federalist revolt, which was severely repressed.

3. *Confessions d'un révolutionnaire*, 82.

4. Translator's note: For Proudhon, a social phenomenon is spontaneous when it takes place solely because of its internal determination, without the intervention of external determination.

effective role of the state with the theory of its decline by linking it to two successive historical phases of society: the military
phase, in which the collective goal is war, requiring a dominating
state led by the feudal caste; and the industrial phase, in which
the goal is production, requiring the elimination of the state as a
force for repression. Proudhon does not fail to adopt this opposition and to recall the monarchy's warlike character, but he cannot limit himself to this indication: for him, the state must be
understood in its relation to the social totality, independently
of the particular forms it takes, from autocracy to representative
democracy.

The possibility of the state lies in the very nature of society as
the real subject and creator of a force. As soon as humans come
together, develop diverse industries among themselves, create
ongoing relations, and impose conditions of solidarity on each
other, a "natural group" is formed that constitutes itself as a city,
as an autonomous social organism.[5] At this level there is still no
state or government, yet collective life develops in full spontaneity; humans are not united by an external constraint but only
by an instinctive solidarity related to mutual protection and
production needs: social life is constituted before politics distinguishes itself. Thus solidarity, economic relations, and the
sovereignty of the autonomous group historically precede the
constitution of the state. The assumption of the primacy of social
life must be applied to all societies, however they are organized;
it is not the social that proceeds from the political but rather the
political that proceeds from the social. But if the force of collectivity is originally immanent in society and emanates only from
social activity, it can be appropriated, diverted from its source.
Precisely because the collective force is the ever-renewed labor
of organized people, not a tangible reality, it can be monopolized, alienated, snatched from its authors.[6] Politics is to social

5. "Natural group": *Contradictions politiques, Théorie du mouvement con-
stitutionnel au XIXe siècle* [Political Contradictions: Theory of the Constitutional Movement in the 19th Century], 237.
6. "The alienation of the collective force." *De la justice dans la révolution et dans l'église*, 4th étude, vol. 2, 266.

life what capital is to labor: an alienation of the collective force.
Here the goal is not to define the public means of production or
distribution and the public services that, while not dependent on
group autonomy, contribute to common activity. Rather, it concerns the central power, governments as holders of a particular
authority over citizens and the different parts of the social body,
an authority that experience will show can become oppressive
and external to the social body.

This preliminary definition points toward the criticisms that
Proudhon will direct against all theories he suspects of individualism or statism. He will reproach Rousseau for a complete distortion of the notion of the social contract: rather than defining
the social relationship established between humans at the level
of exchange and production, Rousseau merely seeks the nature
of the political contract, as if it were the basis for collective life.
The questions thus raised now concern only the alienation of
freedom and submission to common law, as if the social problem would necessarily be resolved under different forms of constraint.[7] Similarly, as early as 1848 Proudhon would rage against
the democrats who claimed to have achieved the social revolution by means of a political revolution, and he would emphasize the mystifying character of such a doctrine: since the state
is only the alienated expression of the forces of collectivity, a
change in government personnel cannot bring about the social
consequences that it boasts of having obtained. More seriously,
an exclusively political reform, whose effect would be to increase
government power and initiative, would have consequences
directly opposed to those hoped for: giving more power to the
state would reinforce the monopolization of collective forces
for the benefit of a minority, thereby fostering reactionary and
counterrevolutionary forces. The ignorance common to these
attempts and theories lies in misunderstanding the monopolization carried out by the state and the true nature of the social:
people continue to believe that social life comes from power,
whereas it is precisely power that imprisons life and prevents it

---

7. *Idée générale de la révolution*, 187–95.

from flourishing and developing. The recognition of real social life, its spontaneous organization, and its own movement will lead to the demand for the anarchist liberation of social forces, at odds with any statist theory.

1. Critique of States

The relationship of economic exploitation is simultaneously a social relationship of subjection. As *The System of Economic Contradictions* underlines, the principle of property is one of authority: in affirming the absolute right to possess and monopolize the collective force, the propertarian principle establishes the subordination of nonowners by owners. It is not only property's consequences that generate inequality and authority, but its very essence that defines and ensures the owner's despotism.[8] This principle is fully developed in bourgeois capitalism, where relations of authority are inscribed in the foundations of economic life, in the workshop: if the propertarian principle contains the germ of the social relation of subordination, it is ultimately realized in the organization of labor. It is there that the division arises between entrepreneurs, who possess both tools and power, and workers, who can only sell their hands, their labor power. This socioeconomic subordination occurs in each of the "epochs" of the system and is reinforced as it develops: through the division of labor, workers lose control of their activity; through mechanization, they find themselves subordinated to technologies that supersede them; through monopoly, they find themselves subjected to a power against which any partial struggle would be futile. The development of the capitalist regime, in its technological and social forms, thus carries out a subordination, inscribed within the relation of property: as the entrepreneurial capitalist becomes the master of labor, he becomes the master of people.

---

8. "Property is the right to use and abuse, in a word, despotism." *Système des contradictions*, vol. 2, 212.

It is in this economic relation of exploitation and subordination that we must seek the roots of the political despotism
inherent in capitalism.[9] The concentration of property and the
conflicts that it necessarily provokes between capital and labor
lead to an alliance of the owners against the workers, growing
inequality between classes, and consequently the constitution
of a constraining public force. Political despotism develops
both as a response to social instability and as an expression of
the appropriation of collective forces. Wealth inequality and the
subordination of ranks generate latent economic conflict and
unrest in the social body. Faced with this insurmountable instability, it becomes necessary to organize a public force, an authority, before which all interests must be erased and to which every
will must submit. Relations of conflict require a strong power
to be established with the aim of disciplining the nation, keeping the lower classes in poverty, combating their agitation, and
defending hierarchies and privileges. Capitalist anarchy requires
a constraint that stifles its conflicting social consequences.[10] At
the same time, the scale of the powers concentrated in the hands
of capitalist entrepreneurs allows them to take direct power over
the state and make it serve their interests: under Louis-Philippe
the state was only an alliance of the bourgeois against the workers; under the Second Empire it essentially became an instrument
of industrial and financial feudalism. In this monopolization, the
proprietors receive the complicity and support of the old hierarchies such as the church and the army, but while the state then
becomes the alliance of these combined forces, its despotic character and its very existence as a repressive force remain based on
economic inequality and the social forms of capitalist property.

This critique of the capitalist state confirms the principle
that the characteristics of politics are derived from economic
forces and social relations. The despotism of the capitalist state

---

9. "From time immemorial, the political constitution has been the
reflection of the economic organism, and the destiny of states has fluc-
tuated according to the qualities and defects of this organism." *Manuel du
spéculateur à la Bourse*, vol. 11, 25.

10. *De la justice dans la révolution et dans l'église*, 4th étude, vol. 2, 177-78.

does not stem from particular modalities of national representation but from the very foundations of society. The outcome
of this critique cannot therefore be a simple revision of political forms: it must be a fundamental transformation of socioeconomic relations.

Thus, Proudhon could only adopt a firmly critical attitude
toward the Banquets' Campaign that was developing in 1847:
since the fundamental goal of this agitation was merely electoral
reform, this campaign seemed of little interest to him, and, since
it diverted attention toward false problems, it was harmful.[11] He
only entered the political battle after the February Revolution,
when he could hope that the republic, instead of sticking to constitutional reforms, would transform itself into a social republic.[12]
But this was again to violently combat the so-called democratic
tendencies of the provisional government and its politics, which
he viewed as regressive.[13]

In March 1848, despite some attempts made to respond to
the real problem of the revolution—the organization of labor—it
was proposed to establish a democracy, without modifying the
bases of the social order, as if the social problem would be solved
by a political reform and in particular by reestablishing universal
suffrage. Against this theory and this illusion, Proudhon develops a virulent critique to show that a democracy, understood in

---

11. Translator's note: The Banquets' Campaign was a series of about
seventy meetings organized throughout France between 1847 and 1848
by the reformers to call for a broadening of the electorate and to oppose
the decisions taken by the conservative government of François Guizot.
Circumventing the ban on political meetings by taking the form of banquets, this campaign spread throughout the country. While the initia-
tors of this campaign simply called for reforms, more radical, republican
ideas ended up imposing themselves. The government chose repression
instead of debate, which led to the revolution of 1848 that brought about
the fall of the monarchy.

12. Translator's note: The civil unrest in France during February of
1848 led to the abdication of King Louis Philippe and the start of the
short-lived French Second Republic (1848–1851).

13. Particularly in articles published in *Le Représentant du Peuple* on
March 22 and March 26, 1848, in *Solution du problème social*, vol. 6, 1–87.

this way, would merely reestablish past hierarchies and social inequality.

The initial vice of democracy thus conceived lies in the notion of representation. It is held that a people cannot directly exercise legislative, executive, and judicial powers, and it is considered sufficient for the people to act by proxy and to give themselves agents to represent them. However, there can be no legitimate, integral representation of the people. At the very moment at which legitimate representation is asserted, women, domestic servants, nearly four-fifths of the people, are excluded from suffrage, and the artificially defined minority, when asked to elect its representatives, can only choose its own masters.[14] In the absence of a popular party and the expression of a collective thought, the day laborers and journeymen, acting under the influence of prejudices and local passions, must elect their bourgeois representatives.[15] Under the mask of democracy, men who possess talent and wealth predominate and immediately reconstitute a new aristocracy. It is vain to expect representative democracy to express the will of the constituents and all the ideas competing in the election; on the contrary, representatives, in theory elected to reconcile all interests, can never represent more than one idea, one interest, and although the National Assembly may better represent the plurality of opinions, it can only declare sovereign the majority opinion. Thus, the opinion of half of the Assembly will be declared the will of the people: the illusion of democracy will be replaced with a real tyranny of the majority. Because of the social relations of hierarchy and division, this majority will once again comprise the privileged members of the regime of property: while apparently seeking democracy, we hand back sovereignty to the privileged at the first step, thereby preventing

---

14. Translator's note: Pierre Ansart dismisses the fact that Proudhon did not seem to consider women as having the capacity to vote. Here is what Proudhon said in 1848: "We do not know whether, among other strange aberrations, the century we are living in is destined to see the emancipation of women realized to some degree. We believe that it is not." *La Liberté*, April 15, 1848).

15. *Solution du problème social*, vol. 6, 48.

any social reform since the only goal of the owner majority will be to ensure that its wealth is preserved. Thus, it will be proven that political reform cannot bring about social reform and that, on the contrary, political reform will come from social reform.

Against this bourgeois democracy, in 1848 Proudhon put forward a republic that would be the authentic expression of the people. In democratic theory, it is assumed that the people do not constitute a unit, that natural groups do not have an existence of their own, and that consideration should be given to isolated individuals; it is assumed that groups cannot have a will and that it is therefore appropriate to substitute representatives for popular sovereignty. This is reasoned within a social system torn apart by conflicts, where wills are contradictory and where the focus is on establishing authority. The concern of democrats, like that of all political revolutionaries, is not to return sovereignty to the people by destroying authority but on the contrary to establish democracy as an authority, thereby making the new power a regressive force. In a republic, the law should be the expression of the unanimous will of the citizens, the representatives should be plenipotentiaries with an imperative mandate that is revocable at will, and the people should think and act as one. But such a republic is only possible if it is based on a new society in which the solidarity of functions replaces hierarchy, labor constantly destroys power, and the only initiative is that of citizens.

These criticisms of democracy are even more valid against the theories of the community, because the community organization of production, the transfer of goods and activities to the community, implies the strengthening of state powers. We know that, according to the Proudhonian critique of the communitarian economy, such an absorption of individual initiatives would lead to a decline in social activity, but an equally sharp critique is offered from the perspective of politics: by claiming to eliminate social inequalities through uniformity of the community, communist doctrine demands the submission of wills and thus reestablishes political tyranny. In order to maintain discipline and the absence of individual freedom, the community must become oppressive and reduce each worker to a new form of servitude. The primacy of the community over the individual, the false theory that individuals must abdicate their differences in unity, is necessarily transformed into an oppressive system. From this point of view, communism reproduces the traditional prejudices of the regime of property and political democracy: the fundamental principle remains the same despite social changes.[16] In fact, feudalism, constitutional monarchy, and bourgeois democracy share the same principle of authority and concern for establishing and respecting authority. Whether the state is an empire, a monarchy, or a democracy, the political relationship remains the same—a relationship of submission to authority—and this fundamental principle that social life could only be ensured by subordination is not called into question. Communism merely adopts this tradition and maintains the same conception of society: instead of basing political authority on the word of God or the will of the ruler, it is based on the sovereignty of the people and the right of the collectivity, but it maintains that power resides in the state and that social life is ensured by this binding power. Rather than considering that the people and individuals can be free and get their sovereignty only from themselves, it makes citizens' rights dependent on the sovereignty of the people and reduces freedom to something that emanates from the collective power. In applying these principles, the theory of community restores a power that is fundamentally identical to the political powers of the past. Thus, contrary to appearances, communism merely contradicts itself by adopting the economic and political model of the regime of property; just as property establishes a monopoly and a relationship of subordination between owners and nonowners, communism envisages an extension of property and its total surrender to a centralizing state.[17] In politics, just as bourgeois capitalism

---

16. Let us recall that this discussion is not directed against Marxist communism, of which Proudhon was not aware. Proudhon criticized his socialist contemporaries, the communist tradition, and more generally any social theory justifying economic unitarism and the strengthening of the state.

17. Translator's note: The idea is that transferring all the means of

corresponds to despotism, communism tends to encompass and destroy individual and local freedoms in the myth of collective freedom by affirming the principle of the individual's subordination to the collective. Despite the changes in economic organization, political power in a communist society would be organized according to the traditional principles of despotism: undivided power, overwhelming centralization, destruction of all individual and local thought or activity "deemed separatist," strengthening of an inquisitorial police force, and restriction of the family.[18] In this compact democracy, which would inevitably turn into an anonymous tyranny, universal suffrage would be organized to serve as a perpetual guarantee of power, and the sovereignty of the people, intended to be the source of power, would be destroyed.[19]

Thus, when Proudhon formulates his critique of the state, he is convinced of his opposition to the whole range of political systems: all of these systems, from autocracy to communist democracy, are identical in his eyes; despite the various reforms and constitutions, they all reproduce the same traditional model, express the same respect for state authority, and re-create new hierarchies. Anarchist theory will not be a new variant in the same series of constitutional forms but rather a general rejection of them, proposing a complete inversion of traditional political relations.

The aim of the revolution is not to discover a new form of authority or to create a new way to subordinate individual liberty to the state; rather, it is power, the state, that must submit to individual liberty.[20] Instead of allowing the state to absorb

---

production into the hands of the state does not abolish ownership but rather concentrates it to the extreme. This would later be called state capitalism.

18. *De la capacité politique des classes ouvrières*, 115.

19. Translator's note: "A compact democracy, apparently based on the dictatorship of the masses, but where the masses only have enough power to ensure universal servitude." *De la capacité politique des classes ouvrière*, 80.

20. *Système des contradictions économiques*, vol. 2, 293.

economic society and collective life, the state must be subjected, subordinated to society. It is therefore of the utmost importance to denounce all the illusions surrounding political power and arrive at a correct theory of the state.

2. Theory of the State

In spite of the plurality of political forms, a theory of the state remains possible because the specific forms that it takes do not alter its fundamental principles. Every state establishes and expresses a social relationship of hierarchy and inequality: it expresses it because the state is subsequent to social organization and depends on the structures of economic society; it establishes it, however, because its presence confirms inequality by reinforcing it. It is an inherently unequal and subordinate relationship since it concentrates authority and requires the submission of its citizens, whether it is autocratic or democratic.

The most common error consists in attributing to the state a reality, a specific force, as if it had its own power, as expressed in the theologies that link power to some transcendent deity. Democrats who expect a government decision to bring about social reform make the same error in hoping that a government will have the power to disrupt economic society. In reality, if the state has any power, it can only come from society as a whole; if it is a force, as we see in war, it is the organ, the custodian of the collective force. In war, the state clearly becomes a power, but this power is only that of society in the plurality of its activities: the state then becomes the expression of this force, "the armed expression of the collective force."[21] Equally, political forces emanate spontaneously from the group and fulfill functions and needs for order and education: by constituting itself politically, the group gives itself disciplinary tools comparable to restrictions imposed on children. This spontaneous, instinctive nature

---

21. *La Révolution sociale démontrée par le coup d'état du deux décembre*, 132.

of the origin of the state explains why the first political systems were created on the model of the family: by the constitution of the family, the father is naturally vested with directing this force resulting from the family group, and when the family expands, grows through slave labor, or becomes a tribe, the father retains his powers and sees his might grow.[22] But from this level, the state's dual nature of spontaneity and alienation emerges, since whereas the group gives itself this authority that ensures its cohesion spontaneously, the father conducts an appropriation of collective forces, and this appropriation has an alienated character because the real relationships are inverted, and the powers that be become the masters of the society from which they emerge. This is what happens when, once society develops beyond tribes, the most powerful family or families seize power and take over the management of collective forces. It may then be that this power, initially established on an alienation, rather than concerning itself with the nation from which it emanates instead aims at continuing its domination and creates a police and military apparatus as a weapon against the nation. The state, which only derives its power from society, turns against it and may cause its demise.[23]

Thus, in its very essence, power finds itself in an ambiguous relationship with the society from which it derives its reality. At the same time, it is only the organ of the collective force, but it is also external to society and appropriates power from it: it is a representation of rights, but it is only their external representation.[24] This relation of externality is reinforced by the mythical character that the state assumes in people's minds: in fact, the state is in itself a myth, since it has no reality other than what it derives from society; it is only a *symbol* of the social, but people bestow it with sacred attributes, and this illusion must be understood as a condition for its existence. Indeed, this phantasmagoria of the

22. *De la justice dans la révolution et dans l'église*, 4th étude, vol. 2, 266.
23. "It is not by their governments that peoples are saved, but that they are lost." *Confessions d'un révolutionnaire*, 86.
24. Ibid., 62.

state results in maintaining obedience and inaction: we saw this in 1848, when the democrats, still victims of the myth of the state, entrusted themselves to a higher power instead of directing their efforts toward a transformation of the foundations of society. In this sense, the state is to social life what religion is to moral life: just as religion is a symbol of values but also an alienation that has the effect of wrenching people's moral will from them, the state, the external representation of social powers, has the effect of diverting society from its own existence. And just as religion is a group creation, an improvisation of the people, so the state is spontaneously surrounded by a religious fervor, a faith that sustains its power. Citizens, uncritically clinging to the myth of the state, make it a superior and, as it were, independent cause. They expect it to protect them and solve their problems, just as believers make their god a reality and expect its beneficial intervention. In both cases, humanity is unaware of what it is looking for and hides the meaning of its creations from itself. The critique of religions has shown that humanity seeks its own ideal in religious allegories and that gods are merely a projection of the human; the critique of the state demonstrates that the state is nothing by itself, that it is only a formula through which society seeks its freedom. Since religion is only a preparation for a higher state in which humanity assumes its own morality, government could only be a step destined to be overcome in an autonomous organization of society.[25]

This fundamental nature of the state—the alienation and appropriation of the collective force—consequently brings with it the necessary logic of its social action. Having only a borrowed existence, the state must constantly appropriate the social force and divert it from its true authors in order to maintain itself: it must necessarily absorb what in fact belongs to creative society, and therefore it naturally tends to subdue and absorb collective forces and, by extension, the whole of society. It is in the nature of the state to reinforce itself by absorbing the forces of collectivity. In fact, every freedom, every uncontrolled initiative,

---

25. Ibid., 61–62.

threatens the state and tends to create or express the limits of its power. In the face of these threats, political power seeks to regain control of what escapes it: if it has to legislate and thus admit a certain limit to its immediate power, it will keep enacting laws so that nothing escapes from its grasp, even indirectly.[26] Thus, the state is motivated by an inner need to monopolize, to centralize, and this centralizing tendency, once begun, tends to grow incessantly, to invade the whole of society. In order to respond to the spontaneous emergence of interests that threaten it, the state must invent new means of control, regulate activities as soon as they appear and thus increase its scope and power at the expense of individual and collective initiatives.[27] This inevitable tendency toward concentration and monopolization is undoubtedly linked to class conflict and the clash of interests, but the unitary state merely confirms these conflicts. Class conflict and the state are in dialectical reciprocity, and the tendency toward centralization expresses and reinforces this social inequality.

By continuing its expansion, the state simultaneously strengthens its authority. Not only is it authority in itself, but it also tends to increase this authority and thus deny and destroy all forms of freedom: its inevitable tendency is toward absorption, the destruction of all forms of autonomy.[28] The state is comparable to a "trap" set for autonomous labor and freedom. This is why political power, contrary to any illusions about political parties and the Jacobin spirit, is counterrevolutionary by nature. The revolution, representing innovation and the tearing down of outdated social constitutions, breaks the forms imposed by power; the centralized state, on the contrary, tends to stifle possibilities for change. Neither the specific intentions of those in power nor alterations to the edifice of government can change this necessity

26. *Idée générale de la révolution*, 204.

27. "Since centralization is expansive, invasive in nature, the remit of the state is continually growing at the expense of individual, corporate, communal and social initiative." *De la capacité politique des classes ouvrières*, 297.

28. "This overwhelming, liberty-destroying concentration . . . ." *Idée générale de la révolution*, 151.

that makes the state a counterrevolutionary force.[29] This shows
the full extent of the error committed by the democrats who in
1848 claimed to be carrying out a revolution but used means
directly opposed to the achievement of their objectives: by calling only for electoral reform, for constitutional change, the fundamental forms of society could in no way be altered, and by
granting new powers to the state and expecting revolutionary
acts to be carried out by the state, the revolutionary forces were
robbed of their possibilities for realization; increasingly powerful obstacles to the social movement were erected, and thus a
counterrevolution was carried out in the name of the revolution.

Between the centralizing state and living society, there is
necessarily a radical contradiction whereby all the features of
society are opposed to those of the state. Social life is made up
of exchanges and mutual relations that are established spontaneously between members: the common law that governs these
relations, permits movement, and ensures circulation is the law
of reciprocity. This law implies equality between the participants,
and relations become more fruitful and dynamic as social contracts are increasingly carried out without constraint and according to the needs of the members concerned. The state, on the
contrary, dictates. Since its inherent law is authority and the use
of constraint, it inevitably replaces free exchange between autonomous subjects with the law of power and thus the negation of
living relations of reciprocity. Similarly, it is the negation of all
freedom: whereas social life is realized through the encounter
of spontaneous acts, the state tends to prohibit any new manifestation that would challenge it. For example, there has been a
constant demand for freedom of the press, for the right to freely
examine and discuss all social and political issues; but there is
necessarily an "incompatibility" between unitary power and freedom of the press: power is inherently hostile to examination and

---

29. "Government is by nature counterrevolutionary; either it resists,
or it oppresses, or it corrupts, or it sanctions. The government does
not, cannot, will never want anything else. Put a Saint Vincent de Paul
in power: he will be Guizot or Talleyrand." *Confessions d'un révolutionnaire*,
284–85.

criticism, and it tends to make itself inviolable like any constituted authority; this intolerance becomes more violent and the contradiction more unbearable the more centralized it becomes, without the antinomy ever disappearing in a unitary system.[30] Moreover, social life is ensured by the plurality of relationships between multiple groups: these groups and "subgroups," some forming, others disappearing, are infinite in number, and this plurality is an essential feature of collective life. Conversely, the state as conceived in the traditional system is unitary and tends to maintain or strengthen its own unity: between society and the state there is a peculiar contradiction between a life that tends to maintain differences in groups and localities and a unitary hierarchy that tends to simplify under a single power. Ultimately, between social life and the state, we find antagonism between the spontaneous and the mechanical, the moving and the immobile: society is not a finished reality; it is engaged in a spontaneous movement, secured by the plurality of exchanges and acts; especially in a revolutionary period, divided forces, still devoid of a shared theory, tend to form and organize themselves into a common practice. More generally, society constantly creates itself, occasionally because it carries out a project almost consciously, more often because it acts without knowing what it carries within itself. Against this creative spontaneity, slow or fast, conscious or unconscious, the state constantly poses its completed forms, its fixed plans, its system. Between living society and unitary political power there are contradictions between the spontaneous and the ordered, the changing and the fixed, creation and repetition.

Political history since the Great Revolution of 1789 confirms the deepening of these contradictions and the inevitable persistence of a centralized state in an unequal society. Of course, from 1789 to 1864, the state experienced numerous reorganizations and fifteen different constitutions, but beyond these changes the principles of authority and hierarchy remained the same: these diverse state forms were part of a homogeneous series even though they led from imperial authority to

30. *De la capacité politique des classes ouvrières*, 316–33.

representative democracy.[31] In fact, by assuming social antagonism and reflecting class inequality, the state continued to pursue
minor changes and reinforced a society riddled with contradictions. Since class antagonism was neither overcome nor erased,
relations of authority were re-created throughout this period,
despite revolutionary efforts and insurrections. The changes of
government and multiple constitutional revisions confirmed that
the main reason behind states' instability was social inequality
and that the deepening of economic contradictions inevitably
made a true social constitution impossible. The four economic
types that Proudhon distinguished in 1853—industrial anarchy,
feudalism, industrial empire, and democracy—correspond to
four political models, the last negating all the previous ones. The
competitive anarchy of the Restoration corresponded to a parasitic state dominated by the bourgeoisie and vested only with
the functions of policing and constraint.[32] Capitalist concentration and the reestablishment of industrial feudalism correspond to a highly centralized state whose economic powers are
reinforced by state monopolies and financial domination: the
Second Empire. Proudhon then predicted that the tendencies
inherent in this system heralded an even more intense political
centralization based on extreme capitalist concentration: the
industrial empire. In fact, the deepening of economic contradictions and social conflicts can only cause an increase in political
powers intended to combat the threat of social war: traditional
prejudices encourage this development in a society in which conflicts can only be resolved through increased concentration; the
monarchical tradition, the myths of the old Jacobin spirit, and
the popular instinct share the same illusions and together favor
the expansion of powers.[33] But all the previous analyses have
shown how much the strengthening of the state is synonymous
with the strengthening of social contradictions: the additional

---

31. *Contradictions politiques*, 198.

32. Translator's note: After Napoleon I fell from power in 1814, the
House of Bourbon was restored to power in France until the July Revolution of 1830.

33. *Manuel du spéculateur à la Bourse*, vol. II, 6.

power given to governments would widen the gap and therefore aggravate the conflict between rulers and ruled. Moreover, if the state defines itself in opposition to life and innovative activity, it defines itself as nonproductive: not only is it an unproductive class, but to the extent that it controls the organization of production, the state burdens it with red tape, makes it more costly, and stifles it. The increasing absorption of the economy by an authoritarian state would thus create an impossible situation from which the industrial republic, positive anarchy, would emerge by dialectical negation.

This fourth term cannot be placed in the same series as the previous ones. Autocracy, constitutional empire, parliamentary monarchy, and representative democracy form a series that can be traced logically from empire to republic: they share the same principles and develop the same law in their specific forms of despotism. Positive anarchy is not another political form: it is the rejection of politics, the radical rejection of any government, aiming to establish a radically new relationship between individuals and groups by eradicating the authoritarian relationship. It appears as a negation, not of one type of government but of the whole series of governments. However, this radical negation does not rule out the possibility that, within despotism itself, productive activity prepares its collapse. Without adopting Saint-Simon's thesis of a complete constitution of the new economic society within state forms, Proudhon notes that relations of authority are challenged by social activity at the very moment they are reinforced. In fact, the development of economic relations and industrial initiatives propagates nonauthoritarian relations between producers on a contractual basis. When these concern large groups, they tend to replace subordination and convert the old authoritarian relations into contractual relations. Similarly, the creation of companies with mutualist characteristics, such as insurance companies, gives rise to the prospect of an organization in which the government would be nothing more than the meeting of interests, an organization in which political authority would be annihilated.[34] The phrase "the workshop will make the government disappear" should not be understood only as the herald of a society in which productive activity has destroyed politics but also as the description of an existing dynamic that constantly drives out authority.[35] In labor itself, to the extent that it necessarily re-creates relations of cooperation, there is a practical critique of authoritarian hierarchy and a process whereby the government is being eliminated. However, this process cannot be powerful enough to make a centuries-old apparatus disappear smoothly.

At the end of this critique of the state, however, there is no reason to conclude that politics is exclusively negative: more accurately, history reveals an increase in the sphere of politics that continues to deepen its negativity and heralds its demise. But the functions performed by the authorities in ancient societies should not be underestimated: they appear vividly in the historical phenomenon of war. In his book devoted to war, Proudhon develops a thesis that did not fail to arouse indignation:[36] opposing, with his usual vehemence, pacifists, jurists, and in general the common opinion that war is always evil and destructive, he shows that in reality war has fulfilled eminently positive functions in the history of civilization. Far from being an accident or an exception, war has been essential to social life and has generated collective exaltation. Using deliberately aggressive phrases, Proudhon links the founding of religions, poetry, and the organization of the social economy and political life to the preparation and conduct of armed struggle. When two nations, unable to resolve their differences, resorted to arms, they made

----

34. *La Révolution démontrée par le coup d'état du deux décembre*, 116.

35. Letter to P. Leroux, *La Voix du Peuple*, December 13, 1849, in *Mélanges*, vol. 19, 36. Translator's note: The full quotation: "A time will come when, since labor is organized by itself, according to its own law and no longer needs a legislator or sovereign, the workshop will make the government disappear."

36. *La Guerre et la Paix. Recherches sur le principe et la constitution du droit des gens* [Investigations on the Principle and Constitution of the Rights of Nations] (1861).

war an act of jurisdiction and expected victory to produce a new social order. However instinctively repugnant it may be to admit these facts, history constantly describes peoples fighting and triumphing over each other and the victors imposing their law. If we take into account not the artificial opinion of jurists and moralists but instead the verdict of the universal conscience, we must recognize that there was always a true right that came from victory, a right of force. At the end of a conquest or the expansion of a nation, the new social fact was established in law, and, if victory confirmed the conqueror's real superiority, this law was accepted by the defeated peoples. This is because law is not an abstraction unrelated to a social group's real powers: equilibrium in society is achieved by the meeting of different social forces, and each force carries within itself its own order and its own law.

These remarks confirm the extreme importance of the state in all ancient societies, since governments were the external representation of law and one of the means to defend and extend a nation's forces, but they also confirm the decline of the state in an industrial society. Indeed, the primary cause of war has always been the lack of means to survive, pauperism: first through looting and then through conquest, people have sought to remedy the scarcity that plagued them. However, in modern nations, plunder and tribute are losing their importance, and external warfare is becoming contradictory and futile. War is concentrated within nations, in governmentalism and economic exploitation, and it is maintained because of economic anarchy and class antagonism. The coming of an egalitarian society would mark the end of external wars just as it would end the era of states.

3. Anarchism

The radical critique of the state leads to its radical negation. The critique has revealed an insurmountable antinomy between freedom—the spontaneity of social life—and political centralization. Whatever accommodation or modification is made to the governmental system, maintaining its principle inevitably

introduces an authority, a principle external to social action. To
maintain the principle of government is to admit that humans
must alienate their freedom in favor of an authority, to admit the
constitution of a superior power in charge of controlling social
life, to affirm the need for the submission and incompetency of
individuals and groups. To introduce authority is also to envisage
the preservation of social inequalities and class conflicts, since
the state is constituted only because of these inequalities and
to prevent their disappearance. The authentically revolutionary demand must therefore not be the reform of the state or the
amendment of political forms but instead the radical disappearance of the state, its extermination, and the establishment of a
society without a government.[37] Anarchist theory is above all this
refusal: the negation of all authority and in particular the negation of the state. The definitions proposed by Proudhon in 1840
emphasize this aspect: anarchism is above all the negation of
power, the denial of governmental sovereignty.[38] Not that anarchy should suggest the notion of disorder: on the contrary, all of
the previous critique overturns the common myth that order is
provided only by government. Rather than establishing order,
the government introduces disorder into social activity by introducing obstacles to social spontaneity and new oppressive controls. The true social order, not imposed on collective life from
outside but resulting from free activity, springs directly from the
collective being and remains proper to, immanent in, the subject
from which it emanates. Anarchy does not therefore designate a
simple critical attitude toward particular or accidental defects of
the state; by denouncing the alienation introduced by any form
of the state, it heralds and designates a real social organization:
positive anarchy, an economic society whose primary characteristic
would be the absence of any government.[39]

---

37. Extermination: "To bring about social reform through the extermination of power and politics." *Système des contradictions*, vol. 1, 345.
38. *Explications présentées au ministère public sur le droit de propriété*
[Explanations Presented to the Public Prosecutor's Office on the Right
of Property] (1842), p. 263, note.
39. "No authority, no government, not even popular: that is the

Thus, anarchist thought marks a historical break with all the state theories of the past and all the falsely revolutionary conceptions of the democrats. Indeed, from the monarchical conception to the democratic conception of direct government, the principles remain the same despite their very different forms. In a monarchy, the ruler, claiming to be the representative of divine right, seizes absolute authority by basing it on revelation; in the system of direct government, the right of authority is entrusted to power, basing it on the sovereignty of the people; but whatever principle is claimed, it is assumed that society is incapable of managing itself, and a power external to collective life is reconstituted, thus respecting the traditional forms of social inequality and injustice. If, on the contrary, we recognize that the state is authoritarian in essence and homologous to social hierarchies, we will recognize that the idea of the revolution is not to reform the state, but instead to replace all the social forms of the past with a new society in which sovereignty would no longer be external to collective life but entirely immanent in it. It is a question of realizing through a new practice what critique has expressed with regard to religious ideas: just as critical rationalism, by questioning the notion of God, has shown that the religious idea was only a human creation that should be returned to its author, revolutionary criticism, by finding the state to be a creation and an alienation of society, points to a society that eliminates power and reconquers what the state diverts from it. Destroying the state would signify and result in the re-appropriation by society of the powers alienated in state externalization.

This negative aspect, the rejection of the state, directly correlates with the organization of economic forces. These two meanings cannot be distinguished: while anarchism designates the critique and negation of the state, it also designates this society in which industrial organization would be realized and replace the government. Just as class inequality and social antagonism made it necessary for a coercive force to intervene, the organization of economic forces would end the hierarchy of powers

---

Revolution." *Idée générale de la révolution*, 199.

and thereby end governmental oppression. Anarchy establishes a social system based solely on the spontaneous practice of industry, in which the free agreement of producers forging reciprocal relations individually or collectively would render politics unnecessary. Such a society would stand in complete opposition to the old societies and establish relations between producers that would necessarily prevent any reconstitution of the state. Anarchy replaces distributive justice, exercised by an authority superior to the contracting parties, with commutative justice, in which the contracting parties mutually engage in equitable exchange and abdicate any claim to government.[40] In all previous societies, the social contract was a social pact whose purpose was to constitute political power: citizens were to abdicate their individual will and submit to a higher authority, and, whatever relationship was thought to have existed between individual will and the general will, the concern was to create an authority to be imposed by constraining individuals. Society fell victim to the prejudice that it does not possess order by itself and that a power must be created with the role of imposing the order that society cannot create by itself. It did not recognize that the urgency to introduce an artificial order was due only to the fundamental disorganization of a divided society. In a contractual society in which economic forces create exchanges of their own accord in reciprocal relations, debated freely and agreed individually, order springs spontaneously from the producers themselves, from their action and their autonomous management.

The revolutionary transition from authoritarian societies to reasoned anarchy does not mark the advent of a historically unprecedented society but rather of a society liberated and finally restored to itself. Indeed, to the extent that there was alienation of the collective force, an *externalization* of the social power, society was not itself, was not in possession of its own order and power. However, beneath the government apparatus and despite the obstacles posed by constraints, economic society silently produced its own organism, its own social constitution,

40. Ibid., 187.

directly opposed to the political constitution.[41] To suppress the state, therefore, is to liberate social life, to allow it to survive and govern itself through its immanent forces. Every form of state oppression is then replaced by the spontaneity of social organizations: economic forces replace political powers; contracts signed by each citizen, each municipality, or company replace laws; professions and special functions replace the old hierarchical classes; the collective force replaces the public force; industrial production companies replace armies; and shared interests replace police coercion.[42] In such an egalitarian and contractual society, not only will there no longer be a government, but social activity and new forms of labor will continue to render the reestablishment of government impossible. If one can still speak of power in such a society, it must be considered as immanent in society as a whole: all individuals and social groups, whether municipalities, cities, or worker companies, are guardians of their own sovereignty, governing themselves mutually and dealing freely with other individuals or groups. In such a society in which autonomous social life destroys power, we can say, borrowing the theological phrase, that "the political center is everywhere, its circumference nowhere."[43]

In the Proudhonian analysis, this political theory is based on the sociological theory of the autonomy and spontaneity of the collective being. Proudhon criticizes government theorists for their ignorance of social reality: they see in society only a *being of reason*, a phrase used to refer to a collection of individuals;[44] far from seeing a real and living being in society, they see only a chaos of distinct individuals. From this initial misunderstanding, they conclude that an external force is needed to maintain artificial cohesion; moreover, they are driven to believe that politics cannot be the object of a science, since there is no natural basis for it, and that it can only be a matter of art. The theory of

---

41. "Its own organism": ibid., 300.
42. Ibid., 302.
43. *De la capacité politique des classes ouvrières,* 198.
44. *Système des contradictions économiques,* vol. I, 123.

the collective being denounces these illusions: if the collective being is a living being, endowed with its own intelligence and activity, it possesses laws and properties that are solely its own. Thus, the solidarity that unites the different members is not the artificial result of an external constraint; it is inherent in social life and emanates directly from its spontaneity. In the same way, the economic laws of the division of labor or exchange do not arise from human conventions: they spring spontaneously from action, appear when they fulfill a role, and are modified as social dynamism develops. Governmentalist theorists, faithful to the common mystification, persist in believing that social transformations can only be achieved through political initiative, as if movement, change, had to come to society through power; this is why in 1848 the democrats demanded an increase in the government's initiative in order to achieve revolutionary objectives. On the contrary, the whole Proudhonian critique of the state concludes that the state tends toward immobility. The statist theory is in fact linked to the religious tradition that rejects social change and progress and opposes it with a stable hierarchy and a set of unchangeable beliefs. However, change does not belong to the state and cannot come from power; on the contrary, it comes from the collective being and occurs spontaneously. It is this spontaneity of the social that anarchy liberates by eliminating the political and intellectual alienation of the past. Through anarchy, society would regain all of its possibilities for autonomous transformation and permanent revision of its constitution. Whereas the state prohibits free social change, either by absolute authoritarianism or by limitations through laws, anarchy, by confirming and realizing the idea of progress, would establish society's ongoing ability to revise its economic forms and its contracts.[45] Positive anarchy is therefore not exactly the establishment of a new order: it is society itself realizing its order and its immanent laws through the action of individuals and communities alone. It marks the disappearance of the alienation and constraints that may have been useful in the past but that lose all purpose once

---

45. *Confessions d'un révolutionnaire*, 223.

society discovers its balances, its laws, and realizes them spontaneously. Anarchy is society itself, a society living and subsisting
by itself.

One of the errors of governmentalism lies in ignorance of
the collective reason. Having denied that society constitutes
a being by itself, it is asserted that common thought can come
to it only from an external source, from the word of a God or
from the authority of a state power; but as the sociology of ideas
will show, from society as a living experience, a general, synthetic thought emerges, different from the partial opinion of
individuals, both as an expression of practice and as a guide for
action. This general reasoning has constantly been mutilated
and fought against by religious and governmental authorities: it
is incompatible with an arbitrary will external to social practice.
Its development and definitive affirmation implies the disappearance of this contradiction between arbitrariness and reason:
indeed, if the common thought carries the demand for a social
constitution and industrial solidarity, economic reform will in
turn give it every chance to express and assert itself. In a society still dominated by authority, the common thought is partially
realized in practice and appears in transactions, but it cannot
yet be expressed explicitly and achieve full self-awareness. It is
only in an egalitarian society that the collective reason, through
economic reform and the organization of universal suffrage
that respects all groups and interests, could expressly assert
itself. Society, previously torn between spontaneous will and
arbitrary will, could move from partial experience to conscious
experience, from spontaneity to reflection. Thus, Proudhon uses
the expressions "positive anarchy" and "reasoned anarchy" to
describe anarchy: positive anarchy, since it is real and based on
the stability of a new economic organization; reasoned anarchy,
since it would be in full harmony with the collective reason. In
other words, while social practice has never been able to achieve
either a full theoretical explanation or a harmony with socially
recognized theories, anarchy in action would cause practice and
theory to converge, with reflection expressing practice and serving as a critical tool.

4. Federalism

The two books in which Proudhon most extensively explains his anarchist conception of society, *Confessions of a Revolutionary* and *General Idea of the Revolution*, were written during the revolutionary period from 1848 to 1852. Directed against conservative threats and the democrats' statist tendencies, these works have a highly polemical character, which Proudhon would later moderate. Indeed, from 1858, more aware of the importance of international political relations, he continues his critique of the centralized state but counters it no longer with the destruction of governments but instead with their restriction within a federal system.[46] From this time, it seems to him that freedoms must be guaranteed not only by denying authority but also as part of a complex organization in which authority and liberty would be limited and mutually counterbalanced. Federalism would respond to this complexity of dialectics, as long as it is conceived not as a simple political system but as a full socioeconomic system in which the many groups would be the free creators of their economic and political relations.

The problem posed to Proudhon, as he is questioning the social constitution of national groups and international relations, concerns both economic and political organization. In the unequal society of the regime of property, politics was constituted in opposition to economic society in order to overcome the class conflicts generated by inequality. Conversely, in a socialist society, where free solidarity would unite individuals and groups, public law should not oppose economic society but should instead accept its principles and simply extend economic organization. Economic principles, contractualism and mutualism, must form the basis of public law and must be reproduced there identically: the dynamic equilibrium established within economic

---

46. Main works on this topic: *La Fédération et l'unité en Italie* [Federation and Unity in Italy] (1862), *Du principe fédératif et de la nécessité de reconstituer le parti de la révolution* [The Federative Principle and the Need to Reconstitute the Party of Revolution] (1863), and (1865).

organization must be re-created in political organization, and economic mutuality is transposed into politics under the term *federalism*.[47] The federal conception of national groups opposes centralizing unitarism with a pluralist vision of society: whereas the monarchical or Jacobin tradition conceives the social good only in the form of absorption of the parts by a unique centralization, federalism is opposed to all centralization and respects the autonomy of specific groups. It is no longer a question of ensuring unity at the price of liberty but of ensuring both unity and liberty in unity.

Federalism implies not only a common form between economic and political organization but also a distinction between the two: it suggests that producer groups, rather than giving up their rights to an authority eager to expand, would retain their economic decision-making powers and consider the state only as a means of expression or stimulation. By establishing the principle of limiting central power by means of particular powers and local groupings, federalism breaks the dogma of the national interest and the common tendency of states toward concentration. No longer representing only the pole of authority, political power ceases to be the master of society and is now just one site of social action among others. Proudhon's statements on this topic in his more specifically anarchist period are still applicable to federalism: the state, organized in the image of economic society and reproducing its essential form, has its powers limited by producers and producer groups, but more precisely it ends up being "subjugated" by economic society as a whole. Rather than appearing as the central organ of society and its only means for cohesion, the functions of the state are merely "sub-functions" of a society now in the hands of the producers.

Proudhon provides an outline of these autonomous centers, which would confine political power to the level of professional

---

47. "Thus, transported into the political sphere, what we have been hitherto calling mutualism or guarantism is now called federalism. In this simple synonym, the whole political and economic revolution opens up in front of us." *De la capacité politique des classes ouvrières*, 198.

groups and local sovereignties. According to a plan drawn up as early as 1848, democratically organized workshops and industrial companies would be driven to federate according to profession and industry, thus constituting a form of centralization at the national level.[48] This federation of industries would ensure groups' need for independence, since relations would be based on contracts between groups, and would meet modern requirements for coordination. But this is only one type of autonomous grouping in a federated society. Considering the relations between local groups, Proudhon stresses the relative independence that different communities and regions must preserve. Contrary to the centralizing tendency that constantly erodes communities' sovereignty, this form of autonomy should be recognized and respected.[49] In federalism, the community, a local and natural group, regains its sovereignty; it has the right to govern itself, administer itself, manage its properties, set taxes, and organize education and policing. It must reconstitute a true collective life, which implies that problems are debated, interests are declared, and internal rules are discussed and chosen. In Proudhon's eyes, this point is decisive: it is not only a question of recognizing a degree of restriction on the state by the presence of groups but also of affirming the plurality of sovereignties and thus the community's real freedom. If only some local freedoms are recognized in a system governed by the rules of centralization, conflicts will occur between communities and the state, and the mightier power will get its way, continuing the history of the decline of communities. Only a federalist organization affirming the principle of the plurality of sovereignties could respect the community's sovereignty and thus restore full collective life to the foundations of society.[50]

Federalism also implies the return to regions and provinces of a share of their autonomy; that is, that the natural groups

---

48. *Programme révolutionnaire aux électeurs de la Seine.*

49. We know the importance that this topic would assume in the Paris Commune in 1871.

50. *De la capacité politique des classes ouvrières*, 285.

united by dialect, customs, or religion would regain this relative autonomy that was absorbed under centralization. The natural group formed by the local community, shared customs, and the linking of interests in fact represent a more vibrant social reality than the artificial groups formed by states. Here too the federalist theory of the state is completely opposed to the unitarist conception, which reasons in terms of force and the reduction of freedoms and, being based on the principle that society does not survive by itself but only by authority, concludes that a state must be established in order to impose discipline and obedience. Since diversity is interpreted as a sign of insubordination, it is thought that unity is achieved only by destroying individuality and establishing a homogeneous and undifferentiated group. Conversely, if we know that a social group exists by itself, ensures its cohesion, lives and thinks like an organic being, and increases its opportunities in line with its freedom, we will conclude that as natural groups gain autonomy, the stability of the nation as a whole would be more secure. The national grouping would therefore no longer be a homogeneous and dominated unity but instead a federation, or more precisely a confederation, of states. Thus, Proudhon was to develop the strongest critiques against the "principle of nationalities" that nevertheless had quasi-unanimous support. Indeed, nationalism, emphasizing national independence and thus the state's unity, may have counterrevolutionary consequences in the name of progress: strengthening the state and centralization tends to give rise to large, artificial groupings, hindering the economic revolution according to the repeatedly emphasized law that centralization tends to prevent social change.[51] Against nationalist and unitarian claims, Proudhon proposes a confederation of regions and provinces, alone able to respect local nationalities. With regard to the dangerous discussions about natural borders, Proudhon criticizes them in principle by showing that borders are generally only artificial political creations: the true limits are not those

---

51. "Nationalism is the pretext they use to dodge the economic revolution." *De la justice dans la révolution et dans l'église*, 4th étude, vol. 2, 289.

decided by a power but rather those that a group has defined and modified according to its development and spontaneous practice.

Federalism would finally apply to relations between peoples, and, just as the monarchy-inspired unitary system carried the need for military confrontation, a confederal organization of states would lead to the establishment of peace. This confederation would be possible if it brought together modest-sized states, themselves internally federated: large states, in which the real links are all the looser given their vast size, always tend to strengthen central powers in order to compensate for their lack of spontaneous unity. Because of their social constitution, states that are too large are driven to centralization and therefore war. Conversely, medium-sized nations could establish relations comparable to mutualist, and thus peaceful, relations. The elimination of war between nations would result from the establishment of a federal pact between nations and, at a deeper level, from the internal federation of each state: the distribution of powers and mutualist reciprocity would wreck the opportunities for domination. Thus, without believing that Europe could constitute a single confederation, Proudhon stresses that the disappearance of wars depends on the establishment of a federal European state.[52]

This political theory is more ideological than sociological. Proudhon knows the power of the economic and ideological tendencies that drive political centralization, and he admits that on this matter the common tendency must be reversed. However, as in all his work, the theory is based on a social theory that must be clarified: it is at this level that one can consider whether Proudhon partly renounced his anarchism in his later writings. We may in fact wonder whether federalism might end up bringing back in a new form what anarchism had radically denied: the political constitution.

Federalism is based on a fundamentally pluralistic reading

---

52. "A great event is already happening, namely that Europe is increasingly becoming a kind of federal state, of which each nation is only a member." Letter to C. Edmond, December 19, 1851, *Correspondance*, vol. 4, 154.

of society and on positive relations between diversity and vitality, unity and oppression. Whether it is productive activity, trade, or political life, Proudhon always believed there is a constant relationship between plurality and movement, the unified and the immobile. Thus it is natural for the centralized state to introduce an obstacle to change, a reactionary element, because of its unitary character. Federalism appears as a technique for respecting plurality and thus social groups' free initiative and freedom. More precisely, pluralism is essential to social reality, freed from its alienation: federalism is not simply a preferable technique likely to bring producers greater welfare or freedom but rather the expression of social reality. Proudhon recognizes that unitarism and federalism have repeatedly manifested in history as two concrete possibilities, but he adds that authoritarian centralization has assumed an artificial character, as underlined by its ill effects. Considered in its living reality, society is both one and many, but it is through its multiplicity that it lives and progresses: social vitality does not come from a guiding center but emerges through encounters—for example, contracts between different producers freely pursuing their interests. Social movement emerges from the very foundations of society and more specifically from the many initiatives taken by producers and producer companies. As long as this plurality of initiatives is respected and finds its means of expression, society can avoid the conflicts and antagonisms that it has consistently run into in the past.

The theory of federalism remains faithful to the Proudhonian project of emphasizing the spontaneity of the collective being as opposed to statist or religious theories. Whether it is to denounce capital's unproductiveness, state conservatism, or religious alienation, Proudhon strives to discover the transformations and creations of the autonomous, immanent social movement. But in his anarchist period, while stressing that social spontaneity comes entirely from the organization of economic forces, he tends to take relations between individuals as a model for this organization. The examples chosen to illustrate the economic contract largely come from private exchanges. In describing federal organization, agro-industrial federation, Proudhon puts greater stress on the relations between groups, just as he emphasizes more strongly than in 1848 the importance of worker companies responsible for managing major industries and works.[53] But, above all, Proudhon introduces the notion of the "natural group," which completes the plurality of spontaneous groupings in geographical terms. Thus, the federal conception puts more emphasis on social reality as being made up of multiple qualitatively different, spontaneously sovereign groupings—geographical, economic, cultural, and political—in which the individual is involved.

In developing this theory of federations and confederations, Proudhon remains faithful to his dialectical method and in particular to his dialectical theory of balances. The spontaneity of different groupings is secured only by establishing relations of balance, in which the expansive tendencies of each will be limited by the autonomy of other groups. Federalism must reinforce this reality of struggles and opposition by seeking only to balance them: far from imposing a stifling synthesis on social life, it must allow forces to fully flourish via a nonhierarchical balancing act. The negative dialectic of federalism would reinforce the pluralistic and antigovernmental character of social spontaneity. However, with political organization, Proudhon introduces a dialectic that he had rejected in his anarchist period, that of authority and liberty.[54] Whereas he had previously expressed a total rejection of authority and asserted that labor activity was by itself a constant protest against authority, he recognized an antinomy in the foundations of federalism in which authority constitutes one of the two terms. The evolution of his thought does not end here: having started with a largely polemical interpretation that granted nothing to political power, with federalism Proudhon reintroduces a local or central authority. However, the concept of authority in the federal organization has a radically different meaning than it had in traditional states: whereas the political contract that was to form the basis of states was made by giving

---

53. *De la capacité politique des classes ouvrières*, 212.

54. "Political order rests fundamentally on two contrary principles: Authority and Liberty." *Du principe fédératif*, 271.

up autonomy, the federative contract would be limited in its purpose, safeguarding the sovereignty of individuals and groups, subject to the special purpose for which it is formed. Federated groups would only commit to governing themselves on the basis of mutualism, cooperating in their economic activities, lending each other assistance in difficulties, and protecting each other against enemies from outside and tyranny from within.[55] Thus conceived, the central power would have no authority external to social life but would simply be the body responsible for coordinating local interests: delegates would not be vested with any special power, their only function being to bring interests together and seek harmony through mutual concessions. The central council then ceases to be a state: it is only the organ of mutuality and constitutes only one of the terms of social activity. Proudhon thus pursues his constant concern for destroying everything that could assume a character external to the social totality. By destroying the state and giving the central power only one particular function among others, we would restore to society everything that it is: destroying alienation would return to social life everything that had been taken away from it.

In this society restored to itself, the state is therefore nothing more than the resultant of interests; however, it adopts the role of initiator. Proudhon, after having asserted during his anarchist period that the authoritarian, centralized state was fundamentally immobilist and unable to contribute to social progress, now believes that a federal, pluralist state could assume an active and relatively creative role. The state cannot replace economic forces and production groups for the execution of works, but it assumes a creative role in activities, economic decisions and projects.[56] Thus, the dialectic between society and state, which in the works of 1848-1852 was the contradictory dialectic of oppression and submission, gives way to a complementary dialectic in which the

---

55. *De la capacité politique des classes ouvrières*, 198.

56. "In a free society, the role of the state or government is essentially that of legislating, instituting, creating, beginning, establishing; as little as possible should it be executive." *Du principe fédératif*, 326.

innovating role of a central council is recognized. The state intervenes only to promote and choose; it must then abstain, but it does have a provisional role of creation.

While this shift marks a correction to earlier political theories, it does not imply a revision of the sociological theories. The denunciation of the centralized state in a regime of property remains in full, as does the analysis of its tendency to expand and concentrate. But Proudhon believes that an institution's nature and needs are completely transformed when it is incorporated in a different overall structure. The fact that the state is necessarily alienating and oppressive in an unequal society does not imply that a central council retains the same character in a different system. The system's overall structure imposes its specific needs on parties and institutions. Class conflict and industrial anarchy require a powerful and oppressive state, just as the federal organization of economic forces and the plurality of sovereignties require a peaceful, non-superior central power. In such a social structure, the very notion of government loses its traditional meaning, its prestige, and its associated myths; it is merely one cog, one function, in an egalitarian society. This historical relativity of the institution again underlines how much political reform remains subordinate. Revolutionary change cannot consist of a simple constitutional revision but must demand an upheaval of society in its general form, in its socioeconomic relations. The organization of social and economic forces will impose new functions on particular institutions and determine their characteristics and operation.

CHAPTER FIVE

Sociology of Knowledge

In affirming the reality of the social being, Proudhon insists on the concepts of collective reason and collective force. The collective being is a force that we know to be fundamentally heterogeneous to the sum of the individual forces; at the same time, it is also an idea, principle, or reason. By these definitions, Proudhon wants to emphasize first of all that social practice cannot be understood as the mere resultant of physical forces and that collective conscious awakenings and theorizations form a component of action. For example, in denouncing Christianity, his critique will stress that it is not a question of refuting a theory, an intellectual system, but rather a mode of being and acting, a social practice. Indeed, a religion is not an abstract theory bereft of any social function: it establishes a practice, justifies a politics, guides action, and participates directly in the general economic and political orientation of a collectivity. Historical understanding and explanation will thus force us to investigate, alongside economic contradictions and developments, the importance of shared theories, illusions, ideas, and ideologies in initiating events and revolutions. In this investigation, Proudhon will not fail to insist on the importance of moral attitudes, convinced that the strictness or deterioration of morals must be considered an important factor in historical becoming. However, this recognition of the importance of theories in social practice is based on a particular interpretation of social reality, an interpretation that gives rise to formulas in Proudhon's writing that are sometimes not easily reconcilable but that nonetheless attempt to articulate an "ideo-realistic" conception of the fabric of society. For Proudhon, to affirm that social reality is indeed dialectical is not only to stress that collective practice is dependent on collective representations, myths, and ideals, or merely to show that social phenomena are contradictory or antagonistic, but on a more profound level to trace a fundamental relationship between social practice and idea, between social structures and the principles that are immanent in them. If the social phenomenon is a fact, a reality, and if an interest is a force with observable effects and consequences, this feature of reality does not exhaust all of its aspects and does not allow us to fathom its essence. Every social fact, whether it concerns a social structure or a practice such as labor or war, is "proper to an idea";[1] it contains its own principle, its own law and its own meaning. The term *idea* is rather poorly suited to this formulation in that it suggests a conscious representation and a duality between a knowing subject and a known object. However, in history, if the idea occurs simultaneously with the practice, subjects taking part in the action are not necessarily conscious of it. There is by no means a correlation between the practice and the awareness of its meaning: people may engage in an action whose real meaning they understand not at all or very incompletely. They may formulate a theory whose essence will be precisely to distort the real relations, such as, for example, in the case of religions. They may also outline limited actions whose idea, whose real meaning, escapes them, as may be the case during a prerevolutionary period: when workers spontaneously organize mutualist societies, they are prefiguring the revolutionary idea in their action without being fully conscious of the implied meanings. They live an idea at the same time as they create it, without yet understanding the full significance of their actions and consequences of the principle that motivates them.

Consequently, the search for and clarification of these ideas will be of paramount importance for revolutionary practice. Understanding their meanings will allow us to reconsider the direction of history, since particular events will be integrated into an overall conception, and to reconsider the present society,

---

1. *La Guerre et la paix*, 9.

since the discovery of principles will allow us to consider the social unit and its transformational possibilities. But it will be even more important to revolutionary thinkers—and this will be their essential function—to extrapolate the ideas immanent in the practical activity of social classes. Indeed, if the idea is initially hidden from people's consciousness, it can be revealed either through the violence of conflicts that force them into awareness, or by clarification on the part of theorists whose function will be to inform people of the meaning of their actions. To bring practice into consciousness, into the idea, is to participate directly in a revolutionary practice, since a class that has reached the level of consciousness and theory has the elements that will guide its activities coherently in order to achieve historical change.

1. Idea and Practice

The relative obscurity of Proudhon's statements on the relations between practice and theory is due to the plurality of the problems tackled, which relate either to the nature of theory or to the varied and possibly contradictory relations between action and idea. Moreover, *idea* can take on different senses that must be distinguished. Thus, Proudhon will be able to propose apparently irreconcilable formulas affirming in turn that practice precedes idea, that practice is itself an idea, and, conversely, that action is an incarnation of the idea.

In the section devoted to labor in *Justice*, Proudhon addresses the philosophical question of the precedence of action, stressing that the response to this problem has direct importance for the social question. Indeed, by affirming the essential duality of idea and practice and the subordination of practice to law, the spiritualistic theory of primitive revelation justified a social order in which the worker was considered to be incapable of creation and condemned to passively receiving truth from an external power. In fact, however, every knowledge, language, science, or philosophy is born from action (and, more precisely, from labor) through the creation of signs and tools.[2] Initial, instinctive activity, carried out prior to any analysis, itself generates signs that directly express spontaneity and that are established in particular between individuals; these signs, which participate directly in acts, encourage reflection and give rise to an initial intelligence.[3] By the attention they give to their works, humans are both creators of signs and their own teachers. In the same way, by spontaneously creating tools, humans give themselves objects that will provide the intelligence with its first element and determine its orientation. By spontaneously creating the first tool, the lever or bar, humans realize and render sensible what will constitute the essence of their thought: the creation of relations, equality, inequality, series, division, balance. Through elementary tools, humans create an object that contains relations, an objective symbol, the materialization of an idea. Thus, the relations that will be the content and the means for reflexive thought, equality and inequality, balance and imbalance, do not come to humans from some transcendent word but from their own instinctive and creative activity. The transition to the analytical method, which constitutes the proper domain of the intelligence, will take place beyond this starting point and once again by means of tools, since tools are both a concrete relation and an instrument of separation. The human intelligence is thus not an inexplicable gift; it results from instinct and action, through the mediation of the object thereby created: it takes the spontaneity of industry as its point of departure and develops through the consciousness of its own works.

2. "The idea, with its categories, is born from action. . . . That means that all so-called a priori knowledge, including metaphysics, arises from labor." *De la justice dans la révolution et dans l'église*, 6th étude, vol. 3, 69.

3. Translator's note: Georges Gurvitch stressed the similarities of Proudhon's epistemology to that of pragmatism in *Proudhon: Sa vie, son oeuvre* (Paris: Presses universitaires de France, 1965). In particular, Proudhon parallels the pragmatist approach in that both understand ideas and reason to be born through action. For more on this relationship, see Stefano Solari, "The 'Practical Reason' of Reformers: Proudhon vs. Institutionalism," *Journal of Economic Issues* 46, no. 1 (2012): 227–39.

These remarks must be extended to all knowledge and to the general relationship between social activity and theories, whether they arise from science, philosophy, or religion; Proudhon formulates the general principle of a sociology of knowledge: rather than considering religion or philosophy as the origin of social organization, we must postulate both an essential connection between social practice and knowledge and the precedence of practice to theory. All the intellectual systems have their "root," their "reason for existence," in collective practice.[4]

However, this precedence does not clarify the content of social practice: it only has the theoretical value of denouncing spiritualistic theories by pointing to this origin of the intelligence, this evolution by which humanity was created. But, in social practice, a constant relation of succession between action and conscious awakening cannot be established since, on the contrary, it will be seen that a theory can precede a practice. It is much more important, after having eliminated spiritualism, to reconsider the nature of the social practice in order to perceive the identity of idea and action. The example of exchange, a fundamental relation that characterizes the very nature of the social, illustrates this identity clearly. Through exchange, participants engage in a concrete practice, carried out through a meeting and a succession of reciprocal activities. But exchange is simultaneously an equation, an operation where the relationship, ideality and reality, is realized. Not that we can contrast an idea with a reality here or seek a relation of succession between one and the other: exchange is both a practice and an abstract relation, a reality and an idea. In exchange, the idea is identical to the act; the action is an idea.[5] Certain awkward phrases suggest that the idea is realized in a particular practice, as if an abstract relation,

---

4. "All the philosophical and religious systems have their root and their reason for existence in society itself." *Deuxième mémoire* [Second Memoir], 121n.

5. "Exchange, this rather metaphysical, algebraic act, so to speak, is the operation by which, in social economy, an idea takes on a body, a form, and all the properties of matter: it is creation ex nihilo." *Système des contradictions*, vol. 2, 71.

arising from an impersonal reason, were to take on material form, but this is only an analogy or a carelessness of style. Proudhon does not intend to say that the practice of exchange can be reduced to a manifestation of ideas—on the contrary, he states that exchange is a human creation arising from labor and needs—but he wants to show, contrary to an interpretation that he calls materialist, that the act of exchange is equally real and ideal, that it consists in, or rather that it is in itself, a logical relation. It is in the sense that he can write that such a practice can be regarded as an "external form of logic."[6]

These remarks must be extended to every social practice and particularly to every economic practice. In *The System of Economic Contradictions*, Proudhon proposes to show, by studying the contradictions of the regime of property, that each economic practice, the division of labor, mechanization, and competition, is the corollary of a logical form. As the division of the labor has analysis as its logical structure, mechanization takes synthesis as its structure, and the structure of competition is the antagonism of terms. Economic facts embody an equivalence of reality and logic.[7] Thus, the relationship between reality and logical forms is completely different from what religion or critical philosophy believed they had discovered. Logic is neither the work of a transcendent spirit nor the expression of human understanding alone, but is the work of society itself, the form of practice. Consequently, Proudhon can write that there is an identity of reason and economic action. However, while he reproduces Hegelian formulations here, in no way does he conclude that the real and the rational are identical: the discovery of a practical logic will not lead him to justify the real but rather to denounce its contradictions.

Participation in a practical and logical form implies neither the formulation of the implicit idea nor consciousness of the lived relationship. Consequently, two meanings must be given to the term *idea*. When Proudhon, in *The Political Capacity of the*

---

6. Ibid., vol. 1, 168–69.
7. "Equivalence of the real and the ideal in human facts." Ibid., 169.

Working Classes, asks if in 1864 the working class has managed to express its own idea, by *idea* he means a theory that would immediately constitute self-awareness of its existence as a class. The working-class idea would in fact be the expression of working-class practice, both the discovery of its existence and the formulation of the revolutionary project. Consequently, the same word has two different senses that must be distinguished: the term *idea* indicates, in the first place, the logical relation that is immanent in social practice or, in other words, its logical essence; it is in this sense that exchange is an idea and that each social practice contains its own meaning. But in the second sense of the term, *idea* indicates any form of knowledge created by human beings, knowledge that they are able to express in language: when the working class manages to formulate its idea in 1864, it expresses the law of its own practice, translates it into words, and justifies it rationally.[8] *Idea* therefore indicates, in the broad sense, any theory, system, belief, myth, or utopia by which human beings give form to their action. In the narrow sense, the term will indicate the theory conforming to the practice, such as the mutualist idea in which the proletariat expresses the law of its being; in the broad sense, *idea* will indicate any theory, true or false, revolutionary or alienating. Thus, a religion is an idea, a certain expression of an unequal and oppressive society that it conveys in its own way.

Consequently, the problem will arise of the relationship to be established between logical forms immanent in practice on the one hand, and explicit theories on the other. The incompatibility between one and the other—practice and awareness of practice—is the most constant form of human experience; and, to the extent that the alienations of state and religion and their myths remain, it is possible to consider all of history as an unsuccessful separation of practice and theory. However, the relations could be infinitely more complex: for example, it may be that during a historical period, a certain clarification is realized in action and a political leader comes to embody and live out the essential

---

8. *De la capacité politique des classes ouvrières*, 90.

idea of their society; or, through the preservation of alienations, a social class, such as the French bourgeois on the eve of 1789, manages to theorize its idea and impose it on the other social classes; or even that there is a decline in theoretical awareness yet a continuation of historical becoming. In this last case there appears the possibility of dissociation between action and theory and autonomy of these two levels: when Proudhon writes that in 1860 there was no longer any conscious revolutionary theory in French society and that the revolutionary movement nevertheless went on, he reveals a complete disparity between the order of things—that is, in the sequence of economic practices—and their theoretical clarification.[9] It may be that in the absence of a coherent conscious awakening, and despite this absence, the social movement continues preparing conditions favorable to future formulations. It may even be that a revolution occurs, such as the Revolution of 1848 in its first weeks, without an idea being clearly proclaimed, produced only by social contradictions and impossibilities: a revolution is then made "without an idea," a revolution in danger of failure.

The task of the revolutionary theorist is situated between this practice that contains its own law and explicit formulation. To participate in the revolutionary act through a labor of theoretical clarification: this is the theorist's role. In his first writings, Proudhon repeatedly states that this creation is a task for a science—social science—and some of his utterances may suggest a complete separation between social practice and scientific knowledge. On the contrary, in *The Political Capacity of the Working Classes*, he expresses the relation of working-class practice to the revolutionary idea dialectically, stressing that practice implies a theory, a law of action, of which the working class becomes conscious by means of theoretical clarification. It is not a question for the working class of waiting for a truth to come from the

---

9. "But today there are no more ideas. . . . The Revolution goes forward, yes, and Progress is achieved, but by force of circumstance and without anyone's initiative." *De la justice dans la révolution et dans l'église*, 5th étude, vol. 2, 471.

theorist's mouth but of extracting from itself its hidden meaning and imposing it by political struggle. The role of theorists must therefore not be overestimated: their work merely participates in a movement that goes beyond them. Thus, when the first socialists, who were not from the working class, posed the social question for the first time, they did nothing but toss ideas around without involving a labor movement under their direction; the working class spontaneously reclaimed some of these ideas, generalized them, and developed them in its own way, turning them into a doctrine.[10] It is the social group itself that must be credited with the inspiration for and creation of its own theory, and this spontaneity is the sign of the agreement between theory and practice. Of course, the work of the theorist cannot be neglected, but it should itself be treated as a form of practice: words inspire action, proclaim a project, and are essential to the success of revolutionary action, but already constitute a practice in themselves. If practice is an idea, then we must say conversely that speech, theoretical clarification, is a form of action.[11]

However, the principle of the identity of social facts and ideas must be further pursued. We know that one social practice—exchange, mutuality—is inscribed in the real according to a logical form, that it carries within itself an ideal relation, but this theory of immanence must be extended to all society, to its organization as a whole. A society, in its divisions and its hierarchies, is at the same time a collective being, a set of practices, and a form that can be expressed in an idea. A society constitutes a totality, organized according to a fundamental and simple form that corresponds to an idea, an intelligible logical form. The Roman idea at its origin can be summarized thus: a patriciate, clientships, a certain system of property; the entire system of the republic arises from this form. Another form in the idea of the Roman Empire: the patriciate reduced to the level of the plebeians, powers concentrated in the hands of an emperor, who was

---

10. *De la capacité politique des classes ouvrières*, 119.

11. "To act is always to think; to say is to do." *Confessions d'un révolutionnaire*, 193.

in turn placed under the control of the praetorians: from this idea, this general form, political centralizations and hierarchies arose. When the revolution occurred in 1789, it carried within itself an order that could be wholly expressed in the notion of human rights: by this principle the nation was declared sovereign, royalty was reduced to a function, the nobility was abolished, and religion was opened up to free inquiry.[12] Thus, the great social systems that history has known—Oriental despotism, the Roman patriciate, papal theocracy, feudalism, bourgeois constitutionalism—constituted coherent and particular systems, different ideas. It is in this sense that Proudhon can say that every society is created and transformed according to an idea, by which he does not mean that society makes itself by means of a theoretical representation—since the idea in question here is only the intelligible form of the whole—but rather that this general form constitutes a society's essence and that its transformation takes place by a reorganization of the structure.

In going from the social totality to its parts, Proudhon retains the same method, since if the social totality is a unity that is both real and logical, then the particular relations established between the parts are integrated into the whole and maintain their characteristics. It is then, in addressing the relations between the terms, that his method stresses the importance of antagonisms in the society of the regime of property and in any society. In his *System of Economic Contradictions*, Proudhon attempts to show that all the terms of economic society are in a relation of antagonism, a dialectical relation, and that the aggravation of contradictions heralds and necessitates the collapse of the regime of property. The theory of the identity of reality and the ideal thus makes this demonstration more persuasive. Indeed, Proudhon proposes to articulate the internal logic of the system, to show how all the parts are antagonistic and how they are integrated into a contradictory whole. Abandoning the historical method, he proposes to describe the proprietary regime in its systematic reality, to describe it "according to the order of ideas" in order to show

---

12. *De la capacité politique des classes ouvrières*, III.

that such a system cannot continue and contains within itself the necessity of its own collapse.[13] He does not preclude any recourse to history, and he would indicate what developments may take place within the system, but the study of the logical structure enables him to show whether these particular developments are either incorporated into the system without fundamentally modifying it, or whether they intensify its contradictions and thus hasten its destruction.

Consequently, we can see the importance that Proudhon was to grant throughout his work to the "extrication" of the revolutionary idea: indeed, he could not imagine that the political struggle was limited to either an everyday practice or to a succession of riots. If it is true that a society is primarily a system, or in other words an idea, it is important above all to know whether the social movement carries the promise of a coherent system and to bring the theory of this new society into consciousness. The revolutionary idea by no means merely indicates a project that happens to be useful for establishing the coherence of action; it indicates both the image of the social relations to be realized and the reality of the relations themselves. To articulate the thought of the revolution or its philosophy will not be to formulate a new abstract theory but rather to discover the general form, the structure, of this society which the social movement, if it is creative, carries within itself. In his final writings, Proudhon exclusively attributes the creation of this idea to the working class, having ascribed it to science prior to 1848. This shift cannot be ignored: however, these two attributions are not contradictory, because we must expect that working-class spontaneity, to the extent that it would express the dynamics of the real society freed from its forms of alienation, would realize in practice what social science had foreseen. By discovering social relations in their reality, social science must be combined with working-class action that restores spontaneity to social life.

* * *

13. *Système des contradictions*, vol. I, 179.

This ideo-realistic or dialectical theory of the social makes it possible to understand how a society creates for itself a theory, a religion, a philosophy. Contrary to spiritualistic and religious explanations, it is important to remember that it is not the religion that makes the human being but rather the human being who makes the religion;[14] but this creation must be understood as the work of a society that constitutes a logical whole. Whatever meaning a religion may have for particular individuals, it is only at the level of an established social reality that we can understand the origin and form of a religion. In religion, society, which comprises a totality of meanings capable of being expressed in a central idea, gives itself a theoretical "translation" of itself, a symbolization. Religion is a symbolic system of society, a deformed image that is ignorant of itself, but is nonetheless an expression in which the critical thinker can discern the features of social practice. Insofar as religion symbolizes moral aspirations, it represents real human needs, and, insofar as it symbolizes unequal social relations, it represents the symbolization of social antagonisms. Proudhon does not conclude that theory should be treated as an epiphenomenal product of a practice that determines it—of course, he sufficiently stressed the major importance of economic relations—but in the social totality, it is less this relation of determination that he retains than relations of analogy between theory and social system. Religion, a social symbol, is an analog or synonym of capitalism.[15] More precisely, the theoretical content intrinsic to its specific organization reflects the economic and political modes of organization analogically. As demonstrated by the critique of the state, political relations are rooted in the economic relations that they express in their own way and consolidate: the same relation of

14. "It is not religion that makes the human being, nor the political system that makes the patriot and the citizen, but, quite to the contrary, the human being who makes religion and the citizen who makes the State." *De la justice dans la révolution et dans l'église*, 12th étude, vol. 4, 492–93.

15. "Capital . . . has as a synonym, in the order of religion, Catholicism." *Confessions d'un révolutionnaire*, 282.

analogy and justification is established between religion and the social totality. We find in Christianity the same organization as in the capitalist economy and politics: the image of higher powers and celestial hierarchies corresponds to the social reality of hierarchical relations, and the myth of a transcendent and absolute power corresponds to oppressive social relations. This emphasizes, to a certain extent, a truth of religion. Proudhon would not stop protesting against the scornful critiques that reduce religions merely to their absurdities or their crimes: being the product of social spontaneity, every religion carries a degree of truth, a deformed image of society, the meaning of which must be explained by rationalizing its causes.[16]

This sociological theory of knowledge or, in other words, this theory of ideologies, also enables us to understand the extreme importance of intellectual systems in social practice. This is a point on which Proudhon insisted very strongly, granting a considerable role to myths, utopias, and explicit formulations, whether arising from religion, philosophy, or metaphysics. Thus it is necessary to underline the social role of the myth of the state in social cohesion and the obstacle it presents to revolutionary action. This myth is a spontaneous creation of "popular idealism" that is all the more powerful to the extent that the people are unenlightened: the people regard themselves as a mysterious unity and want to think of themselves as such because they are afraid of anything that introduces division and plurality. The people give themselves a self-representation that they incarnate in princes and kings, who symbolize the mythical unity, and constitute idols that it will be sacrilege to discuss. This myth is ambiguous, since while the people want to think themselves as a finished totality and entrust themselves to a state, at the same time they distrust it, and this ambiguity results in the recourse to divine right as a transcendent means of control; this has the simultaneous effect of reinforcing the mythical character of the state by lending it sacred endorsement. In another form, this mythology reappears as "popular divine right," whereby an

---

16. *De la création de l'ordre*, 65.

elected assembly is expected to produce a sovereignty endowed again with a sacred, quasi-mystical character.[17] This whole mythology played a considerable and negative role during the 1848 Revolution, during which the people never stopped waiting for government decisions to find a solution to the social problem instead of seeking it in a sweeping reorganization of economic and social relations. The myth of the state leads citizens to give maximum power to the central authority, increase state encroachment, and restrict their own freedom. The tendency of the state to increase its size and the extent of its control results from its own nature and from the social antagonisms that it aims to overcome, but also from this illusion, this mystification to which the citizens adhere and of which they are victims. It is therefore necessary to recognize the historical significance of the myth, a social reality, and examine how it reinforces or combats other aspects of practice.

Thus, utopia must not be considered only as a mistake to be denounced; it must be seen as an element that plays a role in action, and we may say that humans are the victims of their own utopia.[18] This form of illusion, spread either by social reformers or by popular idealism, has the fundamental consequence of diverting collective action from concrete and achievable goals, directing collective thought toward means directly contrary to the ends pursued: in 1848, utopias contributed to the weakening of the revolutionary movement and caused the collective effort to fail. This is why the denunciation of utopias did not solely result from intellectual concerns but constitutes an indispensable social task and an effective political action.

Proudhon is thus led to strongly underline the importance of formulating and disseminating an authentically revolutionary theory. Having recognized the effectiveness of religions, utopias, and various intellectual systems, he is entitled to expect

---

17. *De la justice dans la révolution et dans l'église*, 4th étude, vol. 2, 164.

18. "Utopia . . . as an expression of parties and of sects . . . plays a role in the drama." *Idée générale de la révolution*, 155. "We are victims of a Utopia. Instead of making progress, we spoke, in 1848, of the absolute." Letter to M. Trouessart, August 31, 1853, *Correspondance*, vol. 5, 227.

from a revolutionary idea a cohesion of practice and, to a certain extent, the success of the revolutionary struggle. The shared idea is indeed a tool for social cohesion, enabling a convergence of practices. Studying the conditions in which a social class enters political life, Proudhon suggests in *The Political Capacity of the Working Classes* that the proletariat needs to become conscious of itself and, at the same time, formulate its own theory. The shift to practice requires the assertion of an idea as a guideline for practice: indeed, once the working class becomes conscious of itself, it must "deduce" its practical conclusions from the idea expressed, to find the inspiration for its action in its theory.[19] The bourgeois class unified its fight against the nobility and reorganized political society in 1789 because it had formulated its idea, its project, which was summarized in a principle—human rights— and because it could deduce from this idea the overthrow of the nobility, the freedom of trade, and the abolition of the political powers of the clergy. The coherent expression of revolutionary theory thus constitutes a decisive and necessary moment in the revolutionary process. When a social movement brought about by contradictions occurs without being supported by a theory that meets the requirements of the situation, it cannot go beyond the stage of critique and must retreat in the face of an alliance of reactionary forces.[20]

This last remark reveals that agreement between theory and practice cannot immediately be assumed: practical negation may occur before the inherent goal is discovered, just as the idea may be formulated without yet having given birth to the practice it signals. Identifying the three conditions necessary for working-class political action, Proudhon affirms in turn that this class reached self-consciousness in 1864, that it managed to express its idea, but that it had not yet deduced a practice consistent with its theory. This means that theoretical formulation, however decisive it may be, cannot be treated as the sole condition of revolutionary

---

19. *De la capacité politique des classes ouvrières*, 90.
20. "Social changes are nothing without the intellectual movement." Letter to Pérennès, December 16, 1839, *Correspondance*, vol. I, 166.

practice: it may prompt action, but it does not cause it as a logical necessity. On the contrary, practice can lag behind expression and thus be inconsistent with it.

This possible divorce between theory and practice makes it possible to moderate some of Proudhon's provisional assertions about the social and historical importance of theoretical formulations. Some of his quick judgments attribute a decisive and almost exclusive revolutionary power to the spread of ideas—for example, imagining the drafting of a new catechism that would explain to the people the true meaning of the symbols of Christianity, Proudhon proceeds to imagine that such a work could revolutionize Europe in less than ten years.[21] Moreover, envisioning the consequences of his own work, he hopes on several occasions that it will enable the reconstitution of the revolutionary party. Isolated from their context, these utterances would suggest that theories and awakenings constitute the essential or even the only factors of social change. However, these are only provisional or partial assessments: other texts expressly indicate how illusory it would be to think that knowledge alone could bring about transformation or ensure social cohesion. A social constitution cannot be realized by intellectual consensus alone: it is ensured only by anchoring it within a socioeconomic organization.[22] Proudhon, in fact, explicitly refused to accept the theory of the predominant factor; while he grants that the political constitution is primarily conditioned by the economic organization, this explanation only seems provisional to him: it must immediately be added that the maintenance of the state is also enabled by a mythology shared by the citizens and by the presence of a homologous religion. His concrete analyses primarily concern economic contradictions, class conflicts, state alienation, and political knowledge as parts of the social dynamic, but this list is not exhaustive: elements such as scientific development, the

---

21. *De la création de l'ordre*, 67.

22. "Human beings will pass from discord to harmony, not only by virtue of the knowledge that they will have acquired of their destiny, but thanks to the economic, political, or other conditions that constitute social harmony." *Système des contradictions*, vol. 2, 290.

prejudices of the moment, and the moral attitudes of a class cannot be neglected and must be called upon depending on the situation. Although this conclusion is not made explicit, the historical analyses reveal various social constellations in which these levels of reality may have more or less importance depending on the historical situation; in a revolutionary phase, it may be that the unification of practices, inspired by a common theory, can be accomplished, and that in this case the idea is the decisive social creation: the beginning of the 1789 Revolution was entirely motivated by this conscious will to reconstitute society on the basis of reason alone. But there are also periods of relative quiescence in which the order of things predominates over the order of reasons, in which major transformations occur without either being caused or even accompanied by the corresponding intellectual movement.[23]

This relativity of analyses does not depend only on the empirical observation of the diversity of situations: it is based, in theory, on the conception of social reality. Proudhon can admit, as a general principle of analysis, that the organization of labor sets in place the broad features of the social constitution, but he immediately adds that labor is not a material order, that labor is at once practical and theoretical, work and idea, act and logic. The order of labor is not at the level of reality that would produce a theoretical counterpart; it is in itself an order that has its own logic, its own meaning, and, for example, its own contradictions. In the same way, politics is not merely a collection of incoherent activities; it also has an immanent theory that is expressed more or less clearly and only appears in all its truth to the critical thinker. Thus, social activity is permeated with meanings or, to use Proudhon's word, ideas: the social is "ideo-realistic." Theory thus does not intervene as a distinct factor in a practice that is fundamentally different from itself: it is immanent in the act rather than being an expression of the act. It is thus understood that a theoretical transformation corresponding to

---

23. Proudhon writes, for example, on April 14, 1849, in *Le Peuple*: "We live in a time of great events and small ideas." *Mélanges*, vol. 18, 137.

real practice may permeate action, alter people's attitudes, and thoroughly combine with a revolutionary practice. Moreover, if the theoretical formulation is in agreement with the spontaneous action, we cannot distinguish what is practical from what is theoretical: when speech or writing contribute to collective thought, they are themselves a form of action. The theory of the identity of facts and ideas makes it possible to understand that the act has a logical form and also, therefore, that the idea carries within itself the promise of action and constitutes a form of action in itself.

This theory of the social, which is simultaneously a theory of ideas, explains the importance Proudhon gave to the two fundamental theories that seemed to him to summarize the social contradictions of the mid-nineteenth century: Christianity and revolutionary thought, religion and justice.

2. Religion

It is to the sociology of religions, and particularly to the sociology of Christianity, that Proudhon was to devote his most elaborate work. As an assiduous reader of the Bible, which he constantly annotated, and familiar with the history of religions, he prepared two important works on the origins of Christianity that were published after his death.[24] This extreme interest in religion may be explained by the cultural context of the middle of the nineteenth century and the importance of contemporary debates on these issues, but it is explained more directly by the significance that Proudhon gave to the social idea. If the idea is both the common theory in which consciousnesses find their unity and the general form or structure of society, a reflection on religion will concern not only the thought of individual human beings but also the fundamental relations of society as a whole. To inquire into the idea of Jehovah in the Old Testament is, as he notes in a

---

24. *Jésus et les origines du christianisme* [Jesus and the Origins of Christianity]; *Césarisme et christianisme* [Caesarism and Christianity].

page of his *Carnets*, to inquire into the entire history of the Jewish people, to reconsider a privileged element of a society through which all the general features of the totality will take their form.[25] In the same way, when Proudhon contrasts the church with the Revolution in *Justice in the Revolution and in the Church*, it is less to define two visions of the world than to reconsider the confrontation of two societies through them.

The critique of religion arises from the principle of the creation of religion by human beings: it is, prior to philosophy and scientific knowledge, the first human attempt "to give reason to things," to provide a first explanation while the human mind is still unable to establish well-founded knowledge.[26] Instead of a set of formulas derived from observation, religion creates symbols, concrete images, materializations of the idea. Religion expresses itself in figures and allegories and proposes a symbolization that serves as an explanation for each natural or social fact. But, like any intellectual system, religion has its origin and raison d'être in society itself: its symbols contain both the aspirations of individual human beings and the forms of the society in which they were formulated. Thus, religious representations are linked to a sense of the weakness and impotence of the individual consciousness, but social unanimity in faith sufficiently demonstrates that religion is not only an individual creation. In the same way, one cannot attribute the creation and maintenance of religions to a conspiracy of priests and kings. Religion is a spontaneous creation of the community by which a society creates for itself a representation, a symbolization, of the world and of itself. The divine myth is not an invention of priests to control the crowd; rather, it springs from the people, from society which comes together and expresses itself in an analogous image.

Religious symbolism therefore offers to the critical mind of the mythologist a translation of the temporal: social forms will

---

25. "To narrate the life of Jehovah is to narrate nearly all of Jewish history." *Carnets*, 1853, reproduced in *Écrits sur la religion* [Writings on Religion], 283.

26. "To make sense of things": *De la création de l'ordre*, 46.

be transposed in the symbol but also reproduced in it; for example, a strongly hierarchical society will correspond to a set of religious images in which authority will play an important part.[27] In the same way, a warlike society gives itself a symbolism that glorifies force and violence: if God appears in the Bible in the guise of a war chief, it is because Jewish society symbolized its own bellicose faculties in this image. Society is originally warlike and religious, and myths symbolize this power of the group: at the same time, we might say that war is religious and religion is warlike. Primitive rites, immolation, sacrifice, prayer, and thanksgiving find their origin and meaning in past episodes of violence or fears of violence. But the nature of religion is to be unaware of itself. It is locked in the repetition of its "concrete ideas" whose understanding it forbids by turning the symbol into a truth:[28] for the religious mind, ceremonies and myths are mysteries whose examination it forbids. Religion thus attributes to God what comes from humanity. It ascribes to a supernatural power, whatever it may be, that which in reality can only belong to human beings or to their collective action. This observation holds true not only with respect to Christianity but also with respect to any religion and to socialism itself, if it is made into a religion. All religious knowledge, being in reality only a mythology formulated by human beings and society, creates another universe and separates consciousness from itself. Whereas God is only a "side effect of consciousness," religion introduces otherness, separating consciousness from that which is its own.[29] It leads to the formation of a double consciousness: a "natural consciousness" or real consciousness whose full recognition would destroy any form of religion, and a "theological consciousness," which contains only figurative affirmations.[30] Through this division or

---

27. "The spiritual is indissolubly related to the temporal, which it translates in its own manner. To the religious institution corresponds the political and social institution; the greater the part played by authority in the first, the greater it shall play in the second." *La Guerre et la paix*, 456.

28. *De la création de l'ordre*, 48.

29. *De la justice dans la révolution et dans l'église*, 5th étude, vol. 2, 362.

30. Ibid.

alienation, consciousness, ceasing to know itself in its truth, adores itself and seeks itself in a false image.[31]

Introduced into social action, this alienation symbolizes and reinforces subordination. Proudhon traces a necessary relationship between intellectual alienation and social subordination: when a society creates an ideal principle higher than itself, a transcendent rule that it forbids itself from disobeying, it is inevitably compelled to place respect for the principle above respect for human beings. Religion strips human beings of their rights and their real powers: it attributes to God this justice and freedom that are actually only its own attributes, but this dispossession necessarily involves an inversion, a denaturation of real relations, and a submission to myth. For religion, it is no longer humans who create their own rights and who must, above all, be recognized in the fullness of their dignity. The priest locates the origin of rights, of the good, and of freedom in God; he establishes an external legislator, superior to humans. The priest turns the true creator of rights into a subordinate being: he turns the human being into a believer, just as the statesman turns the citizen into a subject.

Having established this definition of religion, Proudhon believes that he has demonstrated the fundamental relationship between religious thought and its two social consequences: the degradation of humans and the creation of an obstacle to social change. The necessary relationship between religion and social subordination is in any case only one example of the general relation between idealism and inequality. Any theory that glorifies an ideal separate from real practice results in a fragmentation of social forces: when the personal ideal replaces the pursuit of justice, the reign of force replaces social cohesion; when political idealism makes the ruler not just the instrument but also the author of rights, it enables and justifies the absolutism that causes the weakening of social bonds. Religion, a particular form

---

31. "This alienation of the human soul, which, taking itself for an Other, calls out to itself, adores itself . . . without knowing itself." Ibid., 351.

of idealism, reproduces its general movement: by making a transcendent principle the foundation of rights, it necessarily results in humanity being dispossessed of its freedom and dignity. But to this first social characteristic of religion we must add its inevitable negation of history. Proudhon finds an inexorable relation between mythology and the negation of becoming: by creating a symbolism that it turns into a mysterious truth, religion sanctifies myths and prohibits their revision; the law that it imposes includes absolute respect for a timeless truth. It appeals not to reason, which would imply examination and revision, but instead to an unchanging tradition that must be transmitted from generation to generation. In other words, every religion is inherently hostile to discussion and science; it is not an accident that Christianity has continually posed obstacles to the development of the sciences: by affirming a truth external to human intelligence, religion calls us to adhere to an imposed faith and to fear free human reasoning. More generally, a mythology, once established, imposes itself on humans as an immutable truth. While science is necessarily associated with progress and change, religion is necessarily associated with the rejection of change. While science aspires to progress, religion aspires to immutability. Thus it will both justify and reinforce whatever, in a given society, tends toward repetition and conservatism, and we must expect that societies mired in superstitions and mythologies will be the most stagnant. Ancient Egypt, the Byzantine Empire, and the Middle Ages offer examples of societies permeated by religious opposition to progress. Conversely, Greece, Rome, America, and modern Europe demonstrate the creative movement of societies in which religion no longer plays more than a secondary role.[32]

The history of Christianity may serve to illustrate this general theory of religion. Proudhon refuses to attribute the origin of Christianity to a divine will, but he also refuses to regard Jesus as its founder. A phenomenon as important as the creation and diffusion of this universalistic religion can be explained only by a development prior to Christ's arrival and by all of the social, economic,

---

32. *De la création de l'ordre*, 54.

political, and cultural conditions of the Roman Empire.[33] From the complexity of this historical creation, Proudhon primarily singles out three dimensions: Jewish messianism, the failure and the mythological reinterpretation of the message of Jesus, and the reconciliation of messianism and Caesarism in a decadent Rome. Messianism was not originally a religious phenomenon but rather a social aspiration to unify all peoples under a single government, a single law, a single language, a single cult—an aspiration to a unitary reconstitution of the various societies.[34] In this general form, messianism was not absent from the Roman tradition, but it was above all among the Jewish people, shaken by the dramas of conquests and captivities, that it was to acquire its full force and constitute the decisive cause of Christianity. The messianic idea had been formulated several centuries before the birth of Jesus, having attained the status of a collective myth in the prophecies attributed to Daniel. The Roman conquest was to give it an unprecedented intensity while plunging the peoples of Palestine and Asia Minor into a situation of economic disorder and violence. In Jewish society, torn apart by conflict between groups and castes, in which the Pharisees monopolized privileges and the scribes formed an exploitative bureaucracy with the priests' approval, the masses felt the exploitation most keenly and yearned to overturn their conditions. In such a society, the messianic tradition was to be revived with an intensity close to fanaticism: despairing of the present, the crowd cried out for a messiah from whom it awaited the liberation of the territory, the establishment of peace, and the introduction of a power that would dominate foreign peoples. At this time, we can sense that messianic expectations were not bereft of political ambitions and that they could be reconciled with Roman Caesarism, despite the temporary conflicts between them.

---

33. In a few words Proudhon indicates how an explanatory study of the origins of Christianity should begin: "1st Description of the moral, social, religious, economic and political state of the nations under Augustus and Tiberius. Historical summary; Political situation; General expectation." *Jésus et les origines du christianisme*, 550.

34. *Césarisme et christianisme*, Marpon, 1883, vol. I, 5–6.

The Proudhonian interpretation of the personality and message of Christ are thus opposed to the Christian tradition. Jesus would have placed himself at the polar opposite of this messianic expectation: far from recognizing himself as the Messiah, he would have wanted to fight against this mythology by championing a social reform of morals and laws. The message of Jesus, far from being a religious message usable in a political context, would have been a social message with a revolutionary purpose. Proudhon stresses that Jesus's social affiliations led him to share the aspirations of an exploited class: he was not the son of David, as others would insist after his death, but rather the son of an artisan, a "man of the masses," a member of a class dominated by proprietors and priests.[35] He was also a Galilean from an inferior social group, scorned by the people of Jerusalem and the doctors of the law, and was thus particularly sensitive to social oppression. This participation in the trials of the oppressed was to make him feel the need to stand against the social order and to discover the urgency of a revolt against the Pharisees and the priestly caste. It is based on this experience and in this precise social situation that the teaching of Jesus takes form and meaning. As an interpreter of the thought of the masses, Jesus calls neither for a political uprising nor for an inversion of beliefs; he thrusts aside the traps set by theologians and politicians, concentrating all his teachings on moral and social reform, on the "renewal of morals and laws."[36] Of course, he expresses himself in religious language, since he lives in a primarily religious society, but he does not seek to found a new sect. He preaches the abolition of theft and corruption and denounces the exploitation of the people by the rich. He condemns the monopolization of wealth by defending the poor and calling for charity, and he denounces the injustice of slavery and proclaims human equality by preaching equality before God. He avoids attacking Roman oppression, because this revolt is not yet possible, and the call for reform of economic habits goes much further in its consequences than

35. *Jésus et les origines du christianisme*, 536.
36. Ibid., 591.

a simple political opposition. In the same manner, he does not confront priests directly, but by denouncing the rich he disturbs the power of the priesthood and condemns the whole system of priests founded on Mosaism.

Thus, through his moral exhortations, Jesus was calling for a veritable revolution. Contrary to later interpretations, he was little concerned with theology. Born among the poor and asserting equality and justice for all, he was a revolutionary tribune and a socialist *avant la lettre*.[37] His crucifixion and death therefore came as no surprise. The gospel threatened the established order and aroused the hostility of all the traditional hierarchies. The rich were condemned for their privileges; the priests were threatened, perhaps not in terms of their beliefs but, more seriously, in terms of their social dominance; the Romans, while less directly concerned, might worry about a critique that also affected Caesarism. But the masses themselves did not completely understand the revolutionary message: they were not free from the messianic illusion and were partly disappointed by the appeals of a man who refused to announce the construction of a new worldly empire.

The history of Christianity after the death of Jesus was thus more than the history of a lapse of memory: it was that of a gradual betrayal. But this evolution and regression are again explained by social conditions, and it is in terms of the social history of ideas that it must be interpreted. In order to follow this development, it is necessary to study the social relations of the various societies concerned, the political events that overturned previous structures, the cultural influences, the interaction of religions and philosophies, and finally the history and transformations of the collective psyche. The message of Jesus, despite its furious condemnation, failed to disrupt the social relations of Jewish society, and this failure, symbolized by the crucifixion, paved the way for the rejection of the revolutionary nature of the evangelical appeal. The fall of Jerusalem, the destruction of the temple, and the dispersal of the Jews forced

37. Ibid., 540, "Jésus révolutionnaire" [Jesus the Revolutionary].

a revision of the confused memories that had been preserved of the life of Jesus and the legends that had already crystallized around it: since the temple was destroyed and no hope for the reconstitution of a Jewish empire could be maintained, it was because Jesus, who would nonetheless be made into a messiah, had in fact announced the arrival of a spiritual empire and not a temporal or political one. Moreover, contact with non-Jewish groups, and the reality of the new relations that were established with the Gentiles, forced them to reconsider the Jewish character of the early religion and to lend the new religion a universal significance; the cultural dialog with Greek philosophy also lent support to this shift toward a Catholic conception of the religion. Thus, after a few years and particularly after the fall of Jerusalem, the collective psyche and memory managed to integrate and transmute the legendary image of Jesus according to their own model. Jesus had fought against messianism and refused to be regarded as God's messenger, but the collective messianic expectation managed to destroy this part of his teaching and to make him its new messiah. Although he had fought against superstitions and obstinately refused to concern himself with theology, he was turned into an incarnation of the divine, an object of new refinements for the consideration of theologians. But even more seriously, the collective psyche, through several debates and disagreements, almost managed to completely destroy the fundamental intention of the message of Jesus: its revolutionary intention. The word of Jesus was aimed at the critique of institutions and the denunciation of injustice and exploitation, but through a process of deification Jesus was made into a transcendent being, a king, justifying the established order. In theological terms, faith was made the essential virtue, to the detriment of works, whereas Jesus, as a true revolutionary tribune, had only been concerned with practice. This rejection of the original message is particularly visible in the epistles of Saint Paul: Peter still maintained a certain fidelity to essentially moral principles, but Paul imposed a return to theology, faith, and thus obedience and docility toward the social order. Consequently, a reconciliation between the old messianism and

Caesarism was possible, a reconciliation which had in fact been under way before the birth of Jesus.[38]

The last pages of *Caesarism and Christianity* stop at the fall of the Roman Empire and offer only brief comments concerning the feudal period, but the foregoing indications sufficiently underline the continuity between messianism—the more or less mystical assertion of the reunification of all peoples in a single cult and government—and Caesarism, unitary and despotic political organization. Despite their apparent contradiction, messianism came to be reconciled with an oppressive political practice: having become a religion, contrary to the will of the working-class man from Nazareth, Christianity sanctified this new feudal social hierarchy.

Since Christianity has disavowed its origin, rethinking it in the present proprietary regime thus forces us to discover its current meaning. This is the purpose of Proudhon's most extensive work, *Justice in the Revolution and in the Church*: to question the meaning of Christianity at this moment of historical conflict between the proletariat and the bourgeoisie, labor and capital, revolutionary and Christian principles. Of course, religion is ostensibly a theoretical system, a theology, primarily intended to be independent of the temporal order, but the social critique denounces this illusion, restoring religion to its human foundations and its real relationship with the social structure. There does not seem to be a relationship between religious belief and private property, between Christianity and human exploitation; the religious mind feigns to believe that there is no relationship between the truth of a divine word and the existing social order. However, there is no idea that does not have its origins, realization, and practice in society. And Proudhon's thesis is precisely that Christianity, as it is expressed in the middle of the nineteenth century, is the "idea" of this unequal society in which property

---

38. Thus the message of Christ had only a relatively weak influence in the formation of Christianity; in extreme cases, and although it is only partly correct, "we made a Christianity without Jesus." *La Bible annotée* [The Annotated Bible], 401.

monopolizes the bulk of the collective forces, in which the producer is fatally condemned to economic poverty and political
subordination. Christianity constitutes the general theory of this
historically ephemeral society and is involved in it at all levels:
economic, political, legal, intellectual, and moral. The fundamental relationship that Proudhon reveals between the religious
idea and social reality is an analogical relationship. Broadly distinguishing three levels of this reality—economic, political, and
religious—he outlines a fundamental analogy between these
three types of being, enabling their dialectical unity and relations to be understood.[39] Analogical correlations are established
between these three apparently distinct structures, describing
all of the relations of capitalist society in religious doctrines and
practices. Accordingly, the critique of Christianity will take on
a revolutionary function: since it reproduces all social practices
analogically, critiquing it means denouncing the whole of capitalist society in the plurality of its forms and contradictions.

Every religion attributes the principle of truth and rights to
a transcendent being; in doing so, it institutes a separation and a
hierarchy between gods and human beings. It is the nature of the
religious to establish an unequal relationship between the sacred
and the profane, the divine and the human: this unequal and
hierarchical dichotomy will be translated in the political order
by the hierarchy between rulers and ruled and by the particular
hierarchies of privileges. By affirming the transcendence of the
sacred, religion forbids human beings from posing as the creators of their own rights and institutes a relation of authority and
obedience between God and the believer: more generally, the
church thinks in terms of oppositions between knowledge and
ignorance, authority and obedience; since truth and rights come
from God, humans must receive the truth faithfully and abide by
it. This authoritarian relation is analogous to the political principle of the subordination of citizens to the governing powers.

---

39. "Capital, the analogue of which, in the political order, is government, has as a synonym, in the order of religion, Catholicism." *Confessions
d'un révolutionnaire*, 282.

Just as God is absolute, infallible, and the bearer of justice, the ruler is the dispenser of justice and the defender of social life; the believer receives the divine word and must obey the representatives of God, and likewise the citizen awaits and must obey the decision of the political authorities. Thus, religious alienation reflects political alienation analogically: just as the end of humanity does not lie within itself but instead in its future salvation, the end of society does not lie within itself but rather is in the power of the state. The same illusion that divides consciousness and leads human beings to attribute what only comes from themselves to the divine also divides the social body, attributing forces whose real origin lies in collective effort to the authorities. By different means and through divergent theories, religious and political thought are reconciled by definition in the same spirit of despotism.

The same analogical relation links the religious system and the unequal system of private property. In the domain of economic organization, the church pretends not to have a theory of its own and not to take sides, but the spirit that motivates it is entirely in accord with a defense of privilege and a theoretical justification of social exploitation. By systematizing the principle of authority and insurmountable inequality between those destined to command and those destined to obey, the church offers a model similar to the relations between proprietors and workers. Through its theory of original sin, it affirms the inescapable powerlessness of human beings to produce an egalitarian and just social order, and it makes disorder and pain essential conditions of humanity that can only be alleviated by divine grace. Thus, it offers an image of the human condition similar to that described by traditional political economy: it evokes a society in which the inequality of conditions is insurmountable, in which pauperism is inevitable. Just as divine grace is unforeseeable and depends only on a mysterious power, material wealth depends only on the accident of birth or the inevitable disorder of the economy. Just as disorder in the religious world is both inescapable and absurd, economic anarchy is inherent in the economic system and equally senseless.

The extent of these analogies make it possible to understand the scope of the church's influence on capitalist society, an influence all the greater as it pertains to every level of the social and, in a somewhat "occult" manner, directly affects the consciousnesses of individuals.[40] The religious idea is given as the type, the "paradigm" of society as a whole, and it is indeed the sign of an unequal society as well as one of its causes.[41] Proudhon does not at all think that religion must be treated as a secondary or superstructural social phenomenon and that it would be sufficient to note its analogical relations to social structures. On the contrary, he thinks that by serving as an intellectual support for social practice, religion acts both through the theory that motivates it and through the ecclesiastical apparatus charged with inculcating it.

Indeed, the spread of the religious idea entails the constitution of a social body that reproduces its theory in practice. The divine hierarchy in the church corresponds to the hierarchy of ranks, absolute state authority corresponds to the authoritarian power of church elders, and the arbitrariness of the divine corresponds to the arbitrariness of decisions. This social body, despite the weakening of beliefs in nineteenth-century Europe, constantly intervenes in political life to impose its politics and reclaim a power that tends to evade its grasp. The church is considered, because of its doctrines, as the model, the "prototype of government," that must absorb and convert all the others.[42] It also assumes, because of its belief in the absolute preeminence of the divine, the primacy of the spiritual over the temporal—in other words, its own superiority over the civil government. Thus, the policy of the church is necessarily conservative, favorable to the maintenance of hierarchies, centralized powers, and economic oppression, and hostile to the rise of science and reason, to egalitarian and anarchist demands. Proudhon does not fail to recognize the plurality of churches, the nuances of their politics, and the divergences between the high and the low clergy, but he

---

40. *La Révolution sociale démontrée par le coup d'état du deux décembre*, 124.
41. *De la justice dans la révolution et dans l'église*, 4th étude, vol. 2, 197.
42. Ibid., 202.

maintains that despite these minor differences the fundamentally antirevolutionary spirit of the church necessarily prevails; undoubtedly, the Reformation shook the dogma of authority, but, in remaining as a religion, it did not call into question the theoretical and practical foundations of Christianity. For Proudhon, religion cannot be constitutional, much less republican: it could not give human beings their freedom and the responsibility to organize their society without ceasing to be a religion.

However, the action of the church should not be reduced to the struggle of a social instrument concerned with maintaining a certain social organization in its own interest. While this intention does not fail to appear, it is formulated in the name of a coherent doctrine that serves as a basis for the church and its action. Proudhon attributes a particular logic and necessity to the religious idea, as to any idealism: it is the nature of mystical ideas, when they are formulated and accepted, to stifle critical thought in superstitions, to yoke the will, to regiment action, and to absorb all particular interests within an abstract interest.[43] Nor is it only a question of criticizing the circumstantial decisions of a church, but also of radically critiquing the theory that motivates it in order to lay the groundwork for its disappearance.

The necessity of this disappearance arises from the relationship established between authoritarian society and religion.[44] Any autonomous activity of creation, and in particular scientific progress, calls religious dogmas into question: any work of reason is opposed in its very movement to the docility of faith. Rational thought, political freedom, moral emancipation, and demands for rights: all these activities escape religious authority, limit its powers, and turn against it. This gradual erasure heralds a future society in which humans would have to live without religion. Sketching a broad vision of the becoming of societies, and passing from sociology to the philosophy of history, Proudhon

43. *De la justice dans la révolution et dans l'église*, 3rd étude, vol. 2, 19-20.
44. "Human beings are destined to live without religion: a multitude of symptoms show that society, by an interior work, is quickly shedding itself of this now useless envelope." *De la création de l'ordre*, 63.

can thus compare the progressive movement of humanity to a Promethean struggle against God.[45] Humanity, rather than finding its own image in God, affirms itself as God's antagonist in a gradual temporal movement that is opposed to the absolute. Whereas God symbolizes timeless and ahistorical order, societies are made in becoming and through a succession of changes. Whereas the divine symbolizes an infinite and infallible knowledge, humanity creates a finite and continually revised science. Humanity is and must be the antithesis of God. The divine, far from symbolizing the protection of providence, expresses everything that a free society must get rid of: authority, fate, tyranny, class inequality and poverty—in a word, evil.[46]

3. Justice

Against religion, the theory of the unequal and alienated society, Proudhon antithetically puts forward justice, the theory of the egalitarian and anarchist society. Just as religion is the idea and expression of inequality, justice would be the idea and expression of equality. The term *justice* especially causes difficulties in his great work *Justice in the Revolution and in the Church*, where some expressions lend themselves to confusion, seeming to reduce justice to an intellectual representation and base the social organization on an abstract concept. However, this is not Proudhon's intent: faithful to his theory, which he called "ideo-realistic," this new idea refers to a concrete relationship, a new type of social relation that would form the basis of the de-alienated society. Justice is above all a particular type of socioeconomic relation, a

---

45. Translator's note: In Greek mythology, Prometheus molded clay to make humans and then taught them how to survive, including giving them fire stolen from the gods. As punishment, Zeus enchained Prometheus to a boulder where an eagle would painfully eat his liver after it grew back every day. The term *Promethean* implies creativity and originality as well as a disobedience to authority.

46. "God is tyranny and mystery; God is evil." *Système des contradictions*, vol. I, 384.

form of solidarity established between two participants or two groups of participants. But it is known that the reality of a social relation, whether it is a relation of antagonism or reciprocity, is dialectical in nature and corresponds identically to a logical form: the relation can thus be expressed in an idea, and a practice can give rise to an expression, a representation. In this sense, justice is no longer only a practice; it is also an ideal, and it is possible for this representation to precede action. A divorce between theory and practice can then be proclaimed: the revolutionary thinker can trace the broad outlines of the future society, define justice—just relations—insofar as it is in his power to do so, even though a just society has never been realized in the past. But as Proudhon explicitly recalls, if justice can be the subject of a theoretical representation it is exclusively because it is above all a reality, a practice whose idea is only an expression.[47]

The social relation of justice is above all the economic relation of equality and reciprocity, freely established between the contracting parties. Under the concept of justice, Proudhon resumes all the critiques that he had previously formulated against the proprietary regime: whereas private property necessarily establishes a relation of inequality and appropriation between labor and capital, just relations establish equal exchanges between producers and worker companies. What was antagonism and contradiction in the proprietary regime become, in the anarchist economy, equilibrium, balance, a series of reciprocal transactions. The antagonism of wealth and poverty is replaced by a multiplicity of ever-shifting and constantly transformed balances: balances of supply and demand, trade, credit, population; the social economy is based on a vast system of balances or, in other words, equality.[48] In the anarchist economy, this economic relation immediately becomes a social relation of equality: whereas the proprietary regime reproduces the subordination of labor to

47. "This is why we said and repeated so many times that Justice is not only for us an idea; that it is also a reality; that it is in the condition of being beforehand a reality that it can become an idea." *De la justice dans la révolution et dans l'église*, 7th étude, vol. 3, 300.

48. Ibid., 3rd étude, vol. 2, 93.

capital, anarchist reciprocity is carried out through a succession of contracts freely agreed between socially equal worker companies and producers. The balance of transactions, in the absence of the constraints of despotic power and capitalist authority, entails the reconstitution of social relations on the basis of reciprocity among all participants. It is this socioeconomic whole, in its general relations, that most fully expresses the meaning of justice, the concept of egalitarian social relations, spontaneously re-created in the absence of alienating constraints.

It is because justice is this social reality, this practice realized, for example, in mutualist worker companies, that it is also a representation, an idea. In this sense, it is formulated on the theoretical level, outlining an overall vision of society and a practical philosophy. It then allows us to speculate about how to achieve justice, how to discover how equality in social relations and among people could be preserved through education or political life. But Proudhon, faithful to his theory of the immanence of the individual and the collective, adds that justice is still an emotional attitude specific to each individual, a feeling, and a demand by the person to be respected for themselves. Of course, justice does not only originate from this demand by the ego, but only exists and is realized in social relations, presupposing confrontation between people. Just as morality is, in its fulfillment, given to the individual by the social community, in the same way justice, in its fullness, goes beyond the individual person. However, each being experiences themselves as an absolute; they have an immediate feeling of their own dignity, and this intimate feeling is one of the sources of justice and is a faculty immanent in the conscience. While justice cannot be reduced to the needs of the individual, experience gives each person an acute sense of their own dignity and the will to escape from oppression. Thus, justice, while it is realized only in social practice, is rooted in individual needs, in the demand for one's rights, preparing the possibility of an agreement between the individual and collective effort.

Giving a broad and synthetic significance to the idea of justice, Proudhon can conclude that this idea forms the *axis*, the *pivot*, of a society restored to itself, the fundamental form permeating all

social relations and expressing them in their entirety. If any constituted society is organized according to a principle, an essential
relation repeated in different aspects in all the parts of the social
body, the principle of equality and reciprocity will be found at
each level of anarchist society. Justice finds both its realization
and its foundations in the needs of the person, in exchanges
between individuals, in relations of production and in relations
between groups. For the individual, it is not only a representation or even a feeling, but a practical requirement and an imperative faculty, a source of active conduct and effort. In economic
relations, justice is not a mere intellectual representation; it is
the very form of practice or, in other words, the practice itself:
justice is immanent in action or, more precisely, it is the reality of the action itself. In this sense, justice can be called a true
economic force: indeed, by liberating all the material and intellectual powers alienated in the proprietary regime, relations of
balance realize a vitality, a social force higher than those of the
old societies. All of these just, balanced relations have a greater
and more durable power than those of unequal societies: the
history of wars and conquests shows that it is societies that
harbor, if not justice, at least the most fertile and best-defined
relations—relations that are more "right" in the broad sense of
the term—that prevail and impose their jurisdiction on the con-
quered peoples.

Thus, justice, the principle and theory of anarchist society,
is diametrically opposed to religion, the principle and theory
of hierarchical societies. Every religion affirms that the social
principle has its reality and its origin outside social practice and
declares the submission of human beings to the transcendent
principle. Anarchism locates the origin of rights in social practice, awaiting from collective spontaneity alone what religion
awaits from a power, and declares the destruction of all transcendent authority. Religion, in placing what is human outside
of the human, affirms the inequality of people and their necessary
subjugation; revolutionary theory makes humans equal beings
possessing rights in themselves. Religion, through its theory
of original sin and divine grace, makes material inequality the

insurmountable mark of human decline, whereas the revolution
requires an economic organization that makes equality and reciprocity not a mere moral precept but an economic reality. By its
theory of transcendence, religion affirms the value of and need
for a government to impose discipline on a fundamentally dis-
ordered society; conversely, by affirming the spontaneous organization of labor and of economic society, the revolutionary idea
eliminates power and bases social cohesion on the commutative
action of economic forces. In his great work on justice, Proudhon
pursues this antithesis between the church and the revolution at
all levels of individual and social reality: property, the state, education, labor, ideas, conscience, progress, marriage, and morality.
In each of these areas, he finds a radical contradiction between a
society based on the principle of transcendence and an anarchist
society based on the immanence of justice. This contradiction
does not only have a historical significance, emphasizing the transition from a hierarchical society to an anarchist society: if justice
indeed arrives by means of a historical break, Proudhon does not
deny that the old societies have realized relations of justice to a
certain extent. More accurately, as he describes in *War and Peace*,
they have achieved different social rights, resulting from collective action and struggle, including scattered fragments of an egalitarian theory; in this sense, justice is at the same time historical
and ahistorical: historical in its particular forms but eternal in its
more general principle.

The antithesis between religion and the revolutionary idea
has special value as a method of emphasizing the radical character of anarchist critique and showing that a just society can be
built only by the complete elimination of relations of inequality and despotism. The concept of immanence that Proudhon
relates to each problem encountered must be understood in all
its consequences: it implies that nothing must be taken as external to individual and collective practice—that is, that no power,
no absolute authority, can be recognized, and that any restriction
of activity must be consented to by the producers and emanate
directly from their choice. Thus, the theory of justice, while put-
ting greater emphasis on significations than on specific forms of

organization, merely points out the meaning and the requirements of a positive anarchy.

It remains to be shown by what social process this justice could
reach consciousness and how it is constituted spontaneously by
the encounter of individuals. Proudhon constantly stresses that
the collective being was not only a reality and an action but also a
consciousness and a will; he also emphasizes that justice as practice and theory does not find its sufficient origin in the individual. The individual, considered in isolation, cannot fail to assert
themselves absolutely, seeking to dominate in every domain. As
an absolute ego, the human being tends to subordinate everything around them: things and people, truths and feelings.[49] It is
the very law of individuality, thus the law of individual reason, to
pose as an absolute term, to negate resistance, and to assume the
role of an exclusive standard. Thus there is an analogical relation
between the individual reason, which posits itself as the universal principle and center, and the absolutist theories that turn the
social power into a principle of domination. Just as the individual
aims to dominate all things, absolute government aims to dominate all of society and establish state reason as the social reason.
And indeed, in these oppressive societies, what is called public
reason rests only on the likeness of egoisms: far from emerging
from the meeting of all interests, the public reason is formed only
by the sum of individual reasons and differs from them neither in
content nor in form. In such a society, the bureaucrats and the
rich, pooling their will to dominate, make their particular reason
the general rule and impose the absolutism of their interests on
society. Thus, capital imposes itself on economic society without
negotiation, the state asserts itself as an absolute that citizens can
neither master nor control, and justice attaches itself to a sacred
source posing as a command and a duty, not as a right. In these
systems, public reason takes on the form of individual reason and
extends its demand for domination. It is the same when a group
thinks of itself as a complete unit and acts like an individual: when,
in an electoral process, a community votes unanimously and,

49. Ibid., 7th étude, vol. 3, 250.

according to the apt popular expression, "as one," it replaces a discussion that would allow the formulation of the collective reason with an individual feeling that becomes artificially common.[50] In the same way, in the national prejudices and hatred between peoples, a nation, instead of recognizing itself in its diversity, thinks of itself as an individual and replaces collective reality with the fiction of a complete organism. Such a collective feeling by no means expresses the group's reason; it is only an individual feeling amplified by the number of individuals who express it.

Collective reason is thus fundamentally different from individual reason. Whereas the latter imposes itself without debate or is spread by repetition, the former springs only from the clash of opinions and interests. Indeed, collective reason can only begin to form when antagonistic judgments are brought into opposition, when there is an open debate among wills and opinions. This encounter has the immediate effect of destroying the absolutism of individual reasons: before a fellow human, an absolute such as ourselves and our unlimited and domineering demands are immediately checked. Claims must necessarily limit one another—"these two absolutes destroy one another"—leaving behind only the relation of the respective interests about which the debate arose.[51] When two groups with divergent interests clash, discussion imposes the elimination of domination by one of the groups or, in other words, the negation of the absolute. It is thus by mutual contradiction that minds or interests break out of their individual reason and that a collective reason can develop in accordance with the plurality of forces and with social reality.

This encounter of individual reasons is thus not the same as their coalescence: it gives rise to ideas that are not only different from individual demands but also fundamentally heterogeneous and synthetic. The collective reason is greater in power than individual reason in the extent of its forms, but it is also qualitatively dissimilar to it. This elimination of the absolutism of individual reason aptly demonstrates the degree to which collective reason

---

50. Ibid., 270.
51. Ibid., 250.

is not the extension of individual reason but its transformation into a fundamentally different totality. The collective reason is constituted by a movement analogous to that of the collective force. Just as the collective force is the resultant of individual forces, the common reason is the result of individual opinions, and in both cases the results are qualitatively different from the elements that comprise them: just as the gathering of forces gives rise to a power heterogeneous to the sum of those forces, the meeting of wills gives rise to a reason superior to instances of individual reason and capable of checking them.

We must thus recognize a discontinuity between the unlimited claims of the individual and the general will, a potential conflict between individual and collective opinion. But Proudhon reminds us that this fundamental distinction between individual and collective reason does not imply the condemnation or subordination of individuality. On the contrary, the collective reason can be formulated only through the free expression of difference: it is crucial that each should remain what it is, that personalities assert themselves and develop in their uniqueness, and that individual interests should be voiced. Only this open confrontation can bring about the common reason, which no individual could create. Moreover, while the individual demands an unlimited power, they also demand to be respected in their dignity, but this respect comes to them precisely from the reciprocity of wills alone such that, in the supremacy of the common reason, the individual finds a limit but also a recognition of themselves. Whereas individual reason gives rise to hierarchy and despotism, collective reason is fundamentally resistant to any subordination: it only establishes relations, balances, "equations" between the terms present and cannot, by definition, introduce an absolute that would produce a hierarchy. In collective reason, all opinions and all forces are placed in relation to one other, opposed to one another, equally active and free to assert themselves. Collective reason thus does not imply the negation of individual reason— on the contrary, it calls for its affirmation—but it arises from an encounter in which individual reasons shed their absolutism and come to respect a reason superior to themselves.

This constitutive movement sufficiently indicates that the content of collective reason can only be the idea of justice and that its conclusions tend to establish, against all tyranny, an egalitarian society. Whereas individual reason has tended to justify the oppressive modes of capital, the state, and religion, collective reason, affirming only relations, expresses and justifies balances, nonantagonistic oppositions between terms. Thus, in politics, the collective reason is opposed to arbitrary power and validates anarchy; in economics, it expresses and justifies the theory of equilibrium between producer groups. Everything that previously justified the plurality of balances and freedoms—tolerance, reciprocity, the recognition of social rights—emerged from collective reason; everything that justified authority, state power, and religion emerged from absolute reason.

But to attribute to this collective reason any reality transcending the group in which it is formulated would be to reproduce the error of absolutism. Just as the collective force is not a distinct material reality but the very action of the worker group, the collective reason is nothing but the group itself, the industrial society, the academy, the assembly: any meeting of human beings formed to discuss and seek what is right. In any group in which opinions are freely compared, a form of collective reason tends to voice itself. Moreover, we should not expect from this reason a body of doctrines that could be imposed dogmatically. Since religions claimed to possess absolute knowledge, they could establish themselves as unquestionable dogma; on the contrary, since collective reason claims to voice only an ever-changing relationship between ever-shifting terms, it can only ratify becoming and refuse systematization.

This rejection of systems carries a dual conclusion, combining the theses of positive anarchy. As soon as we reject the inventions of the philosophies of transcendence—revelation, authority, discipline, and hierarchy—we deny that public reason can have a priesthood for its organ, a social body distinct from the community of citizens. As soon as we recognize the collective reason only as the resultant of all the particular ideas or reasons that compensate for one another by their reciprocal criticism, we deny that an assembly has the privilege of expressing the social reason; its proper expression is expected from the opinions of all citizens, provided that they are not diverted from their real interests. The theory of collective reason rejects any monopolization of social thought by a privileged body or an absolute state. Moreover, the collective reason, because of its nature, cannot give rise to a definitive intellectual or social system:[52] it expresses changing relationships between equal terms, and thus it cannot, unlike absolutist reason, formulate a definitive system in which each thing is ordered and ranked. For this social reason, nothing can be treated as absolute and untouchable: there exists for it neither primacy nor absolute truth but only social and economic relations in transformation. Every establishment, every social constitution, can be challenged and criticized: the collective reason calls us to regard any human creation as transient and to treat as irremovable only equality itself—in other words, justice.

---

52. "Through the elimination of the absolute, the collective reason is reduced, like algebra, to a series of solutions and equations, which comes down to saying that for society, there is truly no system." Ibid., 265.

CHAPTER SIX

Revolutionary Theory and Practice

The non-polemical study of Proudhonian sociology may allow us to reexamine the relationship between this theory, whose vocation is explicitly revolutionary, and the work of Marx. We know that the orthodox Marxist tradition still considers Proudhon as a theorist of the petite bourgeoisie, incapable of achieving a theory of revolution: according to this tradition, his antistatism is merely the expression of a class threatened by industrial development, and his anarchism is a new version of utopian socialism. On the contrary, we may wonder whether the vigor of Marx's criticisms of Proudhon was not due to the similarity of their concerns, their belonging to the same intellectual movement in which the differences were all the more noticeable because they were small.

In the vast array of nineteenth-century social theories, Proudhon and Marx pursued the same opponents. First of all, they denounced the individualistic assumptions of political economy that led to the separation of the regime of production from the social totality and the denial of the relations between the economy and social relations. As early as 1840, twenty-seven years before the publication of *Capital*, the critique of property aimed to demonstrate that the structure of the regime of property was parallel to the regime of exploitation of the proletariat, and it introduced an insurmountable antagonism between capital and labor. Rethinking the economy thus implies the constitution of a new science that will not only be an economic science, but also a science of society as a whole: a social science in Proudhon's words, a science of history in Marx's words in *The German Ideology*. To this objective, neither traditionalist organicism nor positivism provide an answer that can express the historical and

practical character of social becoming: Proudhon protests violently against traditionalist sociology, which he accuses of confusing social organization for a biological organism. To think of
the social in terms of the organic is to attribute to societies a stability they fundamentally lack. Society is not a natural being that
reproduces itself identically and whose knowledge would allow
us to distinguish a timeless structure; it is a set of mobile solidar-
ities, constantly renewed by human practice. Marx and Proudhon
use the same myth of Prometheus to symbolize the work of liberation that is the history of humanity, a myth that evokes the effort
of people making themselves through labor and against destiny. As Proudhonian anti-theism expresses it, far from obeying
providence or repeating the laws of fate, humanity continues to
transcend what is necessary and natural within itself in order to
bring about new forms of existence through its activity and labor.
Proudhon and Marx are hostile to positivist sociology for the
same reasons: not because they criticize the intention to establish
a social science, since this is in line with their own objectives, but
because they suspect positivism of ignoring social practice and
the possibility for people to radically transform their living conditions. Proudhon rebels against the authoritarian conclusions of
Auguste Comte and accuses him of ascribing to a new spiritual
power what the traditionalists had attributed to absolute monarchical power.

It is therefore up to revolutionary thinkers to create a new
science that is at the same time knowledge of the social totality
and knowledge of its movement, a critique of capitalist society and, in its spirit and in its conclusions, a revolutionary science. The fury of Proudhon's early writings against property is
answered by the caustic fury of *Capital*, with the same intention
not to dissociate explanation and denunciation: no doubt the
critique is often more moralizing in Proudhon's work, but the
same indignation against human denaturation caused by the
capitalist regime can be recognized throughout Marx's work, an
indignation that, while not impassioned, is no less fierce. With
regard to this possibility of associating the description of social
practice with revolutionary critique, Proudhon and Marx base

it on a dialectical understanding of social reality, on the same transformation of the abstract dialectic into a concrete dialectic. Although they propose two different interpretations, the differences should not hide the similarity of their projects. For the author of *The System of Economic Contradictions* and the author of *Capital*, it is a question of showing not only that dialectics is an intellectual method but also that the social movement is dialectical, that it is in the process of development and riddled with contradictions that cause it to mutate. The notion of contradiction plays the dual role of revealing the ruptures in the social body and of pushing toward a knowledge of the totalities. As the title of Proudhon's work suggests, the study of contradictions shows the divisions that bring capital and labor, and owners and producers, into conflict, but it must lead to knowledge of the system as a whole, just as in Marx the study of contradictions must lead to knowledge of the capitalist regime of production as a whole process. In the same way, understanding the dialectical nature of social reality must make it possible to show how people or social classes, engaged in a society that imposes itself on them and defines their affiliation, constantly act on themselves and on the conditions imposed on them. More precisely, the plurality and diversity of dialectics specify the modes of action and the practices available to people: unlike sociological positivism, it is not only a question of recalling that people are both knowing subjects and acting subjects but also of specifying what action, and in particular what revolutionary practice, can and must be carried out by a social class at a given moment in its history. Dialectical study is the study of a social fact and a social practice, leading to clarification of political practices and possibilities.

But to this epistemological connection we must add a similar conception of the social role of theory. As early as 1838, Proudhon defined his intention to establish a politically committed critical knowledge as an instrument of defense and attack for the working classes, and when in 1843 Marx abandoned his liberal positions to take the side of the proletariat, he did so in the same terms and with the intention of helping raise awareness of exploitation. They did not merely consider science as a tool forged arbitrarily for a struggle, but were convinced that true social knowledge is intimately linked to the liberation of the proletariat, since economic contradictions tend to lay the groundwork for a revolution whose agent and main beneficiary would be the working class. At the same time, social knowledge would clarify what the proletariat confusedly carries within itself, and this clarification would contribute organically to the workers' conscious awakening and thus to revolutionary practice. Not only do Proudhon and Marx want to be revolutionary thinkers, but they also want to be spokesmen and, to a large extent, guides for the revolutionary popular classes.

It is these shared intentions that help us understand how Marx could be enthusiastic about Proudhon's work until 1844 and then split from it from 1846 onward. If Proudhon had merely disguised scientific socialism, it would be difficult to understand how Marx could have considered him a leading thinker until then, unless perhaps we believe that Marx was not himself before 1846. Undoubtedly there is a distance between the young Marx and his mature works, but in 1844 the general themes of the critique of political economy and capitalist contradictions and the theories of the emancipation of the proletariat and of alienation, which would later be developed, had already been formulated. The fury of Marx's polemic arises from an awareness of the differences in a common project. In Proudhon's early writings, Marx finds a set of theories that he then promises to develop: social contradiction based on the exploitation of labor, the inception of the proletarian movement, and the virulence that turns economic analysis into a revolutionary appeal. But it was precisely in 1846 that he was irritated to note that the developments proposed by Proudhon were different from those he had expected, and Marx was all the more critical because the topic he was addressing was exactly that for which he had begun to amass material. As Proudhon noted when he read *The Poverty of Philosophy*, Marx was irritated to see Proudhon address before him a subject that he himself had proposed to study.

Thus, the fury of the polemics should not blind us. It is not only their methods and intentions that must be reconciled but also the conclusions reached by Proudhon and Marx in their reading of capitalism. For both of them, it is indeed in the economic regime—in the regime of property or in bourgeois capitalism, in Proudhon's words—that we must look for the crux of social contradictions and the essential dynamics of society's fate. And their most general conclusion is to highlight, through the multiple contradictions of capitalism, a fundamental relationship of conflict and exploitation between capital and labor. Proudhon and Marx do not limit themselves to the protest, commonly repeated around them, against inequality in wealth distribution: they propose to analyze the mechanisms of the capitalist regime, concluding that appropriation is inevitable within the system. Capitalism has resulted in the monopolization of the instruments of labor and the subordination of the workers, but it reproduces, with an inevitability that can be analyzed scientifically, the appropriation of products and inescapably condemns the proletariat to wage labor. It is not only this general intention that *Capital* takes up again but also more precisely the Proudhonian theory of the appropriation of labor: the theory of surplus value provides a commentary on the Proudhonian analysis of capitalist theft by elaborating on it. Both the theory of surplus value and the theory of theft are based on the principle of labor as the sole creator of value, which Proudhon took for granted; for Proudhon and Marx, the problem of profit or aubaine arises in the same terms: given that capital cannot be a creator by itself, and that this is merely a fiction already denounced by the economists, how can the creation of interest and the accumulation of profits be explained? It is exclusively in the process of labor, in the workers' contribution of their force in the process of production, that this mystery of capitalism, the creation of interest, can be discovered. Since labor is the only producer, profit must be part of labor itself, veiled by the surface appearances of the capitalist system. The critic's full attention must be focused on this point: to show how this additional value, which is the foundation of appropriation, is realized in the very act of production. If it can be shown that appropriation is not simply a distribution of profits, whose details could be modified, but also takes place in the very activity of labor, then

it will have also been shown that the capitalist regime is inherently and inevitably a system of exploitation and that exploitation ends through the destruction of this regime of production.
We have seen how Proudhon addressed the problem in socioeconomic terms through the notion of collective force: individual labor is ultimately only a façade validated by the capitalist
legal system; labor contributes to a common effort and generates
a collective force that is masked by the individual aspect of labor.
Marx will say more accurately that the worker provides labor
time, part of which corresponds to the wage and the other part of
which allows the creation of surplus value: this distinction in particular allows a more rigorous analysis of the conflicts between
bosses and workers and will make the reality of exploitation
in the most limited activity more apparent.[1] But the principle
remains the same: to demonstrate how surplus value is created
by monopolization, a theft, carried out directly on the labor force.
As Proudhon asserted, capitalist profit rests on the fact that part
of the labor is unpaid, that workers are the creators of products
that they are forbidden to consume in their entirety. Proudhon
and Marx can maintain this whole theory only by taking the
theory of the natural wage as a given. Indeed, Proudhon notes,
without elaborating further, that the worker's wage merely provides the means of subsistence, and Marx makes wages the means
of renewing the labor force. Despite the accepted variations in
wages, neither Proudhon nor Marx admits that the principle of
the natural wage can be violated, and they only accept variations

---

1. Translator's note: There is a notable difference between Proudhon's theory of exploitation and Marx's theory of exploitation, as it is
usually presented, and it is not certain that Marx presents it "more accurately" than Proudhon. According to Marx, exploitation is defined in
relation to the individual worker, by the non-payment to the worker of
labor time beyond that necessary for their subsistence. For Proudhon, it
is not the work of the individual worker that produces value but rather
the collective and combined work of a given quantity of workers, the idea
being that one hundred workers working together produce more value
than one hundred workers working individually. What the capitalist
appropriates is the value of this combined work, what Proudhon calls an
"accounting error."

around this level. Thus they believe they have demonstrated not only the reality of social exploitation within the regime of property but also, as Proudhon writes, the impossibility of remedying this situation without disrupting the foundations of the economy.

This analysis is immediately expressed in terms of antagonism between social classes and implies an economic definition of this antagonism. Neither Proudhon nor Marx attempted to formulate a rigorous definition of classes, and it may be surprising that, despite granting the bourgeois and working classes such great historical importance they do not bother to define their criteria more precisely. This is because, in their view, economic analysis has already sufficiently determined the characteristics of the classes involved, shown that a class is indeed a social reality, and included the mode of participation in production and the mode of ownership among their criteria. While acknowledging, in their specific analyses, that these criteria do not exhaust the whole reality of classes, they define the bourgeois and working classes respectively as those that hold and those that do not hold the instruments of production, those contributing to production activity or taking away from it. Differences in the levels and sources of income only serve to confirm an opposition inscribed within the general structure of the capitalist economy. Moreover, by defining class as economic class, Proudhon and Marx attribute political and ideological functions to it. Marx asserts more systematically that the economically dominant class is politically dominant—Proudhon, who recognizes a particular dynamic in the centralizing state, indicates that the bourgeois class imposes itself on the state rather than it being the state itself—but the fact remains that in capitalism the state as the organ of the collectivity is only an illusion; in reality, it is the defender of the economic interests of the bourgeoisie or of industrial feudalism.

The possibility of comparing these two sociologies is confirmed in their interpretations of revolutionary action. Although Proudhon does not reduce revolution to a class conflict, he sees class not only as an economic and political reality but also as a collective agent that can bring about social upheaval and make itself the subject of a revolution. To consider the 1789 Revolution would be to seek how the bourgeois class, as a unified and resurgent class, was able to destroy the edifice of feudalism; to consider the end of capitalism would be to seek the conditions under which the working class will be able to intervene as a political and creative class. Consequently, the divergences between Proudhon and Marx about the possible role of the working bourgeoisie should not be overestimated—these divergences must be qualified since in 1848 Marx could consider that the liberal bourgeoisie was at that time the most advanced, and since Proudhon affirmed in his final writings that this bourgeoisie could only follow the workers' impetus—but, above all, they are due to differences of opinion, without the common methodology being called into question. Proudhon and Marx understand the story of classes through the same historical vision: the propertarian or capitalist regime carries within itself, because of appropriation, an insurmountable social rupture that constitutes its law and its condemnation, its "impossibility" according to the first memoir on property. This rupture is simultaneously a struggle, but more precisely it establishes a relationship of domination and subjugation: indeed, for both Marx and Proudhon the proletarian class finds itself deprived of its means of defense and autonomy at the same time as being stripped of its means of production. Proudhon seems to go further than Marx in this description of worker subjugation when he denies that strikes represent an effective tool for workers to defend their wages. But neither did Marx hope that strikes could bring about a change in the working classes' economic situation: on the contrary, the principle of natural wages condemns the proletariat, whatever its economic struggles, to receive only the equivalent of its means of subsistence. Thus, the dichotomy between the bourgeoisie and the proletariat is one of an active class and a dominated class. And what revolutionary writings expect and prepare for is precisely this historical transformation that would permeate the working class and make it, like the bourgeois class on the eve of 1789, the new revolutionary class. Proudhon and Marx subject this internal history of class to a second, silent, and confused history: that of economic tensions. And, despite the simplifying statements about the parallel development of productive forces and revolutionary action, these two histories do not correspond precisely. This shift from subordination to action would no doubt emerge from the aggravation of contradictions, but a class's assertiveness advances or retreats without closely following the same path as the economy. When Proudhon indicates that in 1848 the proletariat posed the revolutionary question of the right to work, he does not try to directly relate this strictly proletarian action to a particular aggravation of economic antagonisms; and when Marx praises the action of the Commune, he considers it as a moment particular to a class, a creative moment of experiment, not as the simple effect of a contradiction. Classes are neither always active nor masters of what they once controlled; and this dual history of the economy and class antagonism dispossesses the bourgeoisie by stripping it of what it believes it controls. Whatever the efforts of the middle bourgeoisie to cling to its weak defenses, and whatever the political attempts of industrial feudalism to gain the power of the state, a silent history unfolds that condemns the old players. Of course, Proudhon would refuse to compare this outcome to fate, and Marx would qualify his prophetic expressions, but they would constantly link the history of classes to the history of economic society and draw a distinction between them.

The use of the same concept of alienation is not a mere convergence of vocabulary, but reveals the same critique of the inhumane consequences of capitalist society and the same general conception of socialist society. And just as an attempt has been made to rethink the whole of Marx's work through this concept, all of Proudhon's thought could be synthesized around his dialectic of alienation. When Marx, in *The Economic and Philosophic Manuscripts of 1844*, takes up the concept of alienation to restore a sociological meaning to it and to examine which specific alienations workers are victims of, he can rightly cite Proudhon's economic works, because the description of proprietary theft can indeed be read as the description of an externalization and alienation. As Proudhon writes, the workers sold their hands, their force, and in this sense the term *alienation* must be given the traditional and legal meaning of a sale to another person, but such a sale only masks a real alienation in the sense of dispossession. Indeed, as expressed by the notion of theft, the workers are, within the production process itself, dispossessed of what they produce; that is, they are dispossessed of their own labor, since the product is none other than their own labor. *The System of Economic Contradictions*, continuing this same analysis, shows that this dispossession amounts to the dispossession of humanity itself since workers, dominated, disqualified, and rejected by the luck of the system, lose all power over their labor after having lost all possession of the instruments. The entire dramatic description of the proprietary regime shows a creation and "externalization" that, far from securing what people have sought, turns against them and destroys their intended goals. It will be an often-repeated theme that, in the proprietary system, functions fulfilled and ends pursued give rise to a complete reversal through a process of degradation, and that the very work of people, apparently reasonable and appropriate, is transformed into an external and destructive force. For both Marx and Proudhon, the goal of an economic revolution would thus be to restore to society what the capitalist system has diverted from it and, by stopping this appropriation, to destroy the human degradation that it causes.

To deny the differences between Proudhon and Marx would certainly be to ignore the originality of their respective theories of political alienation. Since Marx puts greater stress on the relationship between the economically dominant class and the state, he tends to relate political alienation directly to the economic power of the possessing class. Conversely, since Proudhon puts greater consideration on the relation between overall society and the state, between the collective force and its appropriation, he tends to consider political alienation in its specificity and politics in its essence. For him, political alienation is less an effect of economic alienation than another aspect of an overall society alienated in all its forms. Consequently, he generalizes political externalization and looks for different manifestations of it over time: on this point, since he is little concerned with the specifics of history, we might say that he proves to be more of a sociologist while Marx proves to be more of a historian. For each historical type of society, Marx will suggest a reconsideration of the original movement established according to the regime of production: the particularity of the mode of production generates a differentiation of political types. Proudhon thinks, on the contrary, that beyond historical differences the centralizing state repeats an identical model, concealing a dynamic that can be generalized. Similarly, he puts much more emphasis than Marx on the contradiction he believes to be present between the centralizing, oppressive state and economic society. The state monopolizes a force, the collective force, that does not emerge from itself but is able to make it external to society and turn it against society, to use common work against the people who produce it. But we can see that Marx, going beyond the letter of his methodology, admits this possibility of externalization. Describing the French bureaucratic state in *The Eighteenth Brumaire of Louis Napoleon*, he writes that Napoleon III's state made itself independent of French society, suffocating and enclosing it, destroying all freedom and initiative. The relationship established here between governmental power and civil society is no longer one of complementarity but rather one of contradiction, comparable to the Proudhonian scheme. But more generally, and in keeping with the overall problem, Proudhon and Marx share the same inspiration concerning the present and future meaning of the state: despite their very different interpretations which we will highlight next, it should be remembered that the history of the state is told identically by these two authors as the transition from alienation to decay. For both Marx and Proudhon, the preservation of the state in capitalist society is directly linked to a social situation of oppression, in which economic society has not yet broken down the barriers to its full development. As Marx wrote in his early works, social liberation could only come about with the disappearance of the state in its bourgeois forms, its "extermination," as Proudhon put it.[2]

---

2. Translator's note: Proudhon wrote in his notebooks of 1852: "I am in politics to kill it."

And, in the same way, we cannot seriously confuse Proudhon's critique of religious alienation for Marx's. As we saw in
the preceding chapter, Proudhon focuses on this problem, while
Marx merely mentions it. The divergence is essentially due to
the importance of religion in capitalist society. Believing that all
alienation, political and intellectual, is rooted in economic alienation, Marx considers the latter to be fundamental and tends to
see religious alienation as a sign rather than a source of particular social behaviors. Conversely, Proudhon, more attentive to
the analogy of alienations, unrelunctantly affirms the social importance of ideologies: if, as he repeatedly writes, theory is a form of
practice, then there is no reason to separate theory and practice,
and religion directly participates in and influences action. But,
here again, the divergences should not conceal the same movement of thought which links religion directly to social structures,
interprets it as individual and collective alienation, and envisages
a socialist society stripped of religious illusions.

Ultimately, without claiming to draw a full picture of the
complex relations that either unite or separate Marxian and
Proudhonian theory, it is important to stress that both foresee
the same future: the end of capitalism and the establishment of
a socialist society. *Capital* takes up the objective of *The System of
Economic Contradictions*: to demonstrate that the capitalist regime
of production is riddled with unsurmountable contradictions
and that its development tends to reinforce the negative elements that will cause its disappearance. This demonstration must
also show that no partial reform of the system is possible and that
only an economic revolution—a radical reorganization of social
relations and economic structures—will be able to break the contradictions of capitalism. Indeed, this would be a constant theme
of Proudhonian thought and the motive for its struggle against
the democrats: that the revolution consists neither in a change of
political personnel nor in a reorganization of powers but in the
construction of a new economic society based on a de-alienation
of labor. And indeed, for both Proudhon and Marx, this socialist
society would be fundamentally defined by the complete liberation of economic forces: socialism or communism would restore

to labor all its means and possibilities by returning economic society to itself, to the producers alone. The total man evoked by Marx in his early works, the proud and free man evoked by Proudhon, is first and foremost the worker restored to himself, freed from the chains and fetters that class societies have constantly imposed on him and becoming both the model and the master of socialist society.

It is therefore not surprising that Proudhon and Marx encountered the same difficulties and hesitated when faced with the same problems. Wanting to demonstrate the necessity of social becoming toward the collapse of capitalism, they are led to question the validity of such a demonstration and the possibility of affirming, at least for a certain phase of history, the existence of historical determinism. It is remarkable that, on this problem, Proudhon and Marx developed in opposite directions: before the 1848 Revolution, Proudhon did not hesitate to compare economic development to fate, and to describe the series of phases in terms of absolute necessity, as if economic history dominated human practice; conversely, after the revolution, he explicitly cast doubt on the notion of a necessary history and assigned the task of building socialism to a working-class practice. Marx does the opposite: after having insisted on the revolutionary action of the proletariat in his early works, in *Capital* he goes so far as to compare economic development with the necessary movement of the stars. As long as this difficulty is not resolved, the conception of revolutionary practice remains rather problematic: if the contradictions of capitalism necessarily develop and lead to the system's self-destruction, the proletariat will only be led to restore the economic regulations that the bourgeoisie will abandon of its own accord. If, on the contrary, history is confused, made up of crises and relatively uncertain ruptures, then it will be necessary to lend working-class practice a positive and creative content, to consider the proletariat as a will and not only as the negative result of a development. In particular, through the proletariat becoming a conscious class and the development of class consciousness, Proudhon and Marx expect these difficulties to be overcome in practice, but it does not seem that they proposed the same meanings despite using the same words here.

It is indeed within this common language—contradictions, dialectics, classes, social revolution, class consciousness—that conflicts will emerge, rendering the debates all the more acute as the objectives seem to be identical. It was in fact in the problems of revolutionary practice and theory, in the most decisive questions, that the conflicts would be formulated, justifying the passionate nature of the debates.

* * *

In 1848, defining what he called "true revolutionary practice," Proudhon called for autonomous worker emancipation and insisted that mere political reform would constitute deception. At the same time, *The Communist Manifesto* calls for a union of all workers to impose a social revolution from a fundamentally economic upheaval. But while the vocabulary is often identical, it describes two divergent conceptions of revolutionary practice. For Marx, the call for the union of all workers responds to the certainty, expressed in his early writings, that the proletariat's exclusion necessarily makes it a revolutionary class. The class with deep-rooted chains, deprived of all the privileges that still hold back the petite bourgeoisie, cannot rise up without calling into question the very foundations of bourgeois society. The union of the workers would therefore immediately be a revolutionary action that should provoke the social revolution by itself. Conversely, in Proudhon's eyes, the union of the workers is not a sufficient guarantee of their revolutionary will. As we have seen, it is possible that the workers would allow themselves to be dominated by conservative myths and, for example, that they would support a strong power that will appear to them under a demagogic mask. Not only might the working classes become victims of the activities of the bourgeoisie, but they also carry within themselves a plebeian tradition of passivity of which they must rid themselves; we can detect in their recent history what Proudhon calls a popular "instinct" of docility and naive confidence in an authoritarian power, which goes directly against revolutionary objectives and is objectively in line with bourgeois politics. The union of the workers, as Proudhon conceived it, must therefore have a content that needs to be clarified: it must immediately become an economic practice. His thinking on this subject shows the greatest continuity: before 1848, planning the organization of a progressive association, he proposed to call on the producers to emancipate themselves directly by establishing economic relations of mutuality; in 1848, through the Bank of Exchange, he envisaged an autonomous workers' organization called upon to destroy the regime of property, and in 1864 he still stressed economic practices when defining the working-class idea.

While for both Marx and Proudhon the revolutionary struggle can only be led by the producers themselves and aims at the emancipation of labor, it thus receives two different interpretations. For Marx, the struggle must be that of the workers as excluded from bourgeois society and must immediately aim at a political confrontation from which the new economic organization will emerge. For Proudhon, on the contrary, the struggle must be that of the workers as producers and must immediately aim for a new economic organization. The union of the workers must be given a practical and economic meaning, without waiting for a revolution to be achieved: on the contrary, the success of the revolution would be ensured by the dynamism and efficiency of the workers' organization. Proudhon's constant distrust of politics is reflected in this conception of revolutionary practice: far from seeing itself as a party with a fundamentally political purpose, the workers' party must above all separate itself from the bourgeois parties, focus its concerns on the problems of production, and without further delay create the workers' economic organizations that prefigure socialist society.

Proudhon thus signaled a particular trade union history, distrustful of political parties, focusing its concerns on economic struggles and aiming for revolution not through the distraction of politics but through the direct action of the workers. It is surprising that the closest unionism to Proudhonian thought, the revolutionary syndicalism of 1900–1920, had the general strike as its theme of struggle, despite the fact that Proudhon always considered strikes to be ineffective. But this skepticism sheds light on the Proudhonian conception of the workers' struggle. By asserting the vanity of partial strikes, Proudhon wants to call the workers to another form of struggle that would be situated outside bourgeois society from the outset and would directly attack its foundations. He believes that by limiting themselves to particular strikes, the workers disperse their efforts and submit to the conditions imposed by bourgeois capitalism, thus performing a reformist and not a revolutionary task. Because of the power of capitalist economic laws, the workers must free themselves from the system of contradictions and circumvent it through a properly working-class practice based on opposite principles.

Thus, the phrase "revolution from below" has a very precise meaning for Proudhon. For Marx, while the revolution is carried out by the workers, its purpose is to destroy the power of the dominant classes and to seize control of the management of economic society. For Proudhon the notion of revolution from below includes the notion of a revolution carried out at the base and at the level of the producers. It is not simply a question of seizing an apparatus in order to change its orientation but of replacing an exploitative economy with another kind of economy, and this replacement can only take place if the workers themselves create it through their own action. In refusing to instigate a political struggle, Proudhon is inviting a difficult, demanding task that will have the effect of transforming the workers into managers, into leaders, into subjects who are truly productive and conscious of production needs. The Marxian notion of the emancipation of the workers by the workers themselves takes on full significance in Proudhonian thought, for it is not only a brief action by which the working classes would destroy the power that oppresses them but also an indefinite task that would begin before the revolution with the establishment of the first associations and would continue after regaining management of the whole of economic society. We sense that for Proudhon this inherently managerial practice would have a formative effect on the producers: through economic practice, the workers would acquire the knowledge that capital tends to wrest from them, and they would lose the myths and illusions that passivity maintains in them.

The notion around which the opposition between Proudhon and Marx appears most clearly is that of the dictatorship of the proletariat. This revolutionary project was undoubtedly formulated by Marx only cautiously: it can only be defined in relation to its dialectical negation, which would be the withering away of the state. Dictatorship can only be a temporary instrument intended to break the social and ideological barriers erected by the declining classes. In spite of these precautions, here Marx adopts the Jacobin tradition, according to which the success of a revolution depends on a temporary reinforcement of authority. Proudhon did not formulate an explicit critique of this notion: as Marx's work was not known in France at the time, he had no opportunity to critique it, but his conception of revolutionary practice is in itself a critique of the notion of a dictatorship of the proletariat. It is not that any recourse to political authority seemed reprehensible to him: when in 1848 he accepted his appointment as a deputy to the National Assembly and proposed his reform projects, he envisaged that a government supported by the working classes could authoritatively impose a reform of the economy and impose itself by force on the previously privileged classes. Recourse to a temporary dictatorship, provided that it had a genuinely revolutionary objective, was therefore not precluded in Proudhonian thought. However, in the spirit of his work, such a solution can only be viewed with extreme mistrust. As we have seen previously, a dictatorship of the proletariat is not guaranteed to be revolutionary: on the contrary, by the character of unity and docility that the notion of dictatorship involves, there is a danger that the political resignation that Proudhon fears for the working classes will appear. If there is a real taste for dictatorship among the proletariat, it is not the sign of a true revolutionary purpose but of a plebeian instinct for conformity and submission. Moreover, every dictatorship falls within the scope of the incessant criticism of authoritarian powers: in denouncing the uncontrollable tendency of government power to expand and oppress, Proudhon makes no particular exception in favor of proletarian power. Since any centralized power tends to absorb the collective forces within itself and turn them against society, if a power, even a workers' power, established itself as a central authority, it would inevitably tend to reproduce the common defects of the regimes of authority: expansion of the police, bureaucracy, repression of freedoms, and the gradual invasion of economic society. Against the political notion of the dictatorship of the proletariat, Proudhon put forward the economic notion of the organization of labor, expecting working-class practice to impose its idea and its society on the hostile classes through the development of its spontaneous organizations.

Neither Proudhon nor Marx have sufficiently clarified their theory of the proletarian party to be able to compare two definitions term by term. However, on this subject we find two different interpretations corresponding to two conceptions of working-class action. According to Marx, the party is vested with a dual function of coordinating workers' struggles and disseminating proletarian theory. Although Marx does not focus on the historical role of the party, the definition of these two functions confirms the importance of the central organization. Indeed, the coordination of struggles is not spontaneously given in working-class practice, and it is the role of the party to complete it and thus give it political significance. In the same way, revolutionary theory is not explicit and conscious at the level of working-class practices, and the party must participate in the elaboration, defense, and dissemination of revolutionary theories. Thus, the party, and more precisely the central council, plays a role of theoretical and practical stimulus and finds itself vested, to a certain extent, with a leadership role. It is remarkable that Proudhon responded negatively to Marx's proposal to create an intellectual union among socialist theorists in this 1846 letter, which was the occasion of their quarrel. In it, he expressed his instinctive distrust of any centralized organization, even one with a revolutionary purpose. When he talks about the "party of the revolution," it is not to designate a stable political organization but to designate all the people who agree on the same revolutionary theory and are likely to make it a reality. It would indeed be contrary to his conception of revolution to accept that a specifically political organization should have a privileged role in the revolutionary dynamic: the confidence he constantly places in the economic practice of producers limits the role of political leaders by definition. In the same way, he cannot accept that a party is the bearer of authentic revolutionary thought; he recognizes that theories can be formulated by individuals and arrive before working-class practice, but he denies that such formulations are historically effective: for a revolutionary idea to be realized, it must be shared, reconsidered, and transformed by the rising class, and it must truly come from the class itself. Proudhon's general critique of "externalization" should no doubt be applied to the notion of the party: there is a risk that any party will detach itself from economic society, monopolize a portion of the collective forces, and reconstitute a parasitic organism capable of oppressing and hindering social dynamism.

All this discussion of a more political than sociological nature rests on two different conceptions of the proletariat, on two different sociologies of the proletariat. Marx and Proudhon propose the same goal for the revolution—the emancipation of the working class—but in reality the same terms do not have exactly the same meaning. For Marx, the proletarian class is above all the class, forged by capitalist becoming, defined by its exclusion from civil society and whose labor has been transformed into a commodity. The proletariat, having gradually increased in number by the expansion of capitalism and simultaneously rejected, constitutes first and foremost a social force, a force that will be decisive, as a power, in ending capitalist alienation. So there is no reason to attribute to the proletariat an idea that is its own and that comes from its particular practice: the proletariat is not the bearer of an original theory of revolution but is only the conscious subject, the consciousness of capitalism. Its situation of exclusion and painful exploitation reveals the human meaning of capitalism and allows the foundations of the system—class relations and exploitation—to be understood. To grasp the social meaning of capitalism, to understand and feel the reality of exploitation, is at once to want the end of capitalism and therefore the collective appropriation of the means of production. But consciousness is not exactly the creation of a class theory: it is only the act of revealing a future that leads to the demise of capitalism. Equally, the theorist does not have to wonder what the proletariat thinks, and it may be that the workers' conceptions may be completely incorrect. The theorist must essentially reveal this historical movement by which economic decline makes the proletariat the negation of capitalism and makes it the last historical class. The proletariat, a passive object of capitalist development, becomes a subject of history by collectively gaining access to political action.

Conversely, for Proudhon the working classes are the bearers of an original theory and practice. The working class not only embodies self-awareness and consciousness of exploitation, but it also carries within itself what Proudhon calls an *idea*, a particular practice and its corresponding theory. The proletariat is not only this externally constituted social force whose growth would lead to political unification but also a class with an inherent practice, already given in the capitalist system, whose expansion would constitute the revolution. The notion of the "end of politics" must not mislead us: when Proudhon announces the end of politics, he means the extermination of traditional politics—the end of the alienation of collective forces by a centralized and authoritarian state—but he lends the working classes a specific political capacity, a coherent and original socioeconomic practice capable of reorganizing the whole of collective life by its own expansion. The working classes carry an immanent politics within themselves, creating, through their particular modality of practice, a spontaneous community in which consciousness, theory, and practice tend to converge. For Marx, the proletariat is above all a social force whose development pushes the contradictions of capitalism to the extreme, and whose political action will be to realize the dialectical transition from private to collective appropriation. For Proudhon, the proletariat intervenes in history to impose the law of its being, its original and spontaneous practice.

This divergence has a number of practical consequences. Marx stresses the urgency of the unification of forces toward

revolutionary political action and insists on the role of a political party to coordinate struggles. Proudhon, on the contrary,
underlines the urgency of an immediate progression of economic
practices as a means to achieve working-class cohesion and as a
spontaneously revolutionary process. To oversimplify, we could
say that the inspiration of Marx will be found in the Leninist conception of the party, while the inspiration of Proudhon will be
found in the practice of the workers' councils and the soviets.[3]
Marx calls for a revolution defined by the destruction of capitalist structures and of which violence will constitute an almost
necessary means. Proudhon calls for a revolution defined as the
replacement of bourgeois practice by a working-class practice
and in which violence is only one episode: indeed, the success
of the revolution is not assured by the depth of destruction but
rather by the proletariat's degree of maturity. Riots may occur,
the consequences of which may be more harmful than progressive, but what matters is less the violence than the coherence of
working-class practice. Marx gives the revolutionary theorist
the task of explaining capitalist contradictions, and he can consider his most important contribution to be the scientific analysis of capital; Proudhon does not neglect this aspect, but his
main task is defining the revolutionary idea, and he develops
numerous indications on the socialist economy in order to guide

---

3. Translator's note: This is how Georges Gurvitch expressed
himself in 1965 during a colloquium on Proudhon: "I can attest to the
extraordinary penetration of Proudhonian ideas, both among Russian
intellectuals and among Russian workers' unions. For my part, it was
not in France, but in Russia, that I became a Proudhonian, and I came to
France to deepen my knowledge of Proudhon. I therefore bear a direct
personal testimony. The first Russian soviets were organized by Proudhonians, the Proudhonians who came from the left-wing elements of the
Socialist Revolutionary Party or the left wing of Russian social democracy. It was not from Marx that they could take the idea of revolution by
the base soviets, because it was an essentially, exclusively, Proudhonian
idea. As I am one of the organizers of the Russian soviets of 1917, I can
speak with full knowledge of the facts." George Gurvitch, "Proudhon
and Marx," translated by Shaun Murdock, *Journal of Classical Sociology* 22,
no. 2 (2021): 174.

working-class economic practice. Marx calls the proletariat to political action, confident that this action, if it takes place, could only be revolutionary; Proudhon calls the proletariat to political action without being certain that it will be authentically revolutionary, and he must therefore supplement his appeals with a violent critique of certain working-class attitudes and explicitly oppose some working-class projects.

In this Proudhonian perspective, the limitation of revolutionary practice to the proletarian class alone is not necessarily fundamental, and we understand that Proudhon was for a long time imprecise on this subject, often according revolutionary wishes to the middle classes. For Marx, the revolutionary movement stems fundamentally from the situation of exclusion, and we should therefore expect the revolutionary act from the only class that is completely excluded. For Proudhon, authentically revolutionary action must be expected from a class that is oppressed but also capable of organizing economic forces by itself. In this sense, it is not impossible that a working petite bourgeoisie, dispossessed of its instruments by capitalist monopolization, conscious of the necessities of production and capable of participating in it, should have an important role in establishing the regime of socialism.

* * *

It is, to a large extent, arbitrary to attempt to compare the Marxian vision and the Proudhonian vision of the future society term by term. While Marx refuses to provide details on this subject, Proudhon constantly reconsiders this problem and insists on the need to think about the anarchist economy in advance. The main problem for Marx is to know how the revolution will take place; since the content of the revolutionary project is given, at least in its broad outlines, by the historical dialectic and in the negating movement of capitalism, it is not necessary to give a precise image of the future society, a problem that will only arise after the revolutionary act. On the contrary, in Proudhon's eyes the main problem is to know how this society will be, not only because revolutionaries must coordinate their action through a common representation but also because the revolutionary project, in a class in which theory and practice are immanent, is immanent in practice and already implemented.

However, if Marx refuses to clarify this image of communist society, it is also because he takes for granted its fundamental aspect: the socialization of the means of production. The negation of private appropriation that is carried by the movement of historical dialectics sufficiently signals the basic characteristic of the future society: the expropriation of the expropriators, and collective appropriation. Yet we have seen the extent to which, in Proudhon's eyes, this was only false evidence, still dependent on the routines of the regime of property; according to his critique of the idea of community, communism is only the negation of property, the repetition of unitarism and proprietary authoritarianism. To establish socialist society would be to overcome this antinomy by destroying the features common to both terms. And, while Proudhon's criticisms are not actually directed against Marxian collectivism, they are directed against any social theory proposing the centralization of the means of production and the unitary management of the economy, thus anticipating Marxist communism. Indeed, what Proudhon fears in communism is not expropriation but rather the social unitarism that it seeks to establish. He undoubtedly believes it is necessary to socialize property, but without replacing the regime of property with a despotic unification. Having shown that any centralization is, by its very nature, invasive and oppressive, Proudhon concludes that a unitary management of the economy would result not only in a decline in individual freedoms but also a decline in economic dynamism.

Against the communist dogma of unity, he puts forward, in all areas, the principle of pluralism and the relative autonomy of different groups. If Proudhon insists at such length on the notions of balance, mutualism, and the abandonment of synthesis, it is because by these notions he intends to designate a socialist system that, instead of aiming for total social unification, would seek to establish unity in diversity, to respect independence in cooperation. And if the social question is much more complex than the communist utopia supposes, it is precisely because it is necessary to reconcile the plurality of groups with their mutual cooperation, the autonomy of decisions with the need for exchanges. The theory of mutualism explicitly aims to avoid any reduction to unity and to guarantee maintaining the plurality of producer groups and associations. With the notion of mutualism replacing that of community, it is affirmed that relations will be established between centers of production that are at the same time distinct and united by relations of exchange, and that the principle of economic society is not the fusion or identity of forces but the free and balanced organization of living forces. Moreover, pluralism should not be understood only in the economic sense of the term: while the most important social groups may be economic groups such as workers' associations, Proudhon insists that natural groups such as communities should also have relative independence and autonomy to manage themselves. In this way, society would find itself composed of multiple groups—natural, local, provincial, producer and consumer groups—whose diverse relationships, exchanges, and noncontradictory antagonism would ensure mobility and, as Proudhon writes, full social vitality.

Thus, while abandoning some of his furious invective and acknowledging the relative utility of a central state, Proudhon retains the term *positive anarchy* and its essential meaning in his later writings. Essentially this notion refers to a society in which decisions would be taken by the groups themselves, by the producers themselves. In the case of independent producers such as farmers, the individual producer would organize production without any collective control, receiving from society only guarantees and insurance protecting them against possible risks; in the case of associated producers, the workers would jointly decide on the organization of production or appoint delegates to a "council."[4] The term *anarchy* has a negative value to indicate that

---

4. Translator's note: The agrarian question for Proudhon is a long-term strategic reflection. He observes that peasants are fiercely attached

decisions should not be taken by a body outside and superior to the groups directly responsible: here Proudhon means that proprietary authoritarianism must not be replaced by a nationalization of the economy, replacing capitalist oppression with state oppression. The end of authority referred to by the term anarchy supposes that no power superior to the producers as a whole can be reconstituted that would necessarily entail a new appropriation of collective forces. On the other hand, anarchy has a positive value to indicate that social vitality would be ensured only by the meeting and dynamic balance of the decisions and activities of the different producer groups. Indeed, anarchy does not mean that producers would decide on the nature and means of their production without any standards: it means that decisions would be taken exclusively on the basis of the requirements of other producers or consumers.[5] The disappearance of external authorities would commit producers to a relationship of reciprocity or contract, and the dynamism of the economy would be established solely on the basis of these spontaneously agreed upon contracts. Anarchism cannot therefore be confused with individualism: not only are decisions not individual, they are collective, but from the theory of collective reason we know that collective opinion arises from individual opinions and their fundamental transformation

---

to the land and that it makes no sense to talk about collectivizing it. He believed that peasants who own their land should be able to pass it on to their children as a possession but that at the end of the "redemption" of the land rent, the ownership of the land reverts to the commune. He also wanted to create incentives for the peasants to work together, with the question of ownership being postponed until a later date. Proudhon understood that the social revolution against the peasantry could not succeed.

5. Translator's note: Proudhon advocated the application of mathematics to political economy. His ambition was to turn political economy into "an exact and mathematical science," in the words of Sainte-Beuve. Economic accounting "will give political economy, considered in its mechanisms of production and distribution, the scientific apparatus to express the balance of resources and jobs, the economic cycle, and the operations of production, distribution and financing carried out between the different economic agents." Jean Bancal, *Proudhon, pluralisme et autogestion* (Paris: Aubier-Montaigne, 1970).

through confrontation with others. Even in the case of isolated producers who seem to have maximum independence, decisions are always responses to the economic situation and the decisions of other producers or consumers. The dynamism of the economy is guaranteed by the liberation of individual energies, but it is only based on the potentially competitive meeting of individuals and groups.

Proudhon thus raised, with unique skill, the problem of economic management, a problem whose seriousness Marx had not foreseen. Focusing his attention on the collapse of the capitalist regime, Marx indicated only that in a classless society the economy would be managed according to a concerted plan with a view to satisfying all participants. Marx did not ask who would make the decisions and manage the economy in a socialist society, assuming that in a de-alienated society decisions could not be in contradiction with the collective interest. Proudhon, on the contrary, poses the question and does so all the more urgently because he fears that a central power, whether a state or a party, could reconstitute an oppressive apparatus, destroying the individual freedom and spontaneity of producers. He fears the formation of a "compact democracy" in which arbitrary power, while claiming to express the will of the masses, would only destroy it. Against this risk, he proposes a pluralist system where the management of the economy would remain in the hands of the producers, where decisions would be taken at different levels: at the level of independent producers by the producers themselves, at the level of workers' companies by workers' councils, and at the national level by the temporary delegates of the producers. He adds that no organ, even a national one, should be vested with the power to control opinions and impose a common way of thinking: the spontaneity of collective reason requires that diverse opinions should be expressed, brought face to face, thereby revealing objective conflicts and antagonisms. It is not from a complete and destructive synthesis of antinomies that social dynamism would emerge: it is only through dynamic tensions and balances that social spontaneity could develop and express itself.

In underlining the notions of unity and dictatorship of the proletariat, Marx heralded the creation of single parties, administrative and economic centralization, and the Leninist conception of the workers' party. Proudhon, insisting on worker spontaneity and autonomous management, heralded and highlighted the creation of workers' councils, revolutionary syndicalism, and current attempts at self-management. By understanding the importance of the problem raised, we can better comprehend the difficulties Proudhon encountered and that such a novel attempt was bound to arouse irreconcilable hostilities.

Proudhon Throughout History

The history of Proudhonism is strangely marked by approvals and condemnations, enthusiastic readings and indignant rebuttals.[1] While so many nineteenth-century political thinkers are referenced by scholars without arousing particular passions, Proudhon remains a strangely irritating author, as if he somehow remains present and threatening. While historians and scholars calmly try to assess his place in history, his name continues to elicit strong reactions, both positive and negative. And even in scholarly research we cannot fail to notice approving and disapproving attitudes, as if he still needed to be defended or attacked. Before the collapse of the communist regimes, the various resurgences of Proudhonism at different times in this long history have given rise to emotional returns as much as intellectual and political rediscoveries, while official communist ideology has presented a more sinister picture.[2] How can we explain the particularly emotional character of this history of Proudhonism, and what does this signify?

This intensity of emotion toward Proudhon's theories is not recent, and we may say that it was expressed throughout the writer's life. As early as 1840, the first memoir on property was received with keen interest among the working classes, where his opening phrase ("Property is theft") quickly became a familiar slogan. But it also provoked anger from the members of the

---

1. This essay originally appreared as Pierre Ansart, "Proudhon à travers le temps," *L'Homme et la société*, no. 123–124 (1997).

2. On the history of Proudhonism and these "returns" to Proudhon, compare "Proudhon, l'éternel retour," *Mil neuf cent, Revue d'histoire intellectuelle*, no. 10 (1992).

Suard Academy, and then, when his second memoir was published, concern from the justice system. *The System of Economic
Contradictions* attracted admiring and approving readers but
sparked the wrath of Marx. In 1848 Proudhon was regarded
as a prominent defender of the popular classes, and the results
of his election to the National Assembly in June show that the
trust he had gained did not only come from the artisans. But the
events of June that shattered popular hopes also harmed trust
in the people's spokesman, and in 1850 the moderates, who had
once participated in the February Revolution, turned against
Proudhon whom they saw as a disturbing annoyance.[3] After having been followed and discussed, he quickly became known as
"l'homme-terreur." The story of enthusiasm and anger does not
end there: Proudhon, welcomed without hesitation by the citizens of Brussels in 1858, had to flee the city four years later following a violent protest against him. In 1861, his book *War and
Peace* provoked indignation and, furthermore, a complete misunderstanding. The following year, his opposition to Italian unity
attracted very little approval and almost universal animosity.

  Marx's successive attitudes are exemplary of the fury of these
reactions, although they may be interpreted in different ways.
We know that Marx initially expressed extreme admiration for
the first memoir, and that he regarded Proudhon as an authentic
representative of the revolutionary movement,[4] before pillorying
him and giving him the infamous epithet "petit bourgeois."[5] But

3. "[With] the boldness of Mr. Proudhon's proposals . . . , the challenge thrown at all beliefs, all received opinions, inspired violent indignation. . . . Proudhon suddenly gained a reputation, among a small but
growing circle, that attracted greater revulsion than sympathy." Daniel
Stern, *Histoire de la Révolution de 1848* (Paris: Lacroix, 1880), xvii.
  4. "But Proudhon makes a critical investigation—the first resolute,
ruthless, and at the same time scientific investigation—of the basis of
political economy, private property. This is the great scientific advance
he made, an advance that revolutionizes political economy and for the
first time makes a real science of political economy possible." Karl Marx
and Friedrich Engels, *La sainte famille* (Paris: Éditions sociales, 1969),
42.
  5. Karl Marx, *Misère de la Philosophie* (Paris: Costes, 1960).

the history of these contradictory emotions did not end in 1847: the fervent admiration expressed in *The Civil War in France* is also a tribute to Proudhon, since in it Marx praises precisely the communalism and federalism that Proudhon had systematically theorized nearly a decade earlier.

Among these impassioned returns to Proudhonism, we must also include the dramatic period of the Paris Commune.[6] Whereas the twenty years of the Second Empire gave no indication that a federalist movement was possible, the insurrection of March 1871 was driven by popular enthusiasm, and a historic return to Proudhon's federalist hopes and his pluralistic conception of a new social order could clearly be discerned.

After 1880, two great impassioned returns to Proudhon could be contrasted: one positive, that of anarcho-syndicalism; the other negative, that of communist ideology, which would make Proudhonism the symbol of evil. Of course, anarcho-syndicalism's return to Proudhon is based on political explanations and supporting arguments, but it was also charged with feeling and emotion.[7] Georges Sorel, Gaétan Pirou, Célestin Bouglé, Georges Dolléans, and others treat the rediscovery of Proudhonism as a "resurrection" and as the revival of someone once forgotten. It was a revival not made without horrified cries,

---

6. Translator's note: During the 1870-71 Franco-Prussian war, the Second French Empire (1852-1870) collapsed, and Napoleon III went into exile. France's Third Republic (1870-1940) was constituted, followed by France's surrender in January 1871. In the wake of the defeat, socialist groups and defected French soldiers managed to seize control over Paris and establish the Paris Commune, which lasted from March 18 to May 28, 1871. When the French Army eventually took back control of Paris and disbanded the Commune, they killed an estimated 20,000 people and imprisoned even more, which crippled the socialist movement in France. The fall of the Paris Commune marked the highwater moment of the socialist movement at that time, all of which had occurred in France up to that point. While the socialist movement would be severely weakened in France for decades, it rapidly spread to other parts of the globe (see Edward S. Mason, *The Paris Commune*, (New York: Howard Fertig, 1967).

7. Compare Patrice Rolland, "Le Retour de Proudhon (1900-1920)," *Mil neuf cent, Revue d'histoire intellectuelle*, no. 10 (1992): 5-29.

as Eduard Bernstein testifies in 1900 in the French edition of his work *Evolutionary Socialism*, in which he writes in the preface: "Hence that horrified exclamation by a few Marxists to me. He is resurrecting Proudhon!"[8]

It is indeed as a disturbing resurrection that these defenders experienced this return. In fact, the history of the First International was marked by the struggle of the collectivists and communists against the Proudhonians and Bakunin. Marx's son-in-law, Paul Lafargue, seemed to have declared Proudhon's definitive excommunication. However, a new social movement became involved in other activities, giving new life and presence to yesterday's outcast.

The October Revolution and its descent into the Leninist, then Stalinist state, would inspire a new revival, perhaps more easily explained but no less impassioned.[9] The state bureaucracy was compelled to fight against all forms of opposition, particularly against an anarchism that would contrast its revolutionary promises with the realities of a despotic state. Proudhon thus assumed the diabolical figure of the triumphant revolution's worst enemy. Of all the returns to Proudhon, this is perhaps the most understandable and politically logical: as the Bolshevik Party was tightening its grip on behavior and expression, he who denounced the state and political bureaucracy logically became the iconic enemy and a symbol of dangerous resistance. We can follow the extreme contradictions in Lenin's work with regard to the Proudhonian spirit: in 1902, in *What Is to Be Done?*, advocating the centralized party and bringing professional revolutionaries together in perfect unity, Lenin firmly rejected the Proudhonian and anarchist tendency, but in 1917 the analyses in *The State and Revolution* struck antistate tones that Proudhon would not have

---

8. Eduard Bernstein, *Socialisme théorique et social-démocratie pratique*, translated by Alexandre Cohen (Paris: Stock, 1900).

9. Translator's note: Following the toppling of Tsar Nicholas II of Russia in February 1917, the Bolshevik party capitalized on the unstable situation by leading an armed insurrection in modern-day Saint Petersburg. The country descended into the Russian Civil War (1917–1923) which led to the rise of the Soviet Union.

rejected. It was after seizing power that Proudhonism became a threat and a voice to be stifled.

The collapse of the communist regimes and their legitimizing rhetoric marked a calming of these condemnations and abuses. If one can speak of a new return to Proudhon, it is certainly in a calmer, less-sectarian climate, more conducive to a better assessment of his place in history and of the significance of his work. However, after the great revivals that we have just briefly recalled, this complex body of work continues to occupy a contested place among the great predecessors. We must assume that this turbulent, unfinished history of admiration and condemnation, support and excommunication, is not accidental, and that there are discernible reasons for it, even if these reasons may intersect and contradict each other, which is no surprise when it comes to political sensitivities.

We can hypothesize that the extreme reactions toward Proudhon's work in the past, and in a lesser vein still today, are due to strong, non-accidental reasons. It seems that the critique of the three alienations of property, the state, and religion touches on three fundamental questions of the social order, and that these questions, whatever changes they may have undergone over more than a century, remain open, provoking explicit and implicit stances and reactions. Moreover, while the conditions have changed, the basic emotional reactions toward these three foundations of the social order have a degree of historical continuity, and it is perhaps in this regard that Proudhonian discourse most directly responds to persistent attitudes. At any rate, Proudhon's specific answers, his refusal to believe in simple and inevitable solutions, and his very ambiguities, between optimism and clearheadedness, seem to be in tune with current emotional contradictions.

The critique of property is Proudhon's first theme, and, despite the different versions, it would be a constant theme. A critique of the principle of property and refutation of theories defending it in *What Is Property?* (1840), an analysis of the contradictions generated by the regime of property in *The System of Economic Contradictions* (1846), attempts to solve the problem in

The Federative Principle (1846) and *Theory of Property* (published posthumously): the denunciation of the appropriation of capital is a constant critical theme.

This obsession may seem outdated today. Such critiques are said to belong to a bygone era of capitalist development. How can these condemnations be given credence when communism has been proven to fail and the various forms of socialism seek each other through various models of capital management? However, things are far from being so obvious, and although social suffering linked to the possession and deprivation of property has changed in form and place, it is still no less acute throughout the world than in the 1850s. The occurrence of appropriation remains a focal point for satisfaction and dissatisfaction, enjoyment and envy, attraction and revulsion. Statistics and surveys can measure equality and inequality, the closing or widening of income gaps, but they cannot accurately reflect all of the ever-present desires and irritations surrounding the nagging issue of property.

But is it not this irritation and fundamental dissatisfaction that Proudhon expresses? It has often been rightly noted that the rebellious cry "Property is theft!" was not as original as one might think and that it had been expressed in different terms well before 1840. It should undoubtedly be compared with Jean-Jacques Rousseau's *Discourse on the Origin of Inequality* (1755), which shares its vigor and bitter outrage. We can even see a new formulation of religious indignation against the injustice of the earthly city—Pope Leo the Great had said, before many church fathers, "Usury of money is the death of the soul." But the old and rather archaic nature of this cry in no way weakens its emotional power. What Proudhon expresses in these few words, which he would subsequently continue to theorize, is that, through the property relationship, a particular social bond is called into question and that, as Rousseau had already expressed, the social relationship has necessarily become a power relationship. Can this power relationship be overcome, or must we come up with economic, political, and ideological compromises? This question would constantly be revisited over the twenty-five years of reflection between the first memoir and *The Political Capacity of the Working Classes.*

Proudhon's originality in the social movement of the mid-nineteenth century on this point is to increase outrage against property without, however, providing a simple solution to it. While liberals and conservatives see appropriation either as an incidental or wholly beneficial phenomenon, and the communists see it as a temporary evil that a revolution can erase, Proudhon maintains that it is socially illegitimate, a source of destructive contradictions, but nevertheless that there is no eschatological solution to this torment. He fights against the liberals who hide the violence and suffering linked to property, but he fights no less against the supporters of "community," whose dangerous illusions he condemns.[10] He even defends Roman possession and glorifies peasants' physical ties to the land, which they cultivate all the better and with all the more enjoyment because it belongs to them.

There is thus an apparent intellectual contradiction, but the contradiction is based in fact. It is an economic contradiction, since property allows the healthy accumulation of capital but also causes worker subordination and poverty; it is a social contradiction, since property divides capital and labor and provokes "war" between the two; and it is a psychological contradiction between the enjoyment of the possessors and the suffering of the dispossessed. But, paradoxically, Proudhon's attitude is in no way one of resignation. He does not believe that a political revolution could ever resolve permanent problems whose complexity is a condition of economic functioning, but he nevertheless does not stop seeking realistic means to ease the suffering caused by appropriation without destroying its dynamism, whether through immediate measures such as the Bank of the People in 1849 or through highly elaborate measures such as federalism in 1863.

Citizens are encouraged to face up to the suffering resulting from property, appreciate its fatal nature, and called not to resign themselves to it but to participate in balances and exchanges in

---

10. Proudhon, *Système des contradictions économiques* (1846), ch. 12.

order to circumvent its injustices. Is this peculiar mix of anger and realistic hope so distant from a certain current sensibility?

Proudhon's second passion may be even closer to a certain current sensibility, and is why he is regarded as the "father of anarchism": his denunciation of political alienation. It was during the period of the 1848 Revolution, when the hope for establishing a whole new society was asserted, that Proudhon most vigorously expressed his denunciation of the state, particularly in *General Idea of the Revolution in the Nineteenth Century* (1851), but this critique had been outlined ever since his earliest writings. His later writings, though more moderate on this point, nevertheless continue to denounce state centralization.

Again, beyond the historical conditions and the variety of circumstances, the Proudhonian critique touches on a problem that today's societies have not solved. Citizens' relationships with the state continue to oscillate from trust to hostility, depending on class and social status and according to their conditions and interests, always marked by hopes and disappointments. In France, in particular, this relationship is filled with agitation sustained by partisan promises and disillusion, but no nation completely avoids this twofold relationship, nor can it evade the burdens and controls of state machinery. But is Proudhon's anti-state sensibility not in tune with this contemporary sensibility, at least in environments not directly favored by state structures? Proudhon sketches the broad outlines of an abstract state power motivated by a dynamic whose extent and invasiveness is hidden. Beyond the historical and political explanations, which are not lacking, he paints an image of dull violence that devours its victims, the citizens.[11] His essential characterization of the state—that it appropriates citizens' political will—strongly accords with the experience of today's citizens, who find themselves before an obscure, threatening, and crippling technocracy. Here theoretical analyses and proofs matter less than the emotional intuition that permeates the text and lends it emotional significance. Perhaps

---

11. Compare Proudhon, *Les Confessions d'un révolutionnaire* (1849) and *Idée générale de la révolution* (1851).

this is why pages of Proudhon remain perfectly understandable by contemporary citizens, without the need for explanation or comment. If, for example, today's citizens read or heard this passage on the violence of state control—"To be GOVERNED is to be at every operation, at every transaction noted, registered, counted, taxed, stamped, measured, numbered, assessed, licensed, authorized, admonished, prevented, forbidden, reformed, corrected, punished"—we would expect them to grasp its meaning immediately and recognize his emotional experience. Proudhon also says that state power is fascinating and that it may exercise, whether consciously or unconsciously, a seductive power over uninformed citizens. There is thus a permanent emotional ambiguity with regard to state power, which varies according to social groups and the various interests, but which permeates the whole of civil society.

It is regrettable that Proudhon did not maintain his radical denunciation of the state and believed that he had to seek a balance, a dialectic, between the principle of authority and the principle of liberty.[12] But it is precisely one of Proudhon's essential peculiarities to radically denounce state appropriation and then seek realistic solutions to the dilemma. Here too his critique leads neither to resignation nor to nihilism: according to *The Federative Principle*, the dialectic between authority and liberty cannot be avoided, and everyone must face up to its specific consequences. Are these appeals not largely in tune with a certain contemporary sensibility?

Proudhon's third denunciation, of religion, may have seemed in the eyes of many rationalist or scientifically minded people to be a somewhat outdated polemic. In 1865 Marx recognized Proudhon's book *Justice in the Revolution and in the Church* as a useful work, but only because of the rather backward mind-set, in his view, of the French workers. For him, since religious beliefs were linked to archaic, feudal structures, the development of capitalism had the side effect of dispelling these outdated illusions.

---

12. Proudhon, *Du Principe fédératif de la nécessité de reconstituer le parti de la révolution* (1863).

The robust maintenance and development of religions throughout the world and the resurgence of aggressive fundamentalism and religious sects have led, conversely, to reconsidering religious facts from another perspective. Today there is a strong tendency to link two attitudes that are difficult to reconcile: one consists of recognizing all meanings (political, social, artistic) of religious facts, while the other highlights the risks (war, hatred, terrorism).

This ambiguity is one of the pillars of Proudhon's analysis of religion. Proudhon clearly emphasizes, as it is repeated today, that the philosophies of transcendence give all individual and collective practices shared meanings, a unity that is psychologically reassuring and socially effective. In doing so, as he likes to recount, every religion creates a certain social bond among its followers; it "binds" individuals together by creating a shared imagination. But his argument also leads to showing that this community that links individuals comes at the cost of subjecting people to a principle that is external to them, an alienation that destroys their autonomy. The purpose of his great book *Justice in the Revolution and in the Church* is to set forth all the consequences of this heteronomy, this submission to a transcendent principle, in all aspects: economic, political, and moral. Religion is therefore both respectable and redoubtable, worthy of respect and even worthier of being fought against. It is understandable that because of this critical aspect, Proudhon's work remains irritating or despicable in the eyes of devotees of all persuasions.

But once again the Proudhonian critique does not lead to nihilism. The goal of this denunciation is not to commit to the destruction of beliefs, and in this respect there is considerable distance, for example, between Proudhon and Max Stirner, as the latter indeed noticed. As the title suggests, Proudhon's goal is twofold: of course, the dangers of doctrines of transcendence must be denounced, but more importantly this critique is the starting point of a search for a positive theory of justice. Here again the Proudhonian sensibility in no way leads to resignation but rather to seeking solutions to the different contradictions that are the very substance of life.

If there is therefore a clear affinity between major forms of current common sensibility and Proudhonian analyses, it will not be surprising to note that some proposals made over a century ago resonate strongly today. Without intending to develop them further, two great Proudhonian projects—federalism and the theory of justice—emphasize the link between political sensibility and these projects.

It may be said that the movement now inspiring a reevaluation of European federalism, in endlessly discussed forms, is based on one fear and one hope: the fear of seeing the continuation of conflicts that have caused bloodshed in European nations, and the hope of building a new community with greater economic and political cohesion. Keeping just to these aspects, it can be noted that they reproduce a set of attitudes that also support the Proudhonian federalist project. In the 1860s he saw federalism as a sociopolitical system capable of breaking the despotic, warlike dynamics of the great states, a transnational regime making a return to military confrontations impossible. Similarly, provided that federalism was conceived as an economic and social regime and not only as an interstate arrangement, it would need to completely reorganize socioeconomic balances and exchanges, while also transforming all the old structures. This hope is not absent from current expectations, which does not mean that the true Proudhonian project is now being implemented; on this point, there is a large gap between hope and reality.

It is no less remarkable that a broad reflection on the theme of justice is being developed today, which, of course, seeks different means and ends from Proudhon's.[13] An intuition that motivates current research chimes with Proudhon's theory that the free play of economic forces and social contradictions is not a viable long-term response and will only satisfy the governing and possessing classes. As he repeats in *Justice in the Revolution and in the Church*, the collapse of transcendent beliefs and the system of inequality that they legitimize risks surrendering humanity to its

---

13. The allusion is to the rebirth of the debate marked by John Rawls's *Theory of Justice*, 1971.

troubles, to economic, social, and political violence. This does not imply that new, dangerous forms of transcendence must be invented. On the contrary, we must take stock of economic realities, examine the failures of the regime of property and the social inequalities that it reinforces, and bring the demands of personal conscience up to date in order to define the principles of justice and its applications in different areas of life. For Proudhon, a society cannot be based on illusory principles and become a source of dependence and submission. Nor can it surrender itself solely to the determinisms of economic forces or find peace and freedom within the straitjacket of state order. It requires an ideal and real order, an imagination of what it must be, a principle that guides collective and individual action.

Is this justice being achieved, and can we confidently expect the coming transition from a world of injustice to a world of justice? Proudhon is far from asserting this, and after having at times believed in certain progress, he considers regression to be a historical possibility. Humanity's troubles are too glaring for us to be led astray by the illusion of a just future. We must make a careful assessment of violence and injustice and their fundamental causes, and fear the worst without losing hope. Justice remains the goal to be achieved, the task to be carried out.

Pierre Ansart

Further Reading

Proudhon's works available in English:

Celebration of Sunday (1839 / 2012), https://theanarchistlibrary
.org/library/pierre-joseph-proudhon-the-celebration-of-sunday.

What Is Property? (1840 / 1890), https://theanarchistlibrary.org/
library/pierre-joseph-proudhon-what-is-property-an-inquiry
-into-the-principle-of-right-and-of-government.

The Creation of Order in Humanity (parts missing) (1843 / 2021),
https://theanarchistlibrary.org/library/pierre-joseph-proudhon
-the-creation-of-order-in-humanity.

The System of Economic Contradictions (vol. 1) (1847 / 1888), https://
theanarchistlibrary.org/library/pierre-joseph-proudhon-system
-of-economical-contradictions-or-the-philosophy-of-poverty.

Solution of the Social Problem (parts missing) (1848 / 1927), https://
theanarchistlibrary.org/library/pierre-joseph-proudhon-the
-solution-of-the-social-problem.

General Idea of the Revolution in the Nineteenth Century (1851 / 1923),
https://theanarchistlibrary.org/library/pierre-joseph-proudhon
-the-general-idea-of-the-revolution-in-the-19th-century.

The Philosophy of Progress (parts missing) (1853 / 2011), https://
theanarchistlibrary.org/library/pierre-joseph-proudhon-the
-philosophy-of-progress.

War and Peace (1863 / 2022, AK Press.)

The Federative Principle (parts missing) (1863 / 1979), https://
theanarchistlibrary.org/library/pierre-joseph-proudhon-the
-principle-of-federation.

Selected works of Proudhon's available in English:

Selected Writings of Pierre-Joseph Proudhon (edited by Stewart
Edwards, 1969, Macmillan).

Property Is Theft! A Pierre-Joseph Proudhon Reader (edited by Iain
McKay, 2011, AK Press), https://theanarchistlibrary.org/library/
pierre-joseph-proudhon-property-is-theft.

Index

"Passim" (literally "scattered") indicates intermittent discussion of a topic over a cluster of pages.

abdication, 81n24; working
classes, 71–72, 92–98 passim

G

*General Idea of the Revolution
in the Nineteenth Century*
(Proudhon), 8, 25, 75n8, 84,
124n39, 130, 152n18, 216
God (Christianity), 158, 159,
166–67, 170
Grün, Karl, 3–4
Gurvitch, Georges, 87n36,
142n3

H

Hayat, Samuel, 14
Hegel, G. W. F., 3, 19, 26n9,
39, 40, 144
The Holy Family (Marx and
Engels). See *La Sainte famille*
(Marx and Engels)
human rights, 99, 148, 153

I

idea and practice, 141–56
*Idée générale de la révolution au
XIXe siècle* (Proudhon). See
*General Idea of the Revolution
in the Nineteenth Century*
(Proudhon)
individuality and individual rea-
son, 133, 175–78
International Workingmen's
Association (IWA), 13, 212

J

Jesus Christ, 160–64 passim
July Revolution. *See* French
Revolution of 1830 (July
Revolution)
justice, Proudhon theory of,
170–79

*Justice in the Revolution and in
the Church* (Proudhon), 23,
79n18, 96n56, 141–42,
146n9, 150n14, 157, 159n31,
165, 217–20 passim; on
collective reason, 179n52;
justice in, 170, 171n47; on
middle class, 89n39

L

labor, 37, 44–46 passim, 50–68
passim, 105, 122, 155,
185–93 passim; agricultural
labor, 67–68; capital relation, 69; organization of,
24–27 passim, 45, 58–64
passim, 70, 82, 94–96 passim, 105–9 passim, 122n35,
155, 174, 198. *See also* division of labor
Lafargue, Paul, 10, 212
Lefebvre, Henri: *Sociologie de
Marx*, 2
Lenin, Vladimir, 9–10, 212–13
Leroux, Pierre, 24, 99
Leo, Pope, 214
Louis-Philippe, King of the
French, 81, 86, 108, 109n12
Luxembourg Commission, 100

M

Manifeste des Soixante, 97–98,
100
Manuel du spéculateur à la Bourse
(Proudhon), 97n57, 108n9
Marx, Karl, 2–12 passim, 17–19
passim, 181–207 passim;
Capital, 182, 185, 192, 193;
The Civil War in France, 211;
Communist Manifesto, 194;
*Economic and Philosophic
Manuscripts of 1844*, 189;

17-22 passim, 38-39, 48-57
passim, 63n24, 94, 144, 148,
154n22, 213; on exchange,
143n5; God in, 170n46, 183;
Marx and, 11, 17, 192, 210;
on proletarians, 92n47; on
property, 107

T
Theory of Property (Proudhon), 6,
9, 48n8, 214
"Third Estate" (term), 17n1
Tolain, Henri, 13

U
union of all workers, 194-95
use value and exchange value,
38, 39
utopians and utopianism, 24,
27, 31, 58-60 passim, 152

V
value, 49-60 passim, 80. *See
also* surplus value; use and
exchange value

W
wages, 20, 21, 62, 71, 75, 88,
186, 188
war, 114, 122-23, 134
War and Peace (Proudhon),
158n27, 174, 210
Warning to the Proprietors
(Proudhon). See
Avertissement aux propriétaires
(Proudhon)
What Is Property? (Proudhon),
17, 43, 44n2, 54, 61n22, 68,
73n7, 213
What Is to Be Done? (Lenin), 212
workers' associations and federations, 66, 68, 94, 204

workers' councils and soviets,
201-7 passim
working classes. *See* proletariat

AK PRESS is small, in terms of staff and resources, but we also manage to be one of the world's most productive anarchist publishing houses. We publish close to twenty books every year, and distribute thousands of other titles published by like-minded independent presses and projects from around the globe. We're entirely worker run and democratically managed. We operate without a corporate structure—no boss, no managers, no bullshit.

The **FRIENDS OF AK PRESS** program is a way you can directly contribute to the continued existence of AK Press, and ensure that we're able to keep publishing books like this one! Friends pay $25 a month directly into our publishing account ($30 for Canada, $35 for international), and receive a copy of every book AK Press publishes for the duration of their membership! Friends also receive a discount on anything they order from our website or buy at a table: 50% on AK titles, and 30% on everything else. We have a Friends of AK ebook program as well: $15 a month gets you an electronic copy of every book we publish for the duration of your membership. *You can even sponsor a very discounted membership for someone in prison.*

Email **friendsofak@akpress.org** for more info, or visit the website: **https://www.akpress.org/friends.html**.

There are always great book projects in the works—so sign up now to become a Friend of AK Press, and let the presses roll!

About the editors and translators:

Cayce Jamil (he/him) has a PhD in Public Policy from the University of North Carolina at Charlotte. His research focuses on developing social theory, and he has written on Proudhonian thought and its implications for sociology.

Shaun Murdock (he/him) translates texts on the themes of economy, society, and environment from French, Spanish, Italian, Portuguese, and Catalan into English.

René Berthier (he/him) is a French libertarian and anarcho-syndicalist activist. In 1972, he joined the CGT trade union confederation in the printing industry. It was while working in a large Parisian printing house that he completed a master's degree in English (thesis on William Godwin) at the Sorbonne in 1974. Now retired, he devotes himself to writing in the theoretical and historical field.

Jesse S. Cohn (he/him) is the author of *Underground Passages: Anarchist Resistance Culture, 1848–2011*, translator of Daniel Colson's *Little Philosophical Lexicon of Anarchism From Proudhon to Deleuze*, and cotranslator of Wolf and Abba Gordin's *Why? or, How a Peasant Got Into the Land of Anarchy*. A board member of the Institute for Anarchist Studies, Cohn teaches English at Purdue University Northwest.